Here and Now III

Here and Now III

an approach to writing through perception

FRED MORGAN

HARCOURT BRACE JOVANOVICH, INC.

New York   San Diego   Chicago   San Francisco   Atlanta

COVER PHOTO: Jerome Kresch from Peter Arnold

ISBN: 0-15-535624-0

Library of Congress Catalog Card Number: 78-71067

Printed in the United States of America

for
George Henderson

contents

3

being aware of your surroundings

4

observing a scene

5

getting the feel of action

6

observing a person

7

perceiving emotional attitudes

8

estimating a person

9

identifying with a person

10

perceiving a relationship

11

identifying with an animal

12

looking at yourself

13

examining a desire

14

seeing the whole picture

preface

This book, like *Here and Now* and *Here and Now II*, is made up of fourteen units designed to improve students' writing by developing their perceptions. Each unit deals with a specific area of perception; each includes a short discussion of one aspect of writing, assignments that focus on writing from direct observation, examples from literature and art, and questions that help students understand the selections. By using the material provided in the units as a guide, students may learn to organize the data of their own experience and thus increase their writing skills. The selections show how accomplished writers have handled similar material.

Here and Now III includes those selections and assignments from *Here and Now* and *Here and Now II* that have proved most useful in the classroom, with the addition of some new material. The introduction and the last chapter are entirely new to this edition; and so are several of the literary and artistic selections.

The aim, however, remains the same as in the past: to improve writing through perception. Good thinking and writing cannot grow out of second-hand material, but must be firmly rooted in the ability of students to observe and interpret for themselves. As in the earlier volumes, students are encouraged to begin at the beginning by examining their own surroundings. The pattern remains the same: they start with simple objects and progress toward complex ones, but without departing from first-hand observation and experience. Generalization is encouraged only insofar as it can be soundly based on sensory data. The final chapter focuses on generalization, placing it in the context of an argument, where most students are likely to encounter it. By contrast, the introduction shows the risks inherent in generalization, while illustrating some techniques of narration.

Here and Now III is intended to lead students toward self-confidence based on the discovery that they can perceive and evaluate for themselves; this increased self-confidence will be reflected in their writing.

FRED MORGAN

introduction

observing

The first step in improving your writing is to improve your ability to observe. Like most of us, you probably do not observe things and people around you, or yourself, as well as you could. You may accept too readily the observations of others, writing in ready-made generalities instead of depending on your own senses. Most of us are only half aware of our surroundings.

Think of a tree that you pass by every day, or one in your own yard or near your home. Try to visualize it in its real proportions. How thick is the trunk? How does it taper? How do the lowest branches grow from it? Are they in groups like the spokes of a wheel, or are they stepped? How thick are they? At what angle do they rise or sink? How are the leaves or pine needles arranged? What shape are they, and in what kinds of groups? See if you can draw a fairly accurate picture of the tree on a piece of paper. When you get a chance, look at the tree again.

Or think of a coin. Without looking at it, try to draw or describe a penny or a dime. Can you remember which way the portrait faces? Can you recall all the details? Now look at the actual coin and note what you have missed.

These are tests of your visual observation. Many of us depend on vision and neglect the other senses. Close your eyes. Can you clearly imagine the voice of a person you know well? Can you re-create the smell of a baking cake or the taste of apple cider? Can you feel in your hand the sensation of stroking a particular cat or dog, or the coolness of a knife handle? Can you feel in your body the sensation of running, or must you recall the visual images associated with running?

These experiments may convince you that you are not perfectly in contact with your environment. Few people are. But then, few people are good at writing, good at thinking, or even good at living. Anyone can learn to be. All it takes is practice.

Living, thinking, and writing can all be improved by improving observation.

showing

The following is an unsuccessful student essay. See if you can determine why it is not an example of good writing.

a memorable experience

Our trip to Disneyland last year was an experience I will never forget.

The morning of the great day finally arrived. We all got up bright and early and had breakfast. Then we all worked at getting our things together and packed the car. At nine o'clock we left with great feelings of anticipation in our hearts. The weather was fine, and we all had a wonderful time while traveling. At last we arrived at Disneyland.

After we bought our tickets we rode the monorail all around Disneyland, craning our necks to see the hundreds of wonderful sights below and all around us. It was one of the most thrilling experiences I ever had, and I was sorry when it was all over.

But there were even better things to come. For example, we took a spectacular boat ride down a primitive jungle river and saw many interesting animals on the way. It was just like being in Africa. We also visited a realistic western frontier town where we saw just how people used to live in the Old West. From this experience I gained a lot of knowledge of American history. We had many other experiences like this that were fascinating and educational, and I felt that my visit to Disneyland was one of the most valuable experiences I have ever had.

Tired but happy, we all piled into our car and started the long trek home. On the way we had dinner at a good restaurant, which we all enjoyed, and when we got home I headed straight for bed and sweet dreams of Disneyland.

Does the writer tell you anything about Disneyland that you could not find in advertisements or travel brochures? After reading this essay, do you know anything about the trip that would make it seem different from anyone else's trip to Disneyland?

The writer says that the trip was "an experience I will never forget," yet the student writes as though most of it has been forgotten already. The essay could have been written by someone who had never been to Disneyland. Further, because the writer has nothing to say, the essay contains many *clichés*—meaningless standard expressions, such as "the great day," "bright and early," "better things to come," and "tired but happy."

Who are the members of the writer's family? The essay does not even tell us how many there were. What time of year did they go? We have no hint of what the weather was like except that it was "fine." What does the writer mean, "we all had a wonderful time while traveling"? We know nothing of what they did or saw.

Go through the essay sentence by sentence, asking questions the writer does not answer.

Nearly all the evidence that would back up the writer's general statements is missing. When we read about an experience, we want to know what it was like; we want to share it. The writer has told us a few things but has not *shown* us anything.

Show more than you *tell.*

Let the reader see the picture that you see, hear and smell the things you hear and smell, feel what you feel. Re-create the experience in all its sensory detail.

limiting

But, you may protest, if the whole trip is shown in detail, the student would have to write a hundred pages! True. What should the writer do, then?

This writer should *limit* the subject to a part of the experience and do a good job of describing that part. The monorail trip alone would be enough to write about, or the boat ride, or the frontier town.

Let's say the writer chooses the part of the day that was disposed of in the first three dull sentences of the second paragraph, the starting out. If the writer had *limited* the subject to that part, had *observed* well, and had *shown* us the scene, the essay might have come out something like this:

a memorable experience

Getting my eight-year-old brother Ronnie ready to go on a trip is always a memorable experience. He is the nonconformist in our family and usually has his own ideas. I remember especially the sunny morning last June when we had the problem of getting him ready to go to Disneyland with us.

First I had to get Ronnie out of bed. At a quarter past seven, with the smell of frying bacon already making my stomach growl,

I padded up the stairs in my pajamas and pounded on his door. No response. I shoved the door open against its barricade of dirty clothes, toy cars, roller skates, and plastic guns, holding my breath against the odors of abandoned socks, decaying cookie crumbs, and model airplane glue. Under the covers was a shapeless lump, like a turtle defending itself inside its shell. Knowing the lump to be dangerous, I pinned it down first and then shook it thoroughly. It snarled, hissed, struggled, and finally surrendered.

Getting Ronnie into the tub was no problem, since he was too sleepy to know what was happening to him. But getting him out was another matter. After fifteen minutes of yelling at him I burst into the bathroom to find him lying on his back completely submerged, using Father's best pipe for a snorkel. (This episode cured Father of leaving pipes in the bathroom.) Once I had dragged Ronnie's ears above the surface, a little propaganda about the pancakes cooling on his plate was enough to lure him out.

My problems were not over, however. After we had finished breakfast and Father had the old Dodge warmed up, Ronnie was nowhere to be found. Father called in his best foghorn bass, Mother screamed threats in her most hysterical soprano, and I added my piercing two-finger whistle, but the only result was that old Mr. Picard across the street slammed down his window. Naturally, I was the one delegated to find Ronnie, or else. I searched the house. I peered under beds and into closets, finding my lost baseball mitt and a can of tennis balls, but no Ronnie. I searched the attic, the storeroom, and the back yard. Just as I was returning down the front steps, I heard a suspicious little rustle under the house. On my hands and knees, squinting into the musty darkness, I saw a blur that seemed to move.

"Hey, Ronnie, is that you?"

"Sh-h-h! Don't scare him," the blur whispered irritably.

"*Now* what do you think you're doing?" I yelled, losing patience.

"I was catching Felix, but you spoiled it," Ronnie pouted as he scrambled toward me through the powdery dust. "He wants to go with us." Felix is our purebred alley cat.

It was useless to explain that running under the house wasn't the cat's way of telling us he wanted to go to Disneyland. I just grabbed Ronnie, took him inside, and cleaned him up again. This time I kept his scrawny little neck firmly in my grip until I had him safely in the car.

The purpose of this essay is the same as that of the first one, to communicate an experience. But this one communicates *more* about *less*, and that is one of the reasons it is better. Another reason is that it is full of *specifics*. It *shows* the reader what the experience was like: it could serve as the script for a movie scene.

giving specifics

One kind of poor writing is writing that is too *general*. Good writing makes generalizations, but it supports them with plenty of *specifics*.

A *general* statement covers many instances—such as, "Most cats don't like to ride in cars." We do not know whether such a general statement is valid until we have observed a number of specific examples.

A *specific* statement tells us what has actually been observed: "My old, gray alley cat Felix ran under the house when my brother tried to put him in the car." Many specific observations like this one might convince us that the generalization "Most cats don't like to ride in cars" is valid. Good writers convince their readers by giving them enough specifics on which to base their own judgments.

Some general statements can never be proved because they are expressions of feeling. They are called *opinions*. "Cats make the best pets" is an opinion. No one can prove to you that cats are the best pets; you may just happen to like alligators.

Though opinions can never be proved, they can be supported by evidence designed to win the reader's agreement. The first essay does not convince us that the writer's trip to Disneyland was a memorable experience, but the second one does convince us that getting Ronnie ready for a trip was a memorable experience. The writer convinces us by letting us experience the details of one episode and gives us sights, sounds, smells, and descriptions of scenes.

Good writing, then, contains good evidence accurately observed and clearly presented.

Doesn't good writing also require well-chosen words, clear sentences, and coherent paragraphs? Of course. But you will find that when you know what you want to say, and when you have learned to think in concrete instead of general terms, your expression will begin to improve.

The first stage is improving your powers of observation. The following assignments and readings are designed to sharpen your perception of things around you, of people, and even of yourself in relation to your environment.

Drawing by Dedini; © 1975 The New Yorker Magazine, Inc.

1

enjoying
your senses

Your only contacts with the world are through your senses. Even when you dream or imagine, the materials of your images are shapes, colors, sounds, smells, tastes, textures, and temperatures that have come into your mind through your senses. When you have ideas or beliefs, they are derived from sensory data. Your emotions are based on what goes on inside you, and you feel them as bodily sensations: that is why they are sometimes called "feelings."

You have probably noticed that when people are happy, they are aware of everything around them, and that when they are unhappy, their awareness is dimmed. This connection works the opposite way, too: when you become obsessed with matters that are "on your mind" you become unhappy or bored, and the cure is to get out and *experience* something—go to a movie or a play, enjoy the sensations of running or playing a game, or just walk around observing what is there. Sometimes we grow stale and need more sensory "input."

Many people riding on a bus or subway, or waiting at a stop or standing in a line, have blank looks on their faces as though they are in a trance. They don't look around or listen. They don't know how to live. There is always something to observe, something to entertain you, if you just look for it.

The next time you are riding or waiting, deliberately look for something in your surroundings you haven't noticed before. Listen to the way people are talking, even if you can't hear what they are saying. Watch people's gestures and physical attitudes, the way they sit or stand or hold

7

their heads when they are talking, and ask yourself what these attitudes tell you about them. Observe people's clothing and the way they wear it, and ask yourself, "If I were wearing those clothes in that way, what would my reason be?" Like Sherlock Holmes, try to guess a person's profession by clothing and other clues; are you looking at a printer or a carpenter, a banker or a secretary or an artist? Look at details of old buildings and try to imagine why the architect designed them just that way; identify yourself for a moment with a tree or an animal and imagine what it would be like to *be* that tree or animal at that moment. Put your senses and your mind *into* things. The world will become a livelier place.

keeping in touch

Our way of living overemphasizes vision at the expense of the other senses, as when we drive a car, watch television, or read a newspaper. But these activities do not even encourage sensitivity of vision: we are only half using our eyesight when we use it to avoid obstacles, to get the meaning of a blurred image on a picture tube, or to recognize printed words. Dullness of the other senses is promoted even more by the kind of life we live. We use hearing to receive verbal messages and to listen to music, but we often fail to detect more subtle sounds that have messages for us, such as a slight change of tone in a voice or the delicate song of a bird.

You have the five senses of sight, hearing, smell, taste, and touch. In addition, you have the *kinesthetic* sense, the feeling of movement in your body. (You have only to shake your head to observe it.) But it is the sense of touch that is basic. You do not know what you are seeing until you have touched it, or something like it. That is why a baby's hands are always in motion: it is trying to find out what things are. A pillow looks soft only because you have felt pillows and found them soft; ice looks cold because you have touched ice. When a person behaves unrealistically, you say that person is "out of touch."

In a world where our survival no longer depends on hunting, fishing, or primitive farming, we have to invent ways of keeping our bodies in shape—sports, calisthenics, running, and so on. Likewise, in a world where keen senses are no longer necessary, our senses become flabby and need to be exercised deliberately. As physical exercise makes your body come alive and feel better, so exercise of the senses enlivens your mind and makes you happier.

You may have observed that blind newsdealers can make change instantly, identifying the coins with their fingers. You can too, but it takes more time. Reach into your pocket or purse. How long does it take you to be sure you have a penny instead of a dime? Without looking, see how much you can find out about the penny with your sense of touch. Can you identify the head side? Would you know that it is metal, and if so, how? What other features can you be sure of without looking at the coin?

Develop the habit of keeping in touch. Put your mind in your fingers. Touch can tell you a lot about the things around you.

Of all our senses, the one we most neglect is smell. This neglect is understandable, for we live in a world of exhaust smoke, noxious chemicals, and polluted air. Nevertheless, you should fight to keep your sense of smell alive, for it is a part of your awareness, gives pleasure at times, and evokes memories as none of the other senses do. You have no doubt had the experience of catching a scent that suddenly brought back a scene from your childhood. In the following passage, Thomas Wolfe captures some of the nostalgia of remembered smells.

from Look Homeward, Angel

THOMAS WOLFE

He remembered yet the East India Tea House at the Fair, the sandalwood, the turbans, and the robes, the cool interior and the smell of India tea; and he had felt now the nostalgic thrill of dew-wet mornings in Spring, the cherry scent, the cool clarion earth, the wet loaminess of the garden, the pungent breakfast smells and the floating snow of blossoms. He knew the inchoate sharp excitement of hot dandelions in young Spring grass at noon; the smell of cellars, cobwebs, and built-on secret earth; in July, of water-melons bedded in sweet hay, inside a farmer's covered wagon; of cantaloupe and crated peaches; and the scent of orange rind, bitter-sweet, before a fire of coals. He knew the good male smell of his father's sitting-room; of the smooth worn leather sofa, with the gaping horse-hair rent; of the blistered varnished wood upon the hearth; of the heated calf-skin bindings; of the flat moist plug of apple tobacco, stuck with a red flag; of wood-smoke and burnt leaves in October; of the brown tired autumn earth; of honey-suckle at night; of warm nasturtiums; of a clean ruddy farmer who comes weekly with printed butter, eggs and milk; of fat limp underdone bacon and of coffee; of a bakery-oven in the wind; of large deep-hued stringbeans smoking-hot and seasoned well with salt and butter; of a room of old pine boards in which books and carpets have been stored, long closed; of Concord grapes in their long white baskets.

Yes, and the exciting smell of chalk and varnished desks; the smell of heavy bread-sandwiches of cold fried meat and butter; the smell of new leather in a saddler's shop, or of a warm leather chair; of honey and of unground coffee; of barrelled sweet-pickles and cheese and all the fragrant compost of the grocer's; the smell of stored apples in the cellar, and of orchard-apple smells, of pressed-cider pulp; of pears ripening on a sunny shelf, and of ripe cherries stewing with sugar on hot stoves before preserv-ing; the smell of whittled wood, of all young lumber, of sawdust and shav-ings; of peaches stuck with cloves and pickled in brandy; of pine-sap, and green pine-needles; of a horse's pared hoof; of chestnuts roasting, of bowls of nuts and raisins; of hot cracklin, and of young roast pork; of butter and cinnamon melting on hot candied yams.

Yes, and of the rank slow river, and of tomatoes rotten on the vine; the smell of rain-wet plums and boiling quinces; of rotten lily-pads; and of foul weeds rotting in green marsh scum; and the exquisite smell of the South, clean but funky, like a big woman; of soaking trees and the earth after heavy rain.

Yes, and the smell of hot daisy-fields in the morning; of melted puddling-iron in a foundry; the winter smell of horse-warm stables and smoking dung; of old oak and walnut; and the butcher's smell of meat, of strong slaughtered lamb, plump gouty liver, ground pasty sausages, and red beef; and of brown sugar melted with slivered bitter chocolate; and of crushed mint leaves, and of a wet lilac bush; of magnolia beneath the heavy moon, of dogwood and laurel; of an old caked pipe and Bourbon rye, aged in kegs of charred oak; the sharp smell of tobacco; of carbolic and nitric acids; the coarse true smell of a dog; of old imprisoned books; and the cool fern-smell near springs; of vanilla in cake-dough; and of cloven ponderous cheeses.

Smells must be evoked by naming the thing smelled, but sounds are a different matter. Since words themselves are sounds, we have many words that echo the sounds they describe, words like *hum, squeak, murmur, clang,* and *crash*. In the following poem, Isabella Gardner evokes memories of her childhood through sounds.

Summer Remembered

ISABELLA GARDNER

Sounds sum and summon the remembering of summers.
The humming of the sun
The mumbling in the honey-suckle vine
The whirring in the clovered grass
The pizzicato plinkle of ice in an auburn
uncle's amber glass.
The whing of father's racquet and the whack
of brother's bat on cousin's ball
and calling voices call-
ing voices spilling voices . . .

SUMMER REMEMBERED from *The Looking Glass* by Isabella Gardner. © 1961 by the University of Chicago. Reprinted by permission of the publisher and the author.

The munching of saltwater at the splintered dock
The slap and slop of waves on little sloops
The quarreling of oarlocks hours across the bay
The canvas sails that bleat as they
are blown. The heaving buoy bell-
ing HERE I am
HERE you are HEAR HEAR

listen listen listen
The gramophone is wound
the music goes round and around
BYE   BYE BLUES   LINDY'S COMING
voices calling   calling   calling
"Children!   Children!   Time's Up
Time's up"
Merrily sturdily wantonly the familial voices
cheerily chidingly call to the children   TIME'S UP
and the mute children's unvoiced clamor sacks the summer air
crying Mother   Mother   are you there?

Notice how the poet uses words for their sound value. In the first three lines, what is actually *humming* and *mumbling*? Why the *munching* of waves at the dock? Why does the poet use the word *sloops* instead of *sailboats*? Point out other words that evoke what is happening directly through the use of sound.

class exercise

Turn on your senses separately, one at a time, concentrating on each one until you have nearly exhausted what it can tell you. Describe for others what you experience. Begin with the most basic sense.

Kinesthetic sense. First, sit still and define what your body feels. Then move your head, arms, legs, and body, and try to describe the interior feelings each movement creates.

Touch. Before you use your hands, describe what your skin is aware of. What is touching it, and where, and in what way? Now use your hands to explore things on you and around you—the texture of clothing, skin, and hair; the surface and temperature of the desk you are sitting in, your pen, paper, and the objects in your possession, such as your wallet, purse, coins, and combs. What do you find most interesting to the touch? Try to describe the quality of its surface.

Taste. What kind of taste is in your mouth now? What did you last eat or drink? What did it taste like? Try to describe the sensation in your mouth of, say, breakfast cereal, or spaghetti. Use analogy; that is, think of something the taste resembles, or something it reminds you of.

Smell. What can you smell now in the air? What is the smell like? Hold some objects to your nose: a piece of paper, chalk, a pencil, an eraser; open a wallet or purse and smell the inside; dampen a coin or a key and smell it. What do these smells evoke in your imagination or memory?

Hearing. How many different sounds can you hear right now? How do you know what each one is? Are there any you cannot identify? For each sound, try to find a word that echoes it, such as "the *rustle* of a skirt" or "the *scrape* of a shoe." If you can't find an existing word, make up one, as Isabella Gardner made up "plinkle" for her poem.

Sight. Of course you can't report everything you can see in the room, so take up a simple object such as a pen and explore it thoroughly with your eyes. What are its colors and textures? How do its different parts reflect the light? What are its details and what does each mean? What is each part *like?*

writing assignment

With a notebook and pen, sit on your front porch or step, or on a park bench, or at an open window, or in one of the rooms where you live. Write down a description of each sensation you experience, using one sentence for each sensation. Try to evoke each sensation as clearly as possible with your words: "I hear the guttural bubbling of a pot on the kitchen stove and the faint hollow hiss of the gas burner under it." Don't try to organize your material; just observe and record. After you have written a dozen or so observations, look back to see if you have neglected any one of the senses. Try to make at least two observations using each of the six senses listed in this unit.

1. A picture must communicate entirely through the sense of sight. However, the forms and colors may evoke or suggest other kinds of sensory experience. In this picture, what do the colors suggest about the time of day?
2. What is the weather? What other aspects of the climate are evidenced? How did the artist communicate these things?
3. What kinesthetic feelings are suggested? How are they suggested?
4. What sensations of touch are suggested? (Don't forget those connected with the weather.)
5. What smells might be present in this scene? What might possibly be tasted?
6. What sounds are suggested by the scene?
7. If the picture were a moving one, what movements would be observed? How has the painter suggested them?
8. What are some subjects not actually shown within the confines of the picture that nevertheless you know are part of the scene? What are some elements of these people's life style that you can deduce from evidence in the picture? For example, what would you expect their houses to be like, and what might be inside them?

PLATE I

MAN WITH AXE: Paul Gauguin. Mr. and Mrs. Alexander Lewyt/Robert Crandall
Associates, Inc.

2

employing
your senses

Sharpening your senses is a way of not only increasing enjoyment but gaining knowledge of your environment in order to deal with it. Knowledge of your immediate environment helps you survive; knowledge of the total environment helps humanity survive.

Learning to focus the senses purposefully is essential. Thinking is organizing sense impressions, seeing the whole and its parts in relation to each other. Before you can think well you must observe well. In the following selection, the geologist Nathaniel Southgate Shaler tells us of his first formal lesson in observation. He had been accepted as a pupil by the famous naturalist Louis Agassiz, who was an expert at close observation.

from Autobiography

NATHANIEL SOUTHGATE SHALER

When I sat me down before my tin pan, Agassiz brought me a small fish, placing it before me with the rather stern requirement that I should study it, but should on no account talk to any one concerning it, nor read anything relating to fishes, until I had his permission so to do. To my inquiry "What shall I do?" he said in effect: "Find out what you can without damaging the specimen; when I think that you have done the work I will question you." In the course of an hour I thought I had compassed that fish; it was rather an unsavory object, giving forth the stench of old alcohol, then loathsome to me, though in time I came to like it. Many of the scales were loosened so that they fell off. It appeared to me to be a case for a summary report, which I was anxious to make and get on to the next stage of business. But Agassiz, though always within call, concerned himself no further with me that day, nor the next, nor for a week. At first, this neglect was distressing; but I saw that it was a game, for he was, as I discerned rather than saw, covertly watching me. So I set my wits to work upon the thing, and in the course of a hundred hours or so thought I had done much—a hundred times as much as seemed possible at the start. I got interested in finding out how the scales went in series, their shape, the form and placement of the teeth, etc. Finally, I felt full of the subject and probably expressed it in my bearing; as for words about it then, there were none from my master except his cheery "Good morning." At length on the seventh day, came the question "Well?" and my disgorge of learning to him as he sat on the edge of my table puffing his cigar. At the end of the hour's telling, he swung off and away, saying, "That is not right." Here I began to think that after all perhaps the rules for scanning Latin verse were not the worst infliction in the world. Moreover, it was clear that he was playing a game with me to find if I were capable of doing hard, continuous work without the support of a teacher, and this stimulated me to labor. I went at the task anew, discarded my first notes, and in another week of ten hours a day labor I had results which astonished myself and satisfied him. Still there was no trace of praise in words or manner. He signified that it would do by placing before me about a half a peck of bones, telling me to see what I could make of them, with no further directions to guide me.

class exercise

A piece of chalk might seem an object of little interest to anyone except for its usefulness. For years you have handled chalk and seen it around you. Just because it seems such a simple and familiar thing, you may find it worthwhile to examine the chalk more closely to see if you can gain a stronger sense of its reality.

Examine a fragment of chalk as though you were seeing it for the first time. Try to describe it so that a person who never has seen a piece of chalk could get a clear idea of it.

1. Give your description in the order easiest to follow. Begin with the size, shape, and color; then go on to the more obvious details and, finally, the smaller ones. Whenever you can, proceed from large to small, the way you naturally see an object.
2. Be clear at all times. It is not enough to say, "It is broken off at one end." How does the break look? What is the shape, texture, color of the broken surface? What do these qualities tell us about the nature of the material?
3. Use all your senses. Feel the chalk, smell it, taste it, weigh it in your hand, rub it, test its hardness, listen to the sound it makes when you drop it, crumble it and feel the texture of the powder, wet it and smell it again, put a little ink on it to see how well it can absorb liquid, and so on through every test you can think of.
4. Try to find the best word for each quality. If you can't think of a good word, then look for an *analogy*—something that it is *like*.
5. If there is time, use another subject in the same way, such as a wooden pencil or a piece of paper.

writing assignment

1. Select an object that is complex enough to be interesting but easy to replace, because you will want to take it apart. Some good choices would be a kitchen match, a cigar, a potato, an egg, or almost any kind of fruit: an apple, a banana, a strawberry.
2. Inspect the object closely. Observe its size, dimensions, shape, color, texture, weight, smell, taste, resilience or flexibility—all the qualities you can determine without taking the object apart. Write down notes of your observations as you make them.
3. When you are sure you have exhausted all the possibilities of the object's exterior, begin taking it apart carefully, a little at a time, using all your senses as you go. Find out in detail how it is made. Finally, test its components in every sensible way you can think of: squeeze them, bend

them, scratch them, heat them, soak them—anything that might tell you
something. Keep writing down the results as you go along.

4. Now, when you have finished, rearrange your observations, putting them
    in a logical order that is easy to follow. You can start from large to small,
    then perhaps from end to end. Finally, when you are describing your
    experiments, you can use a time sequence saying, "First I did this and
    found out that; then I tried . . ." and so on.

5. Write your report on the object, following the order you set up. Always
    be sure your reader knows where you are; strive to be clear. At the
    conclusion, add a short paragraph summing up what you have learned
    about the object.

The following is a description of the kind you have been asked to
write. Compare it with yours and test yours against it for clarity, complete-
ness, and logical order.

the lemon

The lemon I hold in my hand is an oval, bright yellow fruit
about the size and weight of a large egg. Its shape is about the
shape an egg would be if it had two large ends, except that at each
end there is a small bump, like a nipple, perhaps a quarter-inch
high and a half-inch across.

Unlike the egg, the lemon is resilient: I can push a dent into
it with my thumb, and when I remove my thumb the dent disap-
pears. When I drop the lemon, it bounces a little, though not as
much as a rubber ball. The sound it makes is a solid "thud." The
surface is shiny but not smooth. It is pocked with tiny round dents
about the size a dull pencil point might make. These dents are not
arranged in any definite pattern, but cover the surface fairly evenly.
The surface is slightly oily to the touch and seems to have no taste.
It does have a smell, however, that I find hard to describe: a little
like fresh leaves or grass, with a slightly acid tinge. By driving my
thumbnail into it, I can make a small break into which a little clear,
oily liquid oozes, followed by a much stronger, fruity smell.

Using my nail more strongly, I find I can tear up a bit of the
skin, uncovering a spongy, white layer underneath. The outer,
bright yellow layer is very thin; the second, white layer seems about
a sixteenth of an inch thick and nearly dry. The little dents on the
outside come through the yellow layer and into the white layer as
small, circular cones that let the light through. The inside of the
skin smells much stronger than the outside, with a sharp odor like
lemon extract.

As I tear more of the skin away, I find that the inside of the lemon is ribbed with bulges about three-quarters of an inch across, running from end to end and hinting that the inside has a definite structure. In order to find out what the structure is, I slice the lemon straight across with a knife and find the inside so juicy that the knife blade comes out dripping. This juice is nearly clear, with a strong, fresh smell and a sour taste. It is not at all oily like the outer skin, and its smell makes my mouth water.

There is indeed a definite structure to the inside. The juice is held in ten sections separated by some sort of membrane or skin. These sections are shaped somewhat like brazil nuts, with the sharp edges toward the center of the lemon and the curved edges forming the bulges I first observed. Where these sections are cut across, they fit together like the slices of a pie. The small core of skin from which they radiate is hollow.

Since most of the juice has not run out of the lemon where I cut it but remains inside the halves, I guess that there must be smaller compartments within these wedge-shaped sections that are still holding it. As I examine the sliced surface more closely, I find that this is true; the juice is held in tiny podlike sacs of transparent membrane. Only the juice in the sacs the knife cut through has run out. However, if I pick up half the lemon and squeeze it, more and more of these little sacs burst and more juice runs out. Holding it close to my ear as I do this, I can hear a kind of squeaking sound made by the bursting sacs.

On the inside of the wedges, next to the hollow core, are a few whitish seeds of different sizes, the largest about an eighth of an inch long. They are shaped like miniature lemons. They are not very hard and can be cut in two; they are solid and white, with a thin, greenish skin.

When I squeeze the juice from the lemon halves into a glass, I find it is somewhat pulpy, probably because the sacs have still smaller compartments inside them to hold the juice. The membrane dividing the lemon into sections remains in place inside the squeezed-out skin.

One of the nipples that was at either end of the lemon has a small green stem sticking out of it. When I pull this off, there seems to be a kind of spongy tube leading from it to the hollow core inside, hinting that water may get into the lemon by this route while it is growing. The opposite nipple is a solid, spongy white material like the second layer of skin and probably serves as an anchor for that end of the tube.

I find that the juice in the glass, mixed with sugar, ice, and a large amount of water, makes a refreshing drink.

sketching assignment

This is an on-the-spot description assignment that asks you to sketch with words the same way an art student sketches with charcoal or pencil. If conditions permit, it may be done during class, outside, with the instructor looking over your shoulder now and then to make suggestions.

Select a tree or any interesting large object that is available—a building, statue, flower bed, old piece of machinery, abandoned car—whatever is available that has some varied form and texture to it. Describe it rapidly, following a clear order but not trying to cover every detail, just giving an impression of those features that seem most characteristic.

At the Gudgers'

JAMES AGEE

the supper

The biscuits are large and shapeless, not cut round, and are pale, not tanned, and are dusty with flour. They taste of flour and soda and damp salt and fill the mouth stickily. They are better with butter, and still better with butter and jam. The butter is pallid, soft, and unsalted, about the texture of cold-cream; it seems to taste delicately of wood and wet cloth; and it tastes 'weak.' The jam is loose, of little berries, full of light raspings of the tongue; it tastes a deep sweet purple tepidly watered, with a very faint sheen of a sourness as of iron. Field peas are olive-brown, the shape of lentils, about twice the size. Their taste is a cross between lentils and boiled beans; their broth is bright with seasoning of pork, and of this also they taste. The broth is soaked up in bread. The meat is a bacon, granular with salt, soaked in the grease of its frying: there is very little lean meat in it. What there is is nearly as tough as rind; the rest is pure salted stringy fat. The eggs taste of pork too. They are fried in it on both sides until none of the broken yolk runs, are heavily salted and peppered while they fry, so that they come to table nearly black, very heavy, rinded with crispness, nearly as dense as steaks. Of milk I hardly know how to say; it is skimmed, blue-lighted; to a city palate its warmth and odor are somehow dirty and at the same time vital, a little as if one were drinking blood. There is even in so clean a household as this an odor of pork, of sweat, so subtle it seems to get into the very metal of the cooking-pans beyond any removal of scrubbing, and to sweat itself out of newly washed cups; it is all over the house and all through your skin and clothing at all times, yet as you bring each piece of food to your mouth it is so much more noticeable, if you are not used to it, that a quiet little fight takes place on your palate and in the pit of your stomach; and it seems to be this odor, and a sort of wateriness and discouraged tepidity, which combine to make the food seem unclean, sticky, and sallow with some invisible sort of disease, yet this is the odor and consistency and temper and these are true tastes of home; I know this even of myself; and much as my reflexes are twitching in refusal of each mouthful a true homesick and simple fondness for it has so strong hold of me that in fact there is no fight to speak of and no faking of enjoyment at all.

---

1. "The Supper" is taken from a book by James Agee with photographs by Walker Evans. What parts of the description could be communicated by a good photograph? What parts could not?
2. How many senses does Agee employ? Point out an example of each.
3. Kinesthetic sensations seem to be the ones least noted. Can you find any that are suggested?
4. What are some aspects of the scene Agee might have observed but which he has not written about here?
5. Where has Agee used analogy to make his description clear?
6. What emotions do you find evoked by this description? Why do you feel these particular emotions?

A Study of Two Pears

WALLACE STEVENS

I

Opusculum paedagogum.*
The pears are not viols,
Nudes or bottles.
They resemble nothing else.

II

They are yellow forms
Composed of curves
Bulging toward the base.
They are touched red.

III

They are not flat surfaces
Having curved outlines.
They are round
tapering toward the top.

IV

In the way they are modelled
There are bits of blue.
A hard dry leaf hangs
From the stem.

V

The yellow glistens.
It glistens with various yellows,
Citrons, oranges and greens
Flowering over the skin.

VI

The shadows of the pears
are blobs on the green cloth.
The pears are not seen
As the observer wills.

---

* A small instructive work.

1. Why does Wallace Stevens find it necessary to say that the pears are *not* flat surfaces with curved outlines?
2. Do pears in any way resemble viols, nudes, or bottles? How are they different from these things? What is Stevens trying to show us by insisting upon what the pears are *not*?
3. Stevens deals mostly with the exact appearance of the pears. Does he suggest any data from other senses? Where?
4. What do you think is the general purpose of the poem, since it claims to be instructive? What is the poem's lesson?
5. What further data could you give about the pears that would continue or emphasize this lesson?

1. In "A Study of Two Pears" Wallace Stevens makes an allusion to painters who abstract the outline forms of pears and draw analogies, probably false, between them and viols, nudes, or bottles. Do you find that Mu Ch'i has falsified his persimmons in a similar way? Why, or why not?

2. There is a relationship between the shade of each persimmon—its lightness or darkness—and its shape. What is this relationship? What does it communicate?

3. Which persimmon is heaviest? Which lightest in weight? How can you tell?

4. Which is greenest? Which ripest? How has the artist communicated these facts?

5. What kind of surface are the persimmons resting on? How is this surface positioned in relation to the eye of the observer? Why did the artist place them toward the bottom of the picture rather than in the center?

6. Imagine yourself painting an equally simple picture of several books that show different degrees of use, from a new one that has never been opened to one with a broken spine and worn binding. How would you communicate these differences?

PLATE II

SIX PERSIMMONS: Mu Ch'i. With the permission of Ryoko-in, Daitokuji

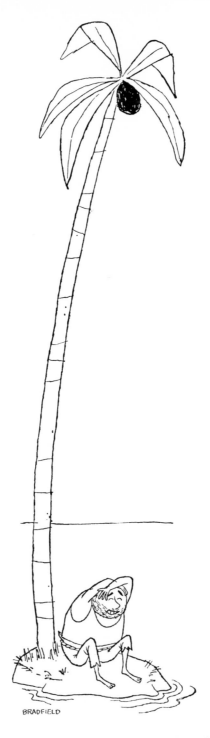

BRADFIELD

3

being

aware

of your

surroundings

The human mind is not a suitcase that will burst from being overfilled. It is more like a computer that builds itself as it goes along, constantly adding new circuits to handle new information. The more information it has, no matter how seemingly useless, the more problems it can solve. Nothing is irrelevant. The mind's capacity to absorb the chaos of experience and make sense of it is unlimited. Intelligence is observing and connecting observations.

As you go through your day, remind yourself every now and then to observe something you haven't noticed before. Look for qualities you have missed: shadows, colors, textures, sounds, and smells. Check out the weather, even when it's not bothering you. Slow down a little while you are eating and taste your food. (If it tastes so bad you don't want to slow down, maybe you shouldn't be eating it.) Work at being in contact with your surroundings, making connections, seeing similarities and differences, observing qualities that unify.

class exercise

In Unit 1 you used the senses one by one, and in Unit 2 you concentrated your senses on one small object. Now expand the scope of your observation, while at the same time keeping your impressions *unified* around central themes. Begin looking at your surroundings as a whole, putting the details together into one complete picture.

Look around the room you are in now, keeping all your senses alert. Decide what feeling the whole scene gives you, your dominant impression of it. Find a word that embodies that impression. Then look (and listen and smell) for the details that caused you to feel that way. You could concentrate on the room itself, or on the people in it, or the two together. For instance, you could have the impression that the room is "old and well-used" and then observe as many details as possible that gave you the impression: worn flooring, chipped and carved desks, cracked paint, and so on. Or you could find the scene "bustling" and note all the busy activities of people around you, from chewing gum to crumpling sheets of paper.

Be prepared to name your impression and support it with several good examples.

writing assignment

1. Spend at least an hour in one place, writing sentences that describe what you are aware of at each moment, much as you did in Unit 1. An hour may seem a long time to spend in this way, but if you concentrate on your sensations for this length of time, you will become aware of things you hadn't noticed before. Keep busy; don't let your mind drift away from the scene around you.
2. As you go along, see if any unified impression is making itself felt. If so, look for more data to reinforce that impression.
3. Do not revise. Just keep observing until you have a substantial number of sentences. Check now and then to see if you are using all your senses.

unity

When you sat for an hour recording your sensations, you were having, in some respects, a *unified* experience. What made it unified? For one thing, the fact that it took place at one time and in one location. But perhaps you can find another, more significant kind of unity in the experience, an inner unity. Look at the list of things you were aware of during the hour and see if you can find some kind of pattern. What kinds of things do you seem to be most aware of? For example, some people might find themselves repeatedly recording their awareness of irritating noises; others might notice visual patterns or colors; and so on. See if you can find three or four sorts of sense impressions you were especially aware of during the hour.

When you have stated one thing that a number of examples have in common, you have made a *generalization*. For instance, you might have seen a dozen cats, in different places and at different times, show enthusiasm for fish; you could *generalize*, then, that cats like fish. Let us say that during your hour you wrote, "I notice a bird flying overhead," "There is a man walking across the street," and "A tree branch is swaying in the wind." If you found such observations in the majority, you could generalize, "I seem to be aware of moving objects more than anything else." This generalization represents a kind of unity given to your experience by your own nature.

Very likely there are several kinds of things that you noticed. Your generalization might go like this: "I seem to be aware of moving objects, loud or sharp sounds, feelings of things touching my skin, and sensations inside my body."

In order to write about an experience, you need to find the generalizations that give it unity, state them, and then give the specific examples that first led you to make these generalizations. In giving the examples, you are showing the reader why you think as you do.

class writing assignment

Organize your sensory observations, giving them as much unity as you can without adding to them. First, write two or three sentences explaining where you were when you made the observations, what time of day it was, what the conditions were, and so on. Then state your generalization in one sentence if possible.

Now, begin a new paragraph telling about the things you noticed most often. Try to remember more about them and how you noticed them, and write a sentence or two about each. Then in another paragraph tell about what you noticed next most often, and so on until you have included all the things you observed.

Finally, before you turn the paper in, look over these several kinds of observations and see if you can discover a generalization about them. Do all these observations have something in common? If you can find this over-all generalization, write it at the end as a summary; if not (and there may be nothing in common to be found), you may want to repeat your original generalization or make a statement about what you learned about yourself while doing the exercise.

sketching assignment

Like the sketching assignment in Unit 2, this one may be done out-doors or in the classroom. But instead of picking out an object to sketch, try to give a quick, lively impression of your surroundings. Again, work from large to small, putting in the general features of the scene first and working down to the smaller things. Be selective: you can't include all the details in a sketch, so choose the more significant ones. Use as many senses as you can.

Big Two-Hearted River: Part II

ERNEST HEMINGWAY

In the morning the sun was up and the tent was starting to get hot. Nick crawled out under the mosquito netting stretched across the mouth of the tent, to look at the morning. The grass was wet on his hands as he came out. He held his trousers and his shoes in his hand. The sun was just up over the hill. There was the meadow, the river and the swamp. There were birch trees in the green of the swamp on the other side of the river.

The river was clear and smoothly fast in the early morning. Down about two hundred yards were three logs all the way across the stream. They made the water smooth and deep above them. As Nick watched, a mink crossed the river on the logs and went into the swamp. Nick was excited. He was excited by the early morning and the river. He was really too hurried to eat breakfast, but he knew he must. He built a little fire and put on the coffee pot.

While the water was heating in the pot he took an empty bottle and went down over the edge of the high ground to the meadow. The meadow was wet with dew and Nick wanted to catch grasshoppers for bait before the sun dried the grass. He found plenty of grasshoppers. They were at the base of the grass stems. Sometimes they clung to a grass stem. They were cold and wet with the dew, and could not jump until the sun warmed them. Nick picked them up, taking only the medium-sized brown ones, and put them into the bottle. He turned over a log and just under the shelter of the edge were several hundred hoppers. It was a grasshopper lodging house. Nick put about fifty of the medium browns into the bottle. While he was picking up the hoppers the others warmed in the sun and commenced to hop away. They flew when they hopped. At first they made one flight and stayed stiff when they landed, as though they were dead.

Nick knew that by the time he was through with breakfast they would be as lively as ever. Without dew in the grass it would take him all day to catch a bottle of good grasshoppers and he would have to crush many of them, slamming at them with his hat. He washed his hands at the stream. He was excited to be near it. Then he walked up to the tent. The hoppers were already jumping stiffly in the grass. In the bottle, warmed by the sun, they were jumping in a mass. Nick put in a pine stick as a cork. It plugged the mouth of the bottle enough, so the hoppers could not get out and left plenty of air passage.

He had rolled the log back and knew he could get grasshoppers there every morning.

Nick laid the bottle full of jumping grasshoppers against a pine trunk. Rapidly he mixed some buckwheat flour with water and stirred it smooth, one cup of flour, one cup of water. He put a handful of coffee in the pot and dipped a lump of grease out of a can and slid it sputtering across the hot skillet. On the smoking skillet he poured smoothly the buckwheat batter. It spread like lava, the grease spitting sharply. Around the edges the buckwheat cake began to firm, then brown, then crisp. The surface was bubbling slowly to porousness. Nick pushed under the browned surface with a fresh pine chip. He shook the skillet sideways and the cake was loose on the surface. I won't try and flop it, he thought. He slid the chip of clean wood all the way under the cake, and flopped it over onto its surface. It sputtered in the pan.

When it was cooked Nick regreased the skillet. He used all the batter. It made another big flapjack and one smaller one.

Nick ate a big flapjack and one smaller one, covered with apple butter. He put apple butter on the third cake, folded it over twice, wrapped it in oiled paper and put it in his shirt pocket. He put the apple butter jar back in the pack and cut bread for two sandwiches.

In the pack he found a big onion. He sliced it in two and peeled the silky outer skin. Then he cut one half into slices and made onion sandwiches. He wrapped them in oiled paper and buttoned them in the other pocket of his khaki shirt. He turned the skillet upside down on the grill, drank the coffee, sweetened and yellow brown with condensed milk in it, and tidied up the camp. It was a good camp.

Nick took his fly rod out of the leather rod-case, jointed it, and shoved the rod-case back into the tent. He put on the reel and threaded the line through the guides. He had to hold it from hand to hand, as he threaded it, or it would slip back through its own weight. It was a heavy, double tapered fly line. Nick had paid eight dollars for it a long time ago.

It was made heavy to lift back in the air and come forward flat and heavy and straight to make it possible to cast a fly which has no weight. Nick opened the aluminum leader box. The leaders were coiled between the damp flannel pads. Nick had wet the pads at the water cooler on the train up to St. Ignace. In the damp pads the gut leaders had softened and Nick unrolled one and tied it by a loop at the end to the heavy fly line. He fastened a hook on the end of the leader. It was a small hook; very thin and springy.

Nick took it from his hook book, sitting with the rod across his lap. He tested the knot and the spring of the rod by pulling the line taut. It was a good feeling. He was careful not to let the hook bite into his finger.

He started down to the stream, holding his rod, the bottle of grasshoppers hung from his neck by a thong tied in half hitches around the neck of the bottle. His landing net hung by a hook from his belt. Over his shoulder was a long flour sack tied at each corner into an ear. The cord went over his shoulder. The sack flapped against his legs.

Nick felt awkward and professionally happy with all his equipment hanging from him. The grasshopper bottle swung against his chest. In his shirt the breast pockets bulged against him with the lunch and his fly book.

He stepped into the stream. It was a shock. His trousers clung tight to his legs. His shoes felt the gravel. The water was a rising cold shock.

Rushing, the current sucked against his legs. Where he stepped in, the water was over his knees. He waded with the current. The gravel slid under his shoes. He looked down at the swirl of water below each leg and tipped up the bottle to get a grasshopper.

The first grasshopper gave a jump in the neck of the bottle and went out into the water. He was sucked under in a whirl by Nick's right leg and came to the surface a little way down stream. He floated rapidly, kicking. In a quick circle, breaking the smooth surface of the water, he disappeared. A trout had taken him.

Another hopper poked his face out of the bottle. His antennae wavered. He was getting his front legs out of the bottle to jump. Nick took him by the head and held him while he threaded the slim hook under his chin, down through his thorax and into the last segments of his abdomen. The grasshopper took hold of the hook with his feet, spitting tobacco juice on it. Nick dropped him into the water.

Holding the rod in his right hand he let out line against the pull of the grasshopper in the current. He stripped off line from the reel with his left hand and let it run free. He could see the hopper in the little waves of the current. It went out of sight.

There was a tug on the line. Nick pulled against the taut line. It was his first strike. Holding the now living rod across the current, he brought in the line with his left hand. The rod bent in jerks, the trout pumping against the current. Nick knew it was a small one. He lifted the rod straight up in the air. It bowed with the pull.

He saw the trout in the water jerking with his head and body against the shifting tangent of the line in the stream.

Nick took the line in his left hand and pulled the trout, thumping tiredly against the current, to the surface. His back was mottled the clear, water-over-gravel color, his side flashing in the sun. The rod under his right arm, Nick stooped, dipping his right hand into the current. He held the trout, never still, with his moist right hand, while he unhooked the barb from his mouth, then dropped him back into the stream.

He hung unsteadily in the current, then settled to the bottom beside a stone. Nick reached down his hand to touch him, his arm to the elbow under water. The trout was steady in the moving stream, resting on the gravel, beside a stone. As Nick's fingers touched him, touched his smooth, cool, underwater feeling he was gone, gone in a shadow across the bottom of the stream.

He's all right, Nick thought. He was only tired.

He had wet his hand before he touched the trout, so he would not disturb the delicate mucus that covered him. If a trout was touched with a dry hand, a white fungus attacked the unprotected spot. Years before when he had fished crowded streams, with fly fishermen ahead of him and behind him, Nick had again and again come on dead trout, furry with white fungus, drifted against a rock, or floating belly up in some pool. Nick did not like to fish with other men on the river. Unless they were of your party, they spoiled it.

He wallowed down the stream, above his knees in the current, through the fifty yards of shallow water above the pile of logs that crossed the stream. He did not rebait his hook and held it in his hand as he waded. He was certain he could catch small trout in the shallows, but he did not want them. There would be no big trout in the shallows this time of day.

Now the water deepened up his thighs sharply and coldly. Ahead was the smooth dammed-back flood of water above the logs. The water was smooth and dark; on the left, the lower edge of the meadow; on the right the swamp.

Nick leaned back against the current and took a hopper from the bottle. He threaded the hopper on the hook and spat on him for good luck. Then he pulled several yards of line from the reel and tossed the hopper out ahead onto the fast, dark water. It floated down towards the logs, then the weight of the line pulled the bait under the surface. Nick held the rod in his right hand, letting the line run out through his fingers.

There was a long tug. Nick struck and the rod came alive and dangerous, bent double, the line tightening, coming out of water, tightening, all in a heavy, dangerous, steady pull. Nick felt the moment when the leader would break if the strain increased and let the line go.

The reel ratcheted into a mechanical shriek as the line went out in a rush. Too fast. Nick could not check it, the line rushing out, the reel note rising as the line ran out.

With the core of the reel showing, his heart feeling stopped with the excitement, leaning back against the current that mounted icily his thighs, Nick thumbed the reel hard with his left hand. It was awkward getting his thumb inside the fly reel frame.

As he put on pressure the line tightened into sudden hardness and beyond the logs a huge trout went high out of water. As he jumped, Nick lowered the tip of the rod. But he felt, as he dropped the tip to ease the strain, the moment when the strain was too great; the hardness too tight. Of course, the leader had broken. There was no mistaking the feeling when all spring left the line and it became dry and hard. Then it went slack.

His mouth dry, his heart down, Nick reeled in. He had never seen so big a trout. There was a heaviness, a power not to be held, and then the bulk of him, as he jumped. He looked as broad as a salmon.

Nick's hand was shaky. He reeled in slowly. The thrill had been too much. He felt, vaguely, a little sick, as though it would be better to sit down.

The leader had broken where the hook was tied to it. Nick took it in his hand. He thought of the trout somewhere on the bottom, holding himself steady over the gravel, far down below the light, under the logs, with the hook in his jaw. Nick knew the trout's teeth would cut through the snell of the hook. The hook would imbed itself in his jaw. He'd bet the trout was angry. Anything that size would be angry. That was a trout. He had been solidly hooked. Solid as a rock. He felt like a rock, too, before he started off. By God, he was a big one. By God, he was the biggest one I ever heard of.

Nick climbed out onto the meadow and stood, water running down his trousers and out of his shoes, his shoes squelchy. He went over and sat on the logs. He did not want to rush his sensations any.

He wriggled his toes in the water, in his shoes, and got out a cigarette from his breast pocket. He lit it and tossed the match into the fast water below the logs. A tiny trout rose at the match, as it swung around in the fast current. Nick laughed. He would finish the cigarette.

He sat on the logs, smoking, drying in the sun, the sun warm on his back, the river shallow ahead entering the woods, curving into the woods, shallows, light glittering, big water-smooth rocks, cedars along the bank and white birches, the logs warm in the sun, smooth to sit on, without bark, gray to the touch; slowly the feeling of disappointment left him. It went away slowly, the feeling of disappointment that came sharply after the thrill that made his shoulders ache. It was all right now. His rod lying out on the logs, Nick tied a new hook on the leader, pulling the gut tight until it grimped into itself in a hard knot.

He baited up, then picked up the rod and walked to the far end of the logs to get into the water, where it was not too deep. Under and beyond the logs was a deep pool. Nick walked around the shallow shelf near the swamp shore until he came out on the shallow bed of the stream.

On the left, where the meadow ended and the woods began, a great elm tree was uprooted. Gone over in a storm, it lay back into the woods, its roots clotted with dirt, grass growing in them, rising a solid bank beside the stream. The river cut to the edge of the uprooted tree. From where Nick stood he could see deep channels, like ruts, cut in the shallow bed of the stream by the flow of the current. Pebbly where he stood and pebbly and full of boulders beyond; where it curved near the tree roots, the bed of the stream was marly and between the ruts of deep water green weed fronds swung in the current.

Nick swung the rod back over his shoulder and forward, and the line, curving forward, laid the grasshopper down on one of the deep channels in the weeds. A trout struck and Nick hooked him.

Holding the rod far out toward the uprooted tree and sloshing backward in the current, Nick worked the trout, plunging, the rod bending alive, out of the danger of the weeds into the open river. Holding the rod, pumping alive against the current, Nick brought the trout in. He rushed, but always came, the spring of the rod yielding to the rushes, sometimes jerking under the water, but always bringing him in. Nick eased downstream with the rushes. The rod above his head he led the trout over the net, then lifted.

The trout hung heavy in the net, mottled trout back and silver sides in the meshes. Nick unhooked him; heavy sides, good to hold, big undershot jaw, and slipped him, heaving and big sliding, into the long sack that hung from his shoulders in the water.

Nick spread the mouth of the sack against the current and it filled, heavy with water. He held it up, the bottom in the stream, and the water poured out through the sides. Inside at the bottom was the big trout, alive in the water.

Nick moved downstream. The sack out ahead of him sunk heavy in the water, pulling from his shoulders.

It was getting hot, the sun hot on the back of his neck.

Nick had one good trout. He did not care about getting many trout. Now the stream was shallow and wide. There were trees along both banks. The trees of the left bank made short shadows on the current in the forenoon sun. Nick knew there were trout in each shadow. In the afternoon, after the sun had crossed toward the hills, the trout would be in the cool shadows on the other side of the stream.

The very biggest ones would lie up close to the bank. You could always pick them up there on the Black. When the sun was down they all moved out into the current. Just when the sun made the water blinding in the glare before it went down, you were liable to strike a big trout anywhere in the current. It was almost impossible to fish then, the surface of the water was blinding as a mirror in the sun. Of course, you could fish upstream, but in a stream like the Black, or this, you had to wallow against the current and in a deep place, the water piled up on you. It was no fun to fish upstream with this much current.

Nick moved along through the shallow stretch watching the banks for deep holes. A beech tree grew close beside the river, so that the branches hung down into the water. The stream went back in under the leaves. There were always trout in a place like that.

Nick did not care about fishing that hole. He was sure he would get hooked in the branches.

It looked deep though. He dropped the grasshopper so the current took it under water, back in under the overhanging branch. The line pulled hard and Nick struck. The trout threshed heavily, half out of water in the leaves and branches. The line was caught. Nick pulled hard and the trout was off. He reeled in and holding the hook in his hand, walked down the stream.

Ahead, close to the left bank, was a big log. Nick saw it was hollow; pointing up river the current entered it smoothly, only a little ripple spread each side of the log. The water was deepening. The top of the hollow log was gray and dry. It was partly in the shadow.

Nick took the cork out of the grasshopper bottle and a hopper clung to it. He picked him off, hooked him and tossed him out. He held the rod far out so that the hopper on the water moved into the current flowing into the hollow log. Nick lowered the rod and the hopper floated in. There was a heavy strike. Nick swung the rod against the pull. It felt as though he were hooked into the log itself, except for the live feeling.

He tried to force the fish out into the current. It came, heavily.

The line went slack and Nick thought the trout was gone. Then he saw him, very near, in the current, shaking his head, trying to get the hook out. His mouth was clamped shut. He was fighting the hook in the clear flowing current.

Looping in the line with his left hand, Nick swung the rod to make the line taut and tried to lead the trout toward the net, but he was gone, out of sight, the line pumping. Nick fought him against the current, letting him thump in the water against the spring of the rod. He shifted the rod to his left hand, worked the trout upstream, holding his weight, fighting on the rod, and then let him down into the net. He lifted him clear of the water, a heavy half circle in the net, the net dripping, unhooked him and slid him into the sack.

He spread the mouth of the sack and looked down in at the two big trout alive in the water.

Through the deepening water, Nick waded over to the hollow log. He took the sack off, over his head, the trout flopping as it came out of water, and hung it so the trout were deep in the water. Then he pulled himself up on the log and sat, the water from his trousers and boots running down into the stream. He laid his rod down, moved along to the shady end of the log and took the sandwiches out of his pocket. He dipped the sandwiches in the cold water. The current carried away the crumbs. He ate the sandwiches and dipped his hat full of water to drink, the water running out through his hat just ahead of his drinking.

It was cool in the shade, sitting on the log. He took a cigarette out and struck a match to light it. The match sunk into the gray wood, making a tiny furrow. Nick leaned over the side of the log, found a hard place and lit the match. He sat smoking and watching the river.

Ahead the river narrowed and went into a swamp. The river became smooth and deep and the swamp looked solid with cedar trees, their trunks close together, their branches solid. It would not be possible to walk through a swamp like that. The branches grew so low. You would have to keep almost level with the ground to move at all. You could not crash through the branches. That must be why the animals that lived in swamps were built the way they were, Nick thought.

He wished he had brought something to read. He felt like reading. He did not feel like going on into the swamp. He looked down the river. A big cedar slanted all the way across the stream. Beyond that the river went into the swamp.

Nick did not want to go in there now. He felt a reaction against deep wading with the water deepening up under his armpits, to hook big trout in places impossible to land them. In the swamp the banks were bare, the big cedars came together overhead, the sun did not come through, except in patches; in the fast deep water, in the half light, the fishing would be tragic. In the swamp fishing was a tragic adventure. Nick did not want it. He did not want to go down the stream any further today.

He took out his knife, opened it and stuck it in the log. Then he pulled up the sack, reached into it and brought out one of the trout. Holding him near the tail, hard to hold, alive, in his hand, he whacked him against the log. The trout quivered, rigid. Nick laid him on the log in the shade and broke the neck of the other fish the same way. He laid them side by side on the log. They were fine trout.

Nick cleaned them, slitting them from the vent to the tip of the jaw. All the insides and the gills and tongue came out in one piece. They were both males; long gray-white strips of milt, smooth and clean. All the insides clean and compact, coming out all together. Nick tossed the offal ashore for the minks to find.

He washed the trout in the stream. When he held them back up in the water they looked like live fish. Their color was not gone yet. He washed his hands and dried them on the log. Then he laid the trout on the sack spread out on the log, rolled them up in it, tied the bundle and put it in the landing net. His knife was still standing, blade stuck in the log. He cleaned it on the wood and put it in his pocket.

Nick stood up on the log, holding his rod, the landing net hanging heavy, then stepped into the water and splashed ashore. He climbed the bank and cut up into the woods, toward the high ground. He was going back to camp. He looked back. The river just showed through the trees. There were plenty of days coming when he could fish the swamp.

---

1. Hemingway employs all the senses to make Nick's experience vivid to the reader. Where do you find the sense of hearing used?
2. Pick out the passages where Hemingway communicates the kinesthetic sense, the feeling of bodily movement, or the sense of the force, weight, or balance of things the body is in contact with.
3. Where do you find use of the sense of touch, the feel of things against the skin?
4. Are any smells suggested?
5. What senses does Hemingway seem to be most aware of? Least aware of?
6. What unifying themes hold the story together? Which of those themes are related to Nick's feelings about his surroundings? How are his observations colored by his feelings? Point out examples.
7. What are some aspects or details of the scene that an observer in a different mood might notice and that Hemingway omits?

Root Cellar

THEODORE ROETHKE

Nothing would sleep in that cellar, dank as a ditch,
Bulbs broke out of boxes hunting for chinks in the dark,
Shoots dangled and drooped,
Lolling obscenely from mildewed crates,
Hung down long yellow evil necks, like tropical snakes.
And what a congress of stinks!—
Roots ripe as old bait,
Pulpy stems, rank, silo-rich,
Leaf-mould, manure, lime, piled against slippery planks.
Nothing would give up life:
Even the dirt kept breathing a small breath.

1. A root cellar is primarily used to store root vegetables and bulbs. What words or expressions in the poem would enable you to deduce this fact?
2. What senses does Theodore Roethke appeal to directly in the poem?
3. What sense impressions does he evoke indirectly?
4. What are some comparisons or analogies that are applied directly? What are some that are implied by the words chosen?
5. What is the unifying impression that binds the details together? Point out how some of the details contribute to making this impression a strong one.

1. *Cafe Terrace at Night* is an Impressionist painting, emphasizing light rather than form. At the same time, it seems to convey the joy of someone who, at a certain moment in a certain place, becomes intensely aware of the surroundings. What are some of the effects to be enjoyed in the scene?
2. What experiences of movement or touch are suggested by the picture? What sounds and smells?
3. One part of the scene—one that we are not usually conscious of when we are in the city—is brought out vividly. What is it? How does its representation here affect our feeling about the scene as a whole?
4. What themes, and what qualities, unify the scene?

PLATE III

CAFÉ TERRACE AT NIGHT: Vincent van Gogh. National Museum Kröller-Müller. Otterlo, Netherlands

4

observing

a scene

When you first enter a room where a party is going on, your impression is one of confusion. But if you stand and observe unnoticed, soon the confusion begins to resolve itself into understandable patterns which you could describe clearly. While you could not describe everything that is going on, you could select those details that would communicate a fairly accurate idea of what the scene is like and what sorts of people are involved.

If you were to write a description of such a scene, your main problems would be continuity and economy. To make clear where and when each thing was happening, you would have to keep in mind the layout of the room and the sequence of time, using such expressions as "over near the fireplace" and "meanwhile, at the kitchen door." And you would have to select those details that give a vivid impression without boring your reader with too many examples. Like the painters of Plates I through V, you would use details that are typical and telling, that stand for the whole.

When writing about a complex subject, write as clearly and economically as you can. Keep your reader oriented, but keep things moving too. The descriptive essay "Laundromat" in this unit is a good example of this kind of writing.

Here are some suggestions of places where you might find lively activity to observe and describe:

> a party
> a bargain basement sale
> a garage sale

a bus or train station
a city bus
an auction
a monkey cage at the zoo

One caution: sports do not work well for this assignment. The action is organized according to rules, and we tend to see it only in relation to the pattern we expect.

class exercise

Variations of the following experiment are sometimes used in psychology classes, with interesting results.

Two volunteers from the class leave the room for a few minutes and plan a brief series of rapid actions, such as a mock pursuit and fight or a bewildering exchange of objects from hand to hand (a pile of books will do). They reenter the room without warning, go through the actions (for no more than ten seconds), and leave quickly. Then, members of the class try to agree on what they saw.

writing assignment

1. Find a place, such as one of those suggested above, where a number of people are engaged in various activities. Carry your notebook and pen.
2. Take notes of what people are doing and what their relationships are with each other. Be sure to note briefly all the following:
    a. *Where* the people are and what position each is in (sitting, standing straight, bending over, walking rapidly, and so on).
    b. *How* each person looks (age, dress, expression, and so on).
    c. *When* each person is acting (meanwhile, a moment later, afterwards, and so on).
    d. *What* each person is doing at that moment (pointing, looking around, and so on).
3. Remain for a short time, not more than fifteen or twenty minutes. Don't try to write everything down; trust your memory for many of the details, but write down enough clues so that you won't forget them.
4. As soon as possible, sit down and organize your description of the scene, adding the details you haven't already written about. Describe the setting briefly; then tell what you saw in a time sequence, from beginning to end.
5. Use as many of the senses as you can; include sounds and smells as well as sights.

economy

Economy means simply saying more with fewer words. This can be done in two ways:

First, you can combine the where, what, how, and when of an action into one sentence: "Meanwhile, bent over the lingerie counter, a red-faced old woman in a gray coat is grabbing a petticoat out of the hands of the girl across from her."

Second, you can select details and actions that are typical and will stand for others. If you used the above sentence, you would not need another like it telling how someone else is grabbing something away from someone.

Of course it should go without saying that economy means leaving out words that don't function. But use moderation in applying this principle. Don't let a passion for economy make your writing sound like a telegram.

class writing assignment

Rewrite your description of a scene for economy. Cull out unnecessary adjectives and adverbs. If you find sentences that are just word exercises, throw them out. See if you can reduce the number of words by one-third without omitting any of the information in your original version and without making your style sound jerky.

Laundromat

SUSAN SHEEHAN

It is one-forty-five on a cold, winter-gray Friday afternoon. There are about a dozen people inside the Apthorp Self-Service Laundromat, between Seventy-seventh and Seventy-eighth Streets on the west side of Broadway. The laundromat is a long, narrow room with seventeen Wascomat washing machines—twelve of them the size that takes two quarters, five of them the size that takes three—lined up on one side of the room, and nine dryers on the other. At the back of the alleylike room, four vending machines dispense an assortment of laundry supplies, which cost ten cents an item, to the younger customers; the older customers (more cost-conscious? more far-sighted?) bring their own soap powders or liquids from home in small boxes or plastic bottles. On the laundromat's drab painted walls are a clock and a few signs: "No Tintex Allowed," "Last Wash: 10 P.M.," "Not Responsible for Personal Property," "Pack As Full As You Want." On the drab linoleum floor are two trash cans (filled to the brim), a wooden bench, three shabby chairs (occupied), and a table, on which a pretty young black girl is folding clothes, and at which a dour, heavyset black woman in her sixties is eating lunch out of a grease-stained brown paper bag. The heavyset woman has brought no clothes with her to the laundromat. The regular patrons believe she has nowhere else to go that is warm, and accept her presence. On a previous visit, she had tossed a chicken bone at someone, wordlessly, and the gesture had been accepted, too, as a reasonable protest against the miserableness of her life.

Half the people in the laundromat have two washing machines going at once. The machines keep them busy inserting coins, stuffing in clothes, and adding detergents, bleaches, and fabric softeners at various stages of the cycle (twenty-five minutes). The newly washed clothes are retrieved from the washing machines and transferred, in a swooping motion, across the narrow corridor to the dryers. No one dares leave the laundromat to attend to other errands while his clothes are drying (at the rate of ten cents for ten minutes, with most things requiring twenty or thirty minutes), because it is known that clothes that have been left to their own devices in the dryers have disappeared in a matter of five minutes.

A middle-aged man whose clothes are in a small washing machine is standing in front of it reading a sports column in the *News*, but most of the other patrons who are between putting-in and taking-out chores seem to be mesmerized by the kaleidoscopic activity inside the machines. In one washing machine, a few striped sheets and pillowcases are spinning, creating a dizzying optical effect. In another, a lively clothes dance is taking place— three or four white shirts jitterbugging with six or eight pairs of gray socks. In a third, the clothes, temporarily obscured by a flurry of soapsuds, still cast a spell over their owner, who doesn't take her eyes off the round glass window in the front of the machine. The clothes in the dryers—here a few towels, there some men's work pants—seem to be free-falling, like sky divers drifting down to earth. The laundromat smells of a sweet mixture of soap and heat, and is noisy with the hum and whir of the machines. There is little conversation, but a woman suddenly tells her teen-age daughter (why isn't she in school at this hour?) that she takes the family's clothes to the self-service laundromat, rather than to the service laundromat right next door to it, where clothes can be dropped off in the morning and fetched in the evening, because everything at the service laundromat is washed in very hot water, which shrinks clothes that have a tendency to shrink. "Here you're supposed to be able to regulate the temperature of the water, but sometimes I punch the warm button and the water comes out ice-cold," she says. "Oh, well, you sort of have to expect things like that. The owner is very nice. He does the best he can."

A middle-aged man wearing a trenchcoat takes a load of children's clothes out of a large washing machine, folds them neatly, and runs out of the laundromat with the damp pile of girls' school dresses and boys' polo shirts and bluejeans over one arm. (What is his hurry? Will the children's clothes be hung up to dry on a rack at home?) A young Japanese boy, who is holding a book covered with a glossy Columbia University jacket, takes a few clothes out of a dryer. They include a lacy slip and a ruffled pale-pink nightgown with deep-pink rosebuds on it. (His girl's? His bride's? Or only his sister's? Is the nightgown's owner at work, putting him through school, or has she become a Liberated Woman and declined to go to the laundromat?) Two little children run down the narrow center aisle playing tag, chanting in Spanish, tripping over laundry carts, and meeting with scowls from the grownups. A washing machine goes on the blink. Someone goes next door to the service laundromat to summon the proprietor, who comes over immediately, climbs on top of the broken machine, reaches behind it, and restores it to working order in no time. He apologizes, in a Polish accent, to one of his regular customers for the scruffiness of the three chairs on the premises. "Six months ago, I brought in here three first-class chairs," he says. "Fifty-dollar chairs. The next day, they were gone."

People come and go, but the population inside the laundromat remains constant at about a dozen. The majority of the customers are blacks and Puerto Ricans who live in nearby tenements and welfare hotels. Most of the whites in the neighborhood live in apartment houses, and have washing machines and dryers in their apartments or in the basements of their buildings, or send their clothes out to local Chinese laundries. One white woman, a blonde in her fifties, says, to no one in particular, that she comes to the laundromat because the laundry room in the basement of her apartment building is not safe. "There have been incidents there," she says meaningfully. "I would love to have my own washing machine, but the landlord says he has to pay for the water, so he won't allow it. I hate coming here and wasting an hour in this depressing place. I wash everything I can by hand at home; that way, I only have to come here with the big things every two weeks, instead of every week. I dream of having my own washing machine and dryer. If I had my own machines, I could fix myself a cup of coffee and a bun, turn on the TV, and sit down in my easy chair; meanwhile, the clothes would all be getting done. It would be heaven."

---

1. No one has explained satisfactorily why we enjoy reading about things we are already familiar with, but we do, just as we enjoy looking at pictures of familiar scenes. Susan Sheehan knows we have seen laundromats. She keeps her description brief and economical to evoke the feel of the scene: if she were writing for people who had never been in a laundromat, what details and explanations would she have to add?
2. What senses does she appeal to? Could she have used any others to advantage?
3. What action verbs does she use?
4. How does she organize her description so it is easy to follow? (You may want to go back to Unit 2 for suggestions.)
5. What words and phrases help you to know where things are and where and when actions occur?

Auto Wreck

KARL SHAPIRO

Its quick soft silver bell beating, beating,
And down the dark one ruby flare
Pulsing out red light like an artery,
The ambulance at top speed floating down
Past beacons and illuminated clocks
Wings in a heavy curve, dips down,
And brakes speed, entering the crowd.
The doors leap open, emptying light;
Stretchers are laid out, the mangled lifted
And stowed into the little hospital.
Then the bell, breaking the hush, tolls once,
And the ambulance with its terrible cargo
Rocking, slightly rocking, moves away,
As the doors, an afterthought, are closed.

We are deranged, walking among the cops
Who sweep glass and are large and composed.
One is still making notes under the light.
One with a bucket douches ponds of blood
Into the street and gutter.
One hangs lanterns on the wrecks that cling,
Empty husks of locusts, to iron poles.

Our throats were tight as tourniquets,
Our feet were bound with splints, but now,
Like convalescents intimate and gauche,
We speak through sickly smiles and warn
With the stubborn saw of common sense,
The grim joke and the banal resolution.
The traffic moves around with care,
But we remain, touching a wound
That opens to our richest horror.

Already old, the question Who shall die?
Becomes unspoken Who is innocent?
For death in war is done by hands;
Suicide has cause and stillbirth, logic;
And cancer, simple as a flower, blooms.

But this invites the occult mind,
Cancels our physics with a sneer,
And spatters all we knew of denouement
Across the expedient and wicked stones.

---

1. "Auto Wreck" is a description of a scene, a description of the observers' reactions to the scene, and a number of comments. Can you separate the three elements?
2. Note the analogies used: "like an artery," "tight as tourniquets," "bound with splints," and so on. Why are these particular analogies used?
3. What lines convey especially vivid visual images? What lines communicate through other senses?
4. Three kinds of organization help to keep the scene clear in our minds. What are they?
5. What general theme, or meaning, binds the whole poem together?

---

1. The painter of *Tombstones* has simplified his presentation of the scene to a comic-book clarity, yet it is an expressive painting that does not lack any significant detail. What is the neighborhood as a whole like? What other "scenes" would you expect to find there?
2. Find a word to describe the emotional attitude of each person in the scene. In each case, how can you tell what that attitude is?
3. What relationships between persons are indicated? Again, how can you tell what they are?
4. What is the unifying theme of the picture? What details contribute to this idea or feeling?
5. Point out some of the artist's economies. Where has he simplified or omitted irrelevant detail in order to make his point more forcefully?

PLATE IV

TOMBSTONES: Jacob Lawrence. 1942. Gouache on paper. 28¾″ × 20½″.
Collection of Whitney Museum of American Art

5
getting
the feel
of action

We perceive action with our bodies as well as with our eyes and ears. Sports fans move as the players move, in their minds if not with their bodies. You move your vocal chords together with those of the singer you are listening to, or even with the sounds of instruments; your fingers or feet tap rhythms in time to the music. When you watch television, you feel the sensation of motion as the camera follows the hero who is chasing the villain.

Much of the fun of watching action is in identifying with it. In describing action, you want to communicate its feeling rather than offer an objective account. The fact that kicking a football involves a sudden contraction of the *rectus femoris* muscle isn't of the slightest interest to the people watching a game or reading about one. They want to be reminded of what it *feels* like to kick a ball.

How can you best convey these kinesthetic feelings? Most writers rely on two devices: clear, economical description of movement, and the choice of strong action verbs, such as *swing, sway, crouch, jump, lunge, stride, stretch,* and hundreds of others. A few well-chosen words get the feel of action across better than do many poorly chosen ones.

Action does not have to be violent to be interesting. Whether a woman sits on the edge of her chair or relaxes with her legs crossed can tell you something about her personality and mood.

class exercise

Most of us have been on a roller coaster or some other machine designed to give the excitement of movement. Try to describe how you feel on such a machine, or how you felt when you were a child on a swing, climbing a tree, or standing on your head. Use the present tense. Describe your feelings, not just the facts. Don't say, "The blood rushes to my head," but try to tell what it feels like to have the blood rushing to your head.

writing assignment

1. Observe a person doing something: a child playing tetherball or climbing on bars; a woman sewing or washing dishes; a man digging or trimming a hedge; someone watering a lawn, making a bed, or shopping.
2. Watch the person's motions carefully and completely, taking notes. If a woman is washing dishes, for example, notice not only what her hands are doing, but also if her feet are moving, how she turns her body, how she moves her head, and so on. Record the sounds and smells that accompany the activity and note the person's reactions to things going on in the environment.
3. Try to find the verbs that best make the actions clear. Use analogy whenever it will help you.

coherence

Coherence is just what the word indicates: the quality of sticking together. In addition to being unified by subject, the parts of your writing should be connected with each other in such a way that the reader can always see how they are related. Here is an example that is unified but lacks coherence.

> Lucretia carries her purse different ways. She lets it hang like a suitcase on the street. When she is in a store, she tucks it under her arm or holds it behind her with both hands. She holds it with her hand when she is fumbling through it at the cash register. She curls her hand around the end and holds it along her arm when she is walking with someone. While talking, she holds it cradled in both arms. She never drops it or leaves it behind.

Analyzing the paragraph, we find there are two elements consistent throughout: the ways Lucretia holds her purse and the situations that determine the way she holds it. To give coherence to the paragraph, we need to (1) restate the first sentence so that it reflects the main idea; (2) express parallel ideas in parallel form; and (3) make clear the relationship of the last sentence to the rest.

Lucretia carries her purse differently in different situations. When she walks alone, she lets it hang like a suitcase. When she is shopping, she carries it under one arm or holds it behind her with both hands. When she is at the cash register, she grips it by the bottom with her left hand while she fumbles through it with her right. When she is walking with someone, she carries it resting along her left arm, with her hand curled around the end. Finally, when she is standing talking, she holds it cradled in both arms. But though she carries it in all these different ways, she never drops her purse or leaves it behind in any situation.

In the next-to-last sentence, we have used a *transitional* expression, "finally," to let readers know that the end of the series is coming, and in the last sentence, we have repeated the expressions "different ways" and "situation" to pull the ideas together. The use of devices to achieve coherence has been exaggerated somewhat in this example, of course, but the point is, *always let your readers know where they are.* Don't surprise them with a sentence that will make them go back to see what on earth that sentence has to do with the previous sentences.

class writing assignment

Look over the notes you took for this unit's writing assignment and see if you can find a generalization that grows out of them naturally. Don't strain for something startling or original; you will probably come up with an idea like, "Making a bed is a complex activity." If such a simple statement doesn't seem to cover all you noticed, add another phrase, such as "and involves many sensory and kinesthetic experiences." Begin your essay with your generalization and go on to support it by organizing your notes into a clear description of the activity. Strive for coherence, always letting your readers know what you are doing, and for clarity, letting them know exactly what is happening and where and when it is taking place.

Contents of the Dead Man's Pockets

JACK FINNEY

At the little living-room desk Tom Benecke rolled two sheets of flimsy and a heavier top sheet, carbon paper sandwiched between them, into his portable. *Inter-office Memo,* the top sheet was headed, and he typed tomorrow's date just below this; then he glanced at a creased yellow sheet, covered with his own handwriting, beside the typewriter. "Hot in here," he muttered to himself. Then, from the short hallway at his back, he heard the muffled clang of wire coat hangers in the bedroom closet, and at this reminder of what his wife was doing he thought: Hot, hell—guilty conscience.

He got up, shoving his hands into the back pockets of his gray wash slacks, stepped to the living-room window beside the desk and stood breathing on the glass, watching the expanding circlet of mist, staring down through the autumn night at Lexington Avenue, eleven stories below. He was a tall, lean, dark-haired young man in a pullover sweater, who looked as though he had played not football, probably, but basketball in college. Now he placed the heels of his hands against the top edge of the lower window frame and shoved upward. But as usual the window didn't budge, and he had to lower his hands and then shoot them hard upward to jolt the window open a few inches. He dusted his hands, muttering.

But still he didn't begin his work. He crossed the room to the hallway entrance and, leaning against the doorjamb, hands shoved into his back pockets again, he called, "Clare?" When his wife answered, he said, "Sure you don't mind going alone?"

"No." Her voice was muffled, and he knew her head and shoulders were in the bedroom closet. Then the tap of her high heels sounded on the wood floor and she appeared at the end of the little hallway, wearing a slip, both hands raised to one ear, clipping on an earring. She smiled at him— a slender, very pretty girl with light brown, almost blonde, hair—her prettiness emphasized by the pleasant nature that showed in her face. "It's just that I hate you to miss this movie; you wanted to see it too."

"Yeah, I know." He ran his fingers through his hair. "Got to get this done though."

She nodded, accepting this. Then, glancing at the desk across the living room, she said, "You work too much, though, Tom—and too hard."

He smiled. "You won't mind though, will you, when the money comes rolling in and I'm known as the Boy Wizard of Wholesale Groceries?"

"I guess not." She smiled and turned back toward the bedroom.

At his desk again, Tom lighted a cigarette; then a few moments later as Clare appeared, dressed and ready to leave, he set it on the rim of the ash tray. "Just after seven," she said. "I can make the beginning of the first feature."

He walked to the front-door closet to help her on with her coat. He kissed her then and, for an instant, holding her close, smelling the perfume she had used, he was tempted to go with her; it was not actually true that he had to work tonight, though he very much wanted to. This was his own project, unannounced as yet in his office, and it could be postponed. But then they won't see it till Monday, he thought once again, and if I give it to the boss tomorrow he might read it over the weekend . . . "Have a good time," he said aloud. He gave his wife a little swat and opened the door for her, feeling the air from the building hallway, smelling faintly of floor wax, steam gently past his face.

He watched her walk down the hall, flicked a hand in response as she waved, and then he started to close the door, but it resisted for a moment. As the door opening narrowed, the current of warm air from the hallway, channeled through this smaller opening now, suddenly rushed past him with accelerated force. Behind him he heard the slap of the window curtains against the wall and the sound of paper fluttering from his desk, and he had to push to close the door.

Turning, he saw a sheet of white paper drifting to the floor in a series of arcs, and another sheet, yellow, moving toward the window, caught in the dying current flowing through the narrow opening. As he watched, the paper struck the bottom edge of the window and hung there for an instant, plastered against the glass and wood. Then as the moving air stilled completely the curtains swinging back from the wall to hang free again, he saw the yellow sheet drop to the window ledge and slide over out of sight.

He ran across the room, grasped the bottom edge of the window and tugged, staring through the glass. He saw the yellow sheet, dimly now in the darkness outside, lying on the ornamental ledge a yard below the window. Even as he watched, it was moving, scraping slowly along the ledge, pushed by the breeze that pressed steadily against the building wall. He heaved on the window with all his strength and it shot open with a bang, the window weight rattling in the casing. But the paper was past his reach and, leaning out into the night, he watched it scud steadily along the ledge to the south, half-plastered against the building wall. Above the muffled sound of the street traffic far below, he could hear the dry scrape of its movement, like a leaf on the pavement.

The living room of the next apartment to the south projected a yard or more farther out toward the street than this one; because of this the Beneckes paid seven and a half dollars less rent than their neighbors. And now the yellow sheet, sliding along the stone ledge, nearly invisible in the night, was stopped by the projecting blank wall of the next apartment. It lay motionless, then, in the corner formed by the two walls—a good five yards away, pressed firmly against the ornate corner ornament of the ledge, by the breeze that moved past Tom Benecke's face.

He knelt at the window and stared at the yellow paper for a full minute or more, waiting for it to move, to slide off the ledge and fall, hoping he could follow its course to the street, and then hurry down in the elevator and retrieve it. But it didn't move, and then he saw that the paper was caught firmly between a projection of the convoluted corner ornament and the ledge. He thought about the poker from the fireplace, then the broom, then the mop—discarding each thought as it occurred to him. There was nothing in the apartment long enough to reach that paper.

It was hard for him to understand that he actually had to abandon it—it was ridiculous—and he began to curse. Of all the papers on his desk, why did it have to be this one in particular! On four long Saturday afternoons he had stood in supermarkets counting the people who passed certain displays, and the results were scribbled on that yellow sheet. From stacks of trade publications, gone over page by page in snatched half hours at work and during evenings at home, he had copied facts, quotations and figures onto that sheet. And he had carried it with him to the Public Library on Fifth Avenue, where he'd spent a dozen lunch hours and early evenings adding more. All were needed to support and lend authority to his idea for a new grocery-store display method; without them his idea was a mere opinion. And there they all lay, in his own improvised shorthand—countless hours of work—out there on the ledge.

For many seconds he believed he was going to abandon the yellow sheet, that there was nothing else to do. The work could be duplicated. But it would take two months, and the time to present this idea, damn it, was *now*, for use in the spring displays. He struck his fist on the window ledge. Then he shrugged. Even though his plan was adopted, he told himself, it wouldn't bring him a raise in pay—not immediately, anyway, or as a direct result. It won't bring me a promotion either, he argued—not of itself.

But just the same, and he couldn't escape the thought, this and other independent projects, some already done and others planned for the future, would gradually mark him out from the score of other young men in his company. They were the way to change from a name on the payroll to a name in the minds of the company officials. They were the beginning of the long, long climb to where he was determined to be, at the very top. And he knew he was going out there in the darkness, after the yellow sheet fifteen feet beyond his reach.

By a kind of instinct, he instantly began making his intention acceptable to himself by laughing at it. The mental picture of himself sidling along the ledge outside was absurd—it was actually comical—and he smiled. He imagined himself describing it; it would make a good story at the office and, it occurred to him, would add a special interest and importance to his memorandum, which would do it no harm at all.

To simply go out and get his paper was an easy task—he could be back here with it in less than two minutes—and he knew he wasn't deceiving himself. The ledge, he saw, measuring it with his eye, was about as wide as the length of his shoe, and perfectly flat. And every fifth row of brick in the face of the building, he remembered—leaning out, he verified this— was indented half an inch, enough for the tips of his fingers, enough to maintain balance easily. It occurred to him that if this ledge and wall were only a yard above-ground—as he knelt at the window staring out, this thought was the final confirmation of his intention—he could move along the ledge indefinitely.

On a sudden impulse, he got to his feet, walked to the front closet and took out an old tweed jacket, it would be cold outside. He put it on and buttoned it as he crossed the room rapidly toward the open window. In the back of his mind he knew he'd better hurry and get this over with before he thought too much, and at the window he didn't allow himself to hesitate.

He swung a leg over the sill, then felt for and found the ledge a yard below the window with his foot. Gripping the bottom of the window frame very tightly and carefully, he slowly ducked his head under it, feeling on his face the sudden change from the warm air of the room to the chill outside. With infinite care he brought out his other leg, his mind concentrating on what he was doing. Then he slowly stood erect. Most of the putty, dried out and brittle, had dropped off the bottom edging of the window frame, he found, and the flat wooden edging provided a good gripping surface, a half inch or more deep, for the tips of his fingers.

Now, balanced easily and firmly, he stood on the ledge outside in the slight, chill breeze, eleven stories above the street, staring into his own lighted apartment, odd and different-seeming now.

First his right hand, then his left, he carefully shifted his finger-tip grip from the puttyless window edging to an indented row of bricks directly to his right. It was hard to take the first shuffling sideways step then—to make himself move—and the fear stirred in his stomach, but he did it, again by not allowing himself time to think. And now—with his chest, stomach, and the left side of his face pressed against the rough cold brick—his lighted apartment was suddenly gone, and it was much darker out here than he had thought.

Without pause he continued—right foot, left foot, right foot, left— his shoe soles shuffling and scraping along the rough stone, never lifting from it, fingers sliding along the exposed edging of brick. He moved on the balls of his feet, heels lifted slightly; the ledge was not quite as wide as he'd expected. But leaning slightly inward toward the face of the building and pressed against it, he could feel his balance firm and secure, and moving along the ledge was quite as easy as he had thought it would be. He could hear the buttons of his jacket scraping steadily along the rough bricks and feel them catch momentarily, tugging a little, at each mortared crack. He simply did not permit himself to look down, though the compulsion to do so never left him; nor did he allow himself actually to think. Mechanically— right foot, left foot, over and again—he shuffled along crabwise, watching the projecting wall ahead loom steadily closer. . . .

Then he reached it and, at the corner—he'd decided how he was going to pick up the paper—he lifted his right foot and placed it carefully on the ledge that ran along the projecting wall at a right angle to the ledge on which his other foot rested. And now, facing the building, he stood in the corner formed by the two walls, one foot on the ledging of each, a hand on the shoulder-high indentation of each wall. His forehead was pressed directly into the corner against the cold bricks, and now he carefully lowered first one hand, then the other, perhaps a foot farther down, to the next indentation in the rows of bricks.

Very slowly, sliding his forehead down the trough of the brick corner and bending his knees, he lowered his body toward the paper lying between his outstretched feet. Again he lowered his fingerholds another foot and bent his knees still more, thigh muscles taut, his forehead sliding and bump- ing down the brick V. Half squatting now, he dropped his left hand to the next indentation and then slowly reached with his right hand toward the paper between his feet.

He couldn't quite touch it, and his knees now were pressed against the wall; he could bend them no farther. But by ducking his head another inch lower, the top of his head now pressed against the bricks, he lowered his right shoulder and his fingers had the paper by a corner, pulling it loose. At the same instant he saw, between his legs and far below, Lexington Avenue stretched out for miles ahead.

He saw, in that instant, the Loew's theater sign, blocks ahead past Fiftieth Street; the miles of traffic signals, all green now; the lights of cars and street lamps; countless neon signs; and the moving black dots of people. And a violent instantaneous explosion of absolute terror roared through him. For a motionless instant he saw himself externally—bent practically double, balanced on this narrow ledge, nearly half his body projecting out above the street far below—and he began to tremble violently, panic flaring through his mind and muscles, and he felt the blood rush from the surface of his skin.

In the fractional moment before horror paralyzed him, as he stared between his legs at that terrible length of street far beneath him, a fragment of his mind raised his body in a spasmodic jerk to an upright position again, but so violently that his head scraped hard against the wall, bouncing off it, and his body swayed outward to the knife edge of balance, and he very nearly plunged backward and fell. Then he was leaning far into the corner again, squeezing and pushing into it, not only his face but his chest and stomach, his back arching; and his finger tips clung with all the pressure of his pulling arms to the shoulder-high half-inch indentation in the bricks.

He was more than trembling now; his whole body was racked with a violent shuddering beyond control, his eyes squeezed so tightly shut it was painful, though he was past awareness of that. His teeth were exposed in a frozen grimace, the strength draining like water from his knees and calves. It was extremely likely, he knew, that he would faint, to slump down along the wall, his face scraping, and then drop backward, a limp weight, out into nothing. And to save his life he concentrated on holding onto consciousness, drawing deliberate deep breaths of cold air into his lungs, fighting to keep his senses aware.

Then he knew that he would not faint, but he could not stop shaking nor open his eyes. He stood where he was, breathing deeply, trying to hold back the terror of the glimpse he had of what lay below him; and he knew he had made a mistake in not making himself stare down at the street, getting used to it and accepting it, when he had first stepped out onto the ledge.

It was impossible to walk back. He simply could not do it. He couldn't bring himself to make the slightest movement. The strength was gone from his legs; his shivering hands—numb, cold and desperately rigid—had lost all deftness; his easy ability to move and balance was gone. Within a step or two, if he tried to move, he knew that he would stumble clumsily and fall.

Seconds passed, with the chill faint wind pressing the side of his face, and he could hear the toned-down volume of the street traffic far beneath him. Again and again it slowed and then stopped, almost to silence; then presently, even this high, he would hear the click of the traffic signals and the subdued roar of the cars starting up again. During a lull in the street sounds, he called out. Then he was shouting *"Help!"* so loudly it rasped his throat. But he felt the steady pressure of the wind, moving between his face and the blank wall, snatch up his cries as he uttered them, and he knew they must sound directionless and distant. And he remembered how habitually, here in New York, he himself heard and ignored shouts in the night. If anyone heard him, there was no sign of it, and presently Tom Benecke knew he had to try moving; there was nothing else he could do.

Eyes squeezed shut, he watched scenes in his mind like scraps of motion-picture film—he could not stop them. He saw himself stumbling suddenly sideways as he crept along the ledge and saw his upper body arc outward, arms flailing. He saw a dangling shoestring caught between the ledge and the sole of his other shoe, saw a foot start to move, to be stopped with a jerk, and felt his balance leaving him. He saw himself falling with a terrible speed as his body revolved in the air, knees clutched tight to his chest, eyes squeezed shut, moaning softly.

Out of utter necessity, knowing that any of these thoughts might be reality in the very next seconds, he was slowly able to shut his mind against every thought but what he now began to do. With fear-soaked slowness, he slid his left foot an inch or two toward his own impossibly distant window. Then he slid the fingers of his shivering left hand a corresponding distance. For a moment he could not bring himself to lift his right foot from one ledge to the other; then he did it, and became aware of the harsh exhalation of air from his throat and realized that he was panting. As his right hand, then, began to slide along the brick edging, he was astonished to feel the yellow paper pressed to the bricks underneath his stiff fingers, and he uttered a terrible, abrupt bark that might have been a laugh or a moan. He opened his mouth and took the paper in his teeth, pulling it out from under his fingers.

By a kind of trick—by concentrating his entire mind on first his left foot, then his left hand, then the other foot, then the other hand—he was able to move, almost imperceptibly, trembling steadily, very nearly without thought. But he could feel the terrible strength of the pent-up horror on just the other side of the flimsy barrier he had erected in his mind; and he knew that if it broke through he would lose this thin artificial control of his body.

During one slow step he tried keeping his eyes closed; it made him feel safer, shutting him off a little from the fearful reality of where he was. Then a sudden rush of giddiness swept over him and he had to open his eyes wide, staring sideways at the cold rough brick and angled lines of mortar, his cheek tight against the building. He kept his eyes open then, knowing that if he once let them flick outward, to stare for an instant at the lighted windows across the street, he would be past help.

He didn't know how many dozens of tiny sidling steps he had taken, his chest, belly and face pressed to the wall; but he knew the slender hold he was keeping on his mind and body was going to break. He had a sudden mental picture of his apartment on just the other side of this wall—warm, cheerful, incredibly spacious. And he saw himself striding through it, lying down on the floor on his back, arms spread wide, reveling in its unbelievable security. The impossible remoteness of this utter safety, the contrast between it and where he now stood, was more than he could bear. And the barrier broke then, and the fear of the awful height he stood on coursed through his nerves and muscles.

A fraction of his mind knew he was going to fall, and he began taking rapid blind steps with no feeling of what he was doing, sidling with a clumsy desperate swiftness, fingers scrabbling along the brick, almost hopelessly resigned to the sudden backward pull and swift motion outward and down. Then his moving left hand slid onto not brick but sheer emptiness, an impossible gap in the face of the wall, and he stumbled.

His right foot smashed into his left anklebone; he staggered sideways, began falling, and the claw of his hand cracked against glass and wood, slid down it, and his finger tips were pressed hard on the puttyless edging of his window. His right hand smacked gropingly beside it as he fell to his knees; and, under the full weight and direct downward pull of his sagging body, the open window dropped shudderingly in its frame till it closed and his wrists struck the sill and were jarred off.

For a single moment he knelt, knee bones against stone on the very edge of the ledge, body swaying and touching nowhere else, fighting for balance. Then he lost it, his shoulders plunging backward, and he flung his arms forward, his hands smashing against the window casing on either side; and—his body moving backward—his fingers clutched the narrow wood stripping of the upper pane.

For an instant he hung suspended between balance and falling, his finger tips pressed onto the quarter-inch wood strips. Then, with utmost delicacy, with a focused concentration of all his senses, he increased even further the strain on his finger tips hooked to these slim edgings of wood. Elbows slowly bending, he began to draw the full weight of his upper body forward, knowing that the instant his fingers slipped off these quarter-inch strips he'd plunge backward and be falling. Elbows imperceptibly bending, body shaking with the strain, the sweat starting from his forehead in great sudden drops, he pulled, his entire being and thought concentrated in his finger tips. Then suddenly, the strain slackened and ended, his chest touching the window sill, and he was kneeling on the ledge, his forehead pressed to the glass of the closed window.

Dropping his palms to the sill, he stared into his living room—at the red-brown davenport across the room, and a magazine he had left there; at the pictures on the walls and the gray rug; the entrance to the hallway; and at his papers, typewriter and desk, not two feet from his nose. A movement from his desk caught his eye and he saw that it was a thin curl of blue smoke; his cigarette, the ash long, was still burning in the ash tray where he'd left it—this was past all belief—only a few minutes before.

His head moved, and in faint reflection from the glass before him he saw the yellow paper clenched in his front teeth. Lifting a hand from the sill he took it from his mouth; the moistened corner parted from the paper, and he spat it out.

For a moment, in the light from the living room, he stared wonderingly at the yellow sheet in his hand and then crushed it into the side pocket of his jacket.

He couldn't open the window. It had been pulled not completely closed, but its lower edge was below the level of the outside sill; there was no room to get his fingers underneath it. Between the upper sash and the lower was a gap not wide enough—reaching up, he tried—to get his fingers into; he couldn't push it open. The upper window panel, he knew from long experience, was impossible to move, frozen tight with dried paint.

Very carefully observing his balance, the finger tips of his left hand again hooked to the narrow stripping of the window casing, he drew back his right hand, palm facing the glass, and then struck the glass with the heel of his hand.

His arm rebounded from the pane, his body tottering, and he knew he didn't dare strike a harder blow.

But in the security and relief of his new position, he simply smiled; with only a sheet of glass between him and the room just before him, it was not possible that there wasn't a way past it. Eyes narrowing, he thought for a few moments about what to do. Then his eyes widened, for nothing occurred to him. But still he felt calm; the trembling, he realized, had stopped. At the back of his mind there still lay the thought that once he was again in his home, he could give release to his feelings. He actually *would* lie on the floor, rolling, clenching tufts of the rug in his hands. He would literally run across the room, free to move as he liked, jumping on the floor, testing and reveling in its absolute security, letting the relief flood through him, draining the fear from his mind and body. His yearning for this was astonishingly intense, and somehow he understood that he had better keep this feeling at bay.

He took a half dollar from his pocket and struck it against the pane, but without any hope that the glass would break and with very little disappointment when it did not. After a few moments of thought he drew his leg up onto the ledge and picked loose the knot of his shoelace. He slipped off the shoe and, holding it across the instep, drew back his arm as far as he dared and struck the leather heel against the glass. The pane rattled, but he knew he'd been a long way from breaking it. His foot was cold and he slipped the shoe back on. He shouted again, experimentally, and then once more, but there was no answer.

The realization suddenly struck him that he might have to wait here till Clare came home, and for a moment the thought was funny. He could see Clare opening the front door, withdrawing her key from the lock, closing the door behind her and then glancing up to see him crouched on the other side of the window. He could see her rush across the room, face astounded and frightened, and hear himself shouting instructions: "Never mind how I got here! Just open the wind—" She couldn't open it, he remembered, she'd never been able to; she'd always had to call him. She'd have to get the building superintendent or a neighbor, and he pictured himself smiling and answering their questions as he climbed in. "I just wanted to get a breath of fresh air, so—"

He couldn't possibly wait here till Clare came home. It was the second feature she'd wanted to see, and she'd left in time to see the first. She'd be another three hours or— He glanced at his watch; Clare had been gone eight minutes. It wasn't possible, but only eight minutes ago he had kissed his wife good-by. She wasn't even at the theater yet!

It would be four hours before she could possibly be home, and he tried to picture himself kneeling out here, finger tips hooked to these narrow strippings, while first one movie, preceded by a slow listing of credits, began, developed, reached its climax and then finally ended. There'd be a newsreel next, maybe, and then an animated cartoon, and then interminable scenes from coming pictures. And then, once more, the beginning of a full-length picture—while all the time he hung out here in the night.

He might possibly get to his feet, but he was afraid to try. Already his legs were cramped, his thigh muscles tired; his knees hurt, his feet felt numb and his hands were stiff. He couldn't possibly stay out here for four hours, or anywhere near it. Long before that his legs and arms would give out; he would be forced to try changing his position often—stiffly, clumsily, his co-ordination and strength gone—and he would fall. Quite realistically, he knew that he would fall; no one could stay out here on this ledge for four hours.

A dozen windows in the apartment building across the street were lighted. Looking over his shoulder, he could see the top of a man's head behind the newspaper he was reading; in another window he saw the blue-gray flicker of a television screen. No more than twenty-odd yards from his back were scores of people, and if just one of them would walk idly to his window and glance out. . . . For some moments he stared over his shoulder at the lighted rectangles, waiting. But no one appeared. The man reading his paper turned a page and then continued his reading. A figure passed another of the windows and was immediately gone.

In the inside pocket of his jacket he found a little sheaf of papers, and he pulled one out and looked at it in the light from the living room. It was an old letter, an advertisement of some sort; his name and address, in purple ink, were on a label pasted to the envelope. Gripping one end of the envelope in his teeth, he twisted it into a tight curl. From his shirt pocket he brought out a book of matches. He didn't dare let go the casing with both hands but, with the twist of paper in his teeth, he opened the matchbook with his free hand; then he bent one of the matches in two without tearing it from the folder, its red-tipped end now touching the striking surface. With his thumb, he rubbed the red tip across the striking area.

He did it again, then again, and still again, pressing harder each time, and the match suddenly flared, burning his thumb. But he kept it alight, cupping the matchbook in his hand and shielding it with his body. He held the flame to the paper in his mouth till it caught. Then he snuffed out the match flame with his thumb and forefinger, careless of the burn, and replaced the book in his pocket. Taking the paper twist in his hand, he held it flame down, watching the flame crawl up the paper, till it flared bright. Then he held it behind him over the street, moving it from side to side, watching it over his shoulder, the flame flickering and guttering in the wind.

There were three letters in his pocket and he lighted each of them, holding each till the flame touched his hand and then dropping it to the street below. At one point, watching over his shoulder while the last of the letters burned, he saw the man across the street put down his paper and stand—even seeming, to Tom, to glance toward his window. But when he moved, it was only to walk across the room and disappear from sight.

There were a dozen coins in Tom Benecke's pocket and he dropped them, three or four at a time. But if they struck anyone, or if anyone noticed their falling, no one connected them with their source, and no one glanced upward.

His arms had begun to tremble from the steady strain of clinging to this narrow perch, and he did not know what to do now and was terribly frightened. Clinging to the window stripping with one hand, he again searched his pockets. But now—he had left his wallet on his dresser when he'd changed clothes—there was nothing left but the yellow sheet. It occurred to him irrelevantly that his death on the sidewalk below would be an eternal mystery; the window closed—why, how, and from where could he have fallen? No one would be able to identify his body for a time, either—the thought was somehow unbearable and increased his fear. All they'd find in his pockets would be the yellow sheet. *Contents of the dead man's pockets*, he thought, *one sheet of paper bearing penciled notations—incomprehensible.*

He understood fully that he might actually be going to die; his arms, maintaining his balance on the ledge, were trembling steadily now. And it occurred to him then with all the force of a revelation that, if he fell, all he was ever going to have out of life he would then, abruptly, have had. Nothing, then, could ever be changed; and nothing more—no least experience or pleasure—could ever be added to his life. He wished, then, that he had not allowed his wife to go off by herself tonight—and on similar nights. He thought of all the evenings he had spent away from her, working; and he regretted them. He thought wonderingly of his fierce ambition and of the direction his life had taken; he thought of the hours he'd spent by himself, filling the yellow sheet that had brought him out here. *Contents of the dead man's pockets*, he thought with sudden fierce anger, *a wasted life.*

He was simply not going to cling here till he slipped and fell; he told himself that now. There was one last thing he could try; he had been aware of it for some moments, refusing to think about it, but now he faced it. Kneeling here on the ledge, the finger tips of one hand pressed to the narrow strip of wood, he could, he knew, draw his other hand back a yard perhaps, fist clenched tight, doing it very slowly till he sensed the outer limit of balance, then, as hard as he was able from the distance, he could drive his fist forward against the glass. If it broke, his fist smashing through, he was safe; he might cut himself badly, and probably would, but with his arm inside the room, he would be secure. But if the glass did not break, the rebound, flinging his arm back, would topple him off the ledge. He was certain of that.

He tested his plan. The fingers of his left hand clawlike on the little stripping, he drew back his other fist until his body began teetering backward. But he had no leverage now—he could feel that there would be no force to his swing—and he moved his fist slowly forward till he rocked forward on his knees again and could sense that his swing would carry its greatest force. Glancing down, however, measuring the distance from his fist to the glass, he saw that it was less than two feet.

It occurred to him that he could raise his arm over his head, to bring it down against the glass. But, experimenting in slow motion, he knew it would be an awkward girl-like blow without the force of a driving punch, and not nearly enough to break the glass.

Facing the window, he had to drive a blow from the shoulder, he knew now, at a distance of less than two feet; and he did not know whether it would break through the heavy glass. It might; he could picture it happening, he could feel it in the nerves of his arm. And it might not; he could feel that too—feel his fist striking this glass and being instantaneously flung back by the unbreaking pane, feel the fingers of his other hand breaking loose, nails scraping along the casing as he fell.

He waited, arm drawn back, fist balled, but in no hurry to strike; this pause, he knew, might be an extension of his life. And to live even a few seconds longer, he felt, even out here on this ledge in the night, was infinitely better than to die a moment earlier than he had to. His arm grew tired, and he brought it down and rested it.

Then he knew that it was time to make the attempt. He could not kneel here hesitating indefinitely till he lost all courage to act, waiting till he slipped off the ledge. Again he drew back his arm, knowing this time that he would not bring it down till he struck. His elbow protruding over Lexington Avenue far below, the fingers of his other hand pressed down bloodlessly tight against the narrow stripping, he waited, feeling the sick tenseness and terrible excitement building. It grew and swelled toward the moment of action, his nerves tautening. He thought of Clare—just a wordless, yearning thought—and then drew his arm back just a bit more, fist so tight his fingers pained him, and knowing he was going to do it. Then with full power, with every last scrap of strength he could bring to bear, he shot his arm forward toward the glass, and he said, *"Clare!"*

He heard the sound, felt the blow, felt himself falling forward, and his hand closed on the livingroom curtains, the shards and fragments of glass showering onto the floor. And then, kneeling there on the ledge, an arm thrust into the room up to the shoulder, he began picking away the protruding slivers and great wedges of glass from the window frame, tossing them in onto the rug. And, as he grasped the edges of the empty window frame and climbed into his home, he was grinning in triumph.

He did not lie down on the floor or run through the apartment, as he had promised himself; even in the first few moments it seemed to him natural and normal that he should be where he was. He simply turned to his desk, pulled the crumpled yellow sheet from his pocket and laid it down where it had been, smoothing it out; then he absently laid a pencil across it to weight it down. He shook his head wonderingly, and turned to walk toward the closet.

There he got out his topcoat and hat and, without waiting to put them on, opened the front door and stepped out, to go find his wife. He turned to pull the door closed and warm air from the hall rushed through the narrow opening again. As he saw the yellow paper, the pencil flying, scooped off the desk and, unimpeded by the glassless window, sail out into the night and out of his life, Tom Benecke burst into laughter and then closed the door behind him.

---

1. In the first few pages of the story there is a good deal about the actions of things—clothes hangers, the wind, the paper, the window sash. What senses are used to communicate these actions?
2. Point out places where the author has used sight, hearing, touch, and the kinesthetic sense to convey the feel of action.
3. What details of the building's structure are used in the description of the action? How do they contribute to the story in each case?
4. Point out some transitional devices that help to give coherence to the story. In addition to these, what are some repeated themes or images that hold the story together?
5. A value judgment is implied in the ending. What is it? Is the generalization supported with enough evidence to be valid?

The Base Stealer

ROBERT FRANCIS

Poised between going on and back, pulled
Both ways taut like a tightrope-walker,
Fingertips pointing the opposites,
Now bouncing tiptoe like a dropped ball
Or a kid skipping rope, come on, come on,
Running a scattering of steps sidewise,
How he teeters, skitters, tingles, teases,
Taunts them, hovers like an ecstatic bird,
He's only flirting, crowd him, crowd him,
Delicate, delicate, delicate, delicate—now!

---

1. The effect of this poem is based largely on the use of words that
   suggest kinesthetic feelings. What are these words? (There are a
   dozen or more.)
2. What analogies are used? Are they good ones? Can you suggest
   better analogies in one or two cases?
3. Probably you have never been stuck on a high window ledge, but
   after reading "Contents of the Dead Man's Pockets" you have a good
   idea of what it would be like. Of course you have seen a baseball
   game. If you had not, would you understand "Base Stealer"?
4. What is the difference, then, between describing an action that is
   familiar to your reader and one that is not? What, or how much can
   you take for granted in the former situation? What devices do you
   have to use to make an unfamiliar action clear?

1. What kinesthetic sensations are evoked by this picture? How has the artist communicated them?
2. Are any other kinds of sensations suggested? If so, what are they and how are they communicated?
3. Has the artist used exaggeration or distortion to help emphasize sensations? If so, where, and what has been altered?
4. The ceiling of the room is not shown. Does this omission contribute to the effect? If so, how?
5. The artist is expressing more than is immediately apparent. There is humorous comment implied through analogy. Can you spot the analogy? What do you think the artist means by it? (It is hinted at by the pair of carcasses and the pair of hams on either side of the butcher.)

PLATE V

THE BUTCHER: Honoré Daumier. Courtesy of the Fogg Art Museum, Harvard University. Grenville L. Winthrop Bequest.

Homo
sapiens

Jerszy Flisak

6

observing
a person

When you look at people, you probably take in a good deal of data about them at a glance and, without analyzing the data, say to yourself, "He looks like a banker" or "She's a lawyer."

At this point, we need to make the distinction between *fact* and *inference*. A *fact* is a direct observation that no one can dispute, such as, "He is wearing a white cap and overalls spotted with paint, and he is carrying a paintbrush and pail." An *inference* is a conclusion that seems reasonable in light of the facts; for example, "He is probably a painter." An inference can be wrong. He might be a bank robber using a disguise to get into a bank.

class exercise

Think of a person you know. Describe that person using only descriptive facts. See if you can lead others in the class to make correct inferences regarding the person's age, occupation, financial status, character, and so on. Do not say, for example, "She is about twenty years old." That is an inference. Describe the factual data concerning her complexion, clothing, movement, and other clues to her age. Work at keeping clear the distinction between fact and inference.

writing assignment

1. Taking a small notebook with you, go to a public place such as a bus station, railway station, city bus, crowded supermarket, or dime store: a place busy enough for you to observe and take notes without attracting your subject's attention.
2. Pick out a person who looks interesting, preferably an older person. Without letting your subject know, observe as closely as you can.
3. Take detailed notes about your subject. First write down a general description, such as you might give to someone who was looking for that person. Then do the detective work: catalogue every detail you can find from which some inference might be made about occupation, financial status, family status, personal habits, home life, and so on. Watch for revealing actions as well as appearances.
4. Now, putting your material in the kind of order you used in the Unit 2 writing assignment, make up an intensive description of the person, including all your inferences and the evidence to support them.

emphasis

Emphasis is calling attention to important things you want your reader to remember; it is making certain parts stand out. If artists want to emphasize something, they put it in the center of the picture, color it more brightly, or make it stand out through contrast.

Poor writers overuse such obvious emphasis devices as underlining, exclamation points, and words like *very, only, absolutely,* and *awfully.* Such words can serve a purpose if they are used sparingly, but there are better methods of achieving emphasis. To emphasize something you can:

1. make short, flat statements. In the first paragraph above, "it is making certain parts stand out" is such a statement.

2. place what is most important at the beginning or end of a sentence, paragraph, or essay. First and last things get attention; things in the middle get lost.

3. give a larger proportion of your writing to what is more important. When you describe people, for example, write most about the things that tell us what kinds of people they are, and cover the other necessary details briefly.

class writing assignment

Rewrite the material you have collected for the writing assignment, organizing it into paragraphs, each one based on a *generalization.* Begin with a paragraph of general description. The generalization that begins your introductory paragraph should reflect the impression the person gives at first glance; for example, "He is a tall, neatly dressed man who probably works indoors." Then round out the paragraph with the simple physical facts that support this generalization, such as height, weight, complexion, and kind of clothes.

Then, using your inferences as generalizations, write two or three more paragraphs about such matters as details of dress and appearance, movements and facial expressions, and reactions to the surroundings. Unify each paragraph by putting in only material that supports the generalization at the head of it, and try to give full and convincing evidence for each of these inferences.

Generalizations on which paragraphs and essays are based are often called *topic sentences* because they represent the topic, or subject, of the paragraph or essay.

At the end of your description, add a brief paragraph in which you summarize the inferences you have made about the person. This will help to emphasize the point of your essay.

Red

NICCOLO TUCCI

A few years ago, a bum killed himself by jumping from one of the masts of the lightship Scotland, which was docked at the foot of Fulton Street. I knew him. He was called Red. No one knew his real name. Among acquaintances, he had a reputation for making long speeches and for having theories that no one understood but that sometimes made people laugh. When he wasn't making speeches, he might remain silent for weeks. On the street, he had for years introduced himself to strangers by saying, "Dime for a cup of coffee?" More recently, he had been saying, "Quarter for a cup of coffee?" He had gradually given up another activity, which he had called "collecting"; in fact, he had given up the whole city, with its immense wealth in newspapers and in objects of all sorts and sizes—umbrellas, electric wires, bulbs, bottles. This had advantages. A bum can travel light. He needn't have a heavy shopping bag weighing him down and cutting his fingers, and he doesn't have to decide whether to discard the newspapers he has carried for months in order to make room for new ones. I first met Red on a beautiful June morning, shortly after sunrise, at the Battery. It was a Saturday. On Saturdays and Sundays, I often walk all the way down-town from Sixty-seventh Street and Madison Avenue, where I live. I enjoy wandering alone through the financial district, which in its abandoned state becomes a place for meditation—like a dead city. The atmosphere lasts well into the afternoon, when tourists walk about aimlessly, as if they were in Pompeii. The fruit store beyond the five-cent turnstiles of the Staten Island Ferry is open on Sundays, and I usually buy myself bananas and pretzels, saving some money in spite of the wasted five cents, because they are cheaper than elsewhere. At any rate, on this particular Saturday, I encoun-tered a bum in Battery Park whose gray hair was glued to the side of his face that he had been sleeping on (obviously in the dirt) and whose clothes were torn at the back, one sleeve hanging loose and showing a brownish-red arm with many scars, the other sleeve tied up with rather clean strings, like a salami. He was clutching a brand-new shoe under his left arm. On his feet were the last remnants of an old pair of shoes, tied together by a similar system of strings. He was whistling a twenties tune called "When My Baby Smiles at Me."

"How do you come to remember that tune?" I asked.

"I was a rich man once," he said cheerfully. "I went to night clubs, and I danced with rich girls to that tune." Then, as if there were a connection between the two things, he showed me the new shoe and said he had found it the day before. He insisted that I appreciate the quality of the leather, the perfection of the finish, the thickness of the double sole. Everything about the shoe pleased him.

"Wonderful," I said. "But where's the other shoe?"

He scouted the horizon—the harbor, with its ships—then looked at the seagulls above us, at the blue shadows of leaves on the asphalt pavement, at the rags on his feet, and said, "Man always strives for the impossible. But hope is one-legged. All it needs is two wings." He started to walk away, and I realized I had made a bad mistake. I ran after him and gave him a dollar, and that was my second mistake, because it was actually ten dollars— all I had in my pocket for the weekend. He took the money without thanking me, and left me.

Later that morning, I found myself in the midst of noises, smoke, and smells; the Brooklyn Bridge, to the north, stood high above me, thun-dering horribly with trucks and cars, which sent the bitter taste of exhaust over the rusty roofs of sheds adjoining the Fulton Fish Market, where empty strainers with bits of rotting fish clinging to them were glittering in the pink sunshine, garbage was burning in the streets, and oil was leaking from a parked truck that was puffing poison in my face. Across the river from me, smokestacks filled the sky with black clouds from which descended invisible cancer for smokers and nonsmokers alike. It wasn't one of those days when the sea manages to pierce the curtain of industrial development and salt it, iodize it, disinfect it.

Oscillating like metronomes, above a white hull, were the masts of the Coast Guard ship Eagle. Suddenly the bum with the shoe under his arm was at my side, saying, "Wouldn't you like to climb up there and feel the sea under your feet? I've never had the sea under my feet. Only the earth".

"That's all we have," I said.

"Don't forget the moon," he said. "Next year, we'll set foot on the moon."

"Not you or I," I said. "A couple of trained mechanics. And the price of their ticket, far exceeding the yearly budget of a large city, will be paid by us in taxes."

"I don't pay taxes," he said. "And I wouldn't if they asked me."

"You pay more for beer, or whatever it is you drink, and for whatever else you buy," I said. "You're being taxed."

"I don't care," he said. "I despise money anyway."

"You are luckier than I am," I said. "I respect money very much. But it seems to despise me."

"Then listen to me," he said. "Don't give it to bums. They are immoral. Especially those who sleep on the benches in Madison Square Park. I wouldn't be seen dead in that place. But also the bums on the Bowery. Don't trust them. They are stupid. They don't think. They have no conversation."

"Thanks for warning me," I said. "I'll make a mental note of that."

"Don't you be so goddam wise," he said.

I looked at him closely. His face was flushed. He seemed to be in a state of extreme anger.

"Do you think the bums can go on picking up after you?" he continued. "I used to collect empty bottles, old newspapers, and everything else. I ruined myself to save the city, but now I've given up."

I looked about me for help. We were alone. At a great distance from us, another bum was sitting in front of a pile of burning garbage.

"Looking for help?" the bum with the shoe said. "Do you need the police? Why don't you use your brain? No, that all goes into making money. So when you meet a man who knows how to talk to you, your money does all the talking and you run away from him."

I said nothing, and turned to go my way.

"Where do you think you are going?" he said. "How about showing me what you are worth. Not in hard cash—I don't give a damn about your cash—but with your head. Why did you talk to me this morning? I was happy and you ruined my happiness. So I need another shoe, eh? Want to see what I do with your damn shoes that come in pairs? This." And he threw the shoe into the filth of the river. Obviously, the loss was painful to him, for he followed the shoe's course intently. I even thought I saw tears in his eyes. I dared not move. "How about that broken glass everywhere in the city?" he said, finally. "You have good shoes. You don't care. God mends my feet for free. All you can think of is to throw another bottle in my path. From rooftops. From windows. You missed my head by an inch last week. And then you cut my back and my arm. See? God mends my arm, but you don't mend my sleeve for free."

"But that's exactly what I was saying," I said. "You pay taxes—more so than anyone else."

"Who throws those bottles from the rooftops?" he said. "Who breaks them in my path?"

"I never threw a bottle in my life," I said. "Besides, I live uptown."

"So it's the Negroes and the Puerto Ricans—is that it?" he said.

"No, the kids," I said. "All kids, of all races and backgrounds. It's their idea of fun. A barbarous idea—new to me. When we were young, these things were unknown."

"Kids don't throw away what they can sell for cash," he said. "But with prices going up every day, bottles worth two cents apiece only a few years ago drop down to zero. They're good enough to be thrown in my path. What's wrong with glass? The one thing that doesn't rot. I have seen bottles in museums, with my own eyes—unbroken through many civilizations. So why don't you pay fifteen cents apiece and keep the kids working and the city clean?" This was before "the environment" and "recycling" had entered everyone's vocabulary.

That was only the beginning of a long conversation that took place over a number of days and covered many subjects, but Red always steered away from any inquiries relating to his origins and to his name. He told me simply to call him Red. I made it a point to walk all the way down to the Battery even on weekdays, because his case fascinated me, even though it irritated me at the same time. I never told him I would be there again the next morning. In fact, I made it clear to him that I was a bit tired of his absurdities, but the next morning I was sure to find him there, and he never seemed surprised to see me come back. I must add that I did give him some money every day. Not as much as the first day—indeed, never more than fifty cents, but fifty cents at five in the morning is a very good beginning for a bum. So one day I decided to tell him that I couldn't go on helping him, because I had to go to Europe and also because I was not the rich man he had imagined. To my great surprise, he not only understood but he offered to help me financially, to the extent of a few hundred dollars. This,

I felt, authorized me to look into his personal finances. If he had all that money, he obviously possessed more than I did, so why didn't he spend it to make himself more presentable? I told him I didn't think people had a right to go around filthy and in rags, and pretend that it was a private matter. The moment I had finished, he said, "But then you agree with me. I cannot ride an image of myself out of this life. And *who am I? What* am I? I haven't opened a book in years." I secretly registered this as an important fact. He had cared for books.

"Why don't you tell me your real name?" I said. "That will help you understand who you are."

By then, we were walking uptown from the Battery. It seemed to me that he was turning morose, and I feared a new outbreak of the anger that had frightened me the first day. To keep him from brooding, I began to elaborate on the reasons an intellectual like him might have for becoming so secretive about his personal identity. "You tend to identify yourself with your intellectual achievement, and, having given this up, you have denied yourself even the use of your own name," I said. "Is that it?"

He said nothing, but he seemed interested. This gave me courage to go on.

"If you knew how little most intellectuals read, and how little they absorb of what they read, even after they have earned the respect of the world, you would realize that they don't deserve it," I said. "Have *I* opened a book in many years? No, and I close my eyes on all the good books I read, because I read them in bed after a strenuous day of lecturing, teaching, correcting papers, listening to the nonsense of others. But that's all irrelevant to our discussion. What is your name?"

He stared at me as if he hadn't heard me.

"Did you hear my question?" I asked.

"Yes, yes, of course," he said. "That's interesting. Go on. So they don't deserve it, you were saying. See? I was listening."

I decided to go on. "Now, dressing up like the others is one sure way to keep your identity hidden, while going around in rags reveals too much of your inner conflicts to people who have no right to pry into your background. Get it?"

He smiled and nodded, staring at the pavement in front of the Chase Manhattan Bank Building. He was obviously thinking.

"Even if you have reasons for keeping your name a secret forever," I said, "it is harder for you to do so in your present condition than it would be as a normal-looking person with a name you had adopted to cover up your past once and for all."

He was now listening with great intensity, and he did look like a hunted criminal trying to flatten himself against a wall so as not to be seen by the police and at the same time fearing every noise from behind the wall.

I thought it best not to show apprehension, but just then my apprehension became greater, because the "wall" at that moment was one of the windows of the Marine Midland Bank, and the night watchmen were right inside. What if they came out and Red had one of his temper tantrums? They had a right to ask what we were doing there, and would I want to take his side? But there was more to worry me. If I feared a summons that would delay my trip to Europe, I was equally afraid of hurting Red's feelings. I knew what to expect from him when he spoke to an audience of one—and a friendly one, at that. Let a watchman threaten him with a nightstick, and God knew what would happen. "Red, please, let's go," I said. "What are you doing there?" He seemed to be listening to the building. His ear was pressed against a metal partition between two windows.

"This building is completely dead," he said.

"What do you mean?" I said. "Can't you see the night watchmen inside? Let's go, Red. It's dangerous."

"Dangerous?" he said. "I don't see why. The building has no voice. I've always known that. Look over there across the street. That was a building with a voice. They are tearing it down. The voice is gone. It's the first thing to go."

I headed for the building across the street, and Red followed me. We just made it, for one of the night watchmen came out.

"Interesting architecture," I said, very loudly. "It's really a shame they are tearing it down."

"The seamen's hotel down there was even better," he said. "They are tearing that down, too. And look at this sign. They put this sign up everywhere."

The sign was the usual warning to trespassers, with promise of a reward to anyone turning in trespassers or leading to their capture. "How do you like that?" he asked me. "We are trespassers, but they are aliens— the ones who are tearing it down. That building that lost its voice—you know what it was called? It was called the Singer Building, and it used to sing every morning with the voices of thousands of birds. And find me a window ledge or a roof where birds can nest along the walls of these new buildings!"

We were now standing under some scaffolding across the street from the Chase Manhattan Bank Building. Another building was coming down. A row of beautifully carved closet doors and shutters had been erected all around the wrecking site, but through fissures here and there we could see what resistance the wreckers were encountering from the ancient masonry. An acrid smell of rotting wood emanated from the half-demolished building. Red sniffed the air. "Smell the breath of the dead?" he asked me. Then he shouted, "Rape and murder, in there!" He went on, in his ordinary voice, "Did you see the crater down this way? That will be the World Trade Center. There were many birds in that area, but they left when the steel cage was built. You can catch buildings in cages but not birds. Tell me, are they doing the same thing to the mansions on Fifth Avenue? Putting them in a cage and killing them?"

"Yes," I said. "But how long has it been since you were in that area?"

"Years, I guess," he said. "Ever since they tore down that beautiful club at the corner of Fifth and Fifty-first, to replace it with Best & Co. Let's go listen to the birds at the U. S. Court House. That's become the last gathering place since the Singer Building began to come down."

We walked up past City Hall, and there, in the grayish morning mist, while the first drops of rain were falling on us, we heard the most wonderful concert of birds, coming from dark corners between windows and stone garlands all along the facade and the side of the Court House. Red stood there in the middle of Foley Square, his legs apart, listening.

After five minutes or so, Red said, "Let's go to the jail."

"To the jail?" I asked.

"Yes, to the jail," he said. "Three blocks from here, on Centre Street."

We walked up Centre Street until we came to the new Tombs. He pointed out to me that hands were moving at almost every window. A group of black women and children soon joined us on the sidewalk. Hands were raised in the rain, answering hands at the windows. A child next to us couldn't identify the window from which his father was calling. His mother tried to direct his eyes toward it but couldn't get him to stay quiet. "It's Saturday morning," Red whispered to me. "They come early for the visit."

We continued uptown on Centre Street. It was really raining now— a cold rain. Red's feet looked purple through his torn shoes.

"You know, here is another stupid thing they do," Red said. "All the streets of New York are full of steam heat, but the pedestrian gets none of it. If I were rich, I would have all the streets heated."

"Wouldn't it be easier to buy yourself a pair of shoes?" I asked.

"It's always easier to think of yourself, first and last, and neglect the rest of suffering mankind," he answered, with anger. "I am thinking of others. And my plan would cost nothing."

"Really?"

"Much less than a day's fighting in Vietnam," he said. "Do you know how much heat is generated by one single bomb? Do you know how much iron is thrown away every hour in Vietnam? And these streets could be paved with iron bars, like those we have just seen. The subways would have light, and we would have heat; then I would have the subway closed down at midnight and the tracks cleaned by people. Just by people—you know? Even by me. I wouldn't mind."

We were walking up Lafayette Street now, and I had decided that I would take a bus at Astor Place, because that is where the Madison Avenue line begins, but Red insisted that we go and walk on the Bowery, which, from the jail, would be quite a detour for me, with all that rain coming down from the sky and up from the earth through my shoes. I was colder than I had almost ever been, even in the winter, because the weather forecast had spoken of an unusually warm day, precipitation probability near zero, wind at a few inches per hour; so here I was in my lightest summer suit, with no raincoat and no umbrella, and with sudden gusts of the nastiest possible wind bringing whiffs of dejection and garbage into my face.

"Why the Bowery, Red? Haven't you had enough of it? I have. Especially this morning."

But he was way ahead of me, walking at an exceptionally energetic pace for him, so I ran after him, in order not to hurt his feelings—all the way from there to Cooper Union, where he suddenly seemed to lose all his strength, just when I was beginning to recapture mine. The bus was there, ready to leave. It meant all the difference between sitting in warm, dry air and standing in the rain, and I boarded it. Once comforted by the heat and transportation, I decided I must do something for Red, even if it seemed impossible. I simply must.

A week or so later, I decided to go downtown and look for Red. I found him listening to buildings, as usual. It was difficult for me to tell whether the shoes and rags he wore were those I had last seen him in or were new ones. He appeared glad to see me—as if he sought friendship. Or, at least, he liked to be seen to have friends by those who were incapable of friendship; namely, the bums on the Bowery. He evidently liked to impress bums and policemen alike by showing them the sight of him, a filthy bum, talking authoritatively to a man from "the other world."

I decided to treat Red as a friend, and told him candidly that I didn't like his suicidal way of living.

"Suicidal?" he shouted, in a fit of anger. "Su-i-ci-dal, *he* says." And he harangued the trees, the seagulls, and the whole Port of New York out to the Statue of Liberty. "I don't believe in suicide," he said. "I don't like those bums who try to be run over by cars in the Bowery. They are stupid. But if you want to kill yourself you'd better not talk about it, or you'll wind up in Bellevue. Just do it before they can get to you. And do it quietly."

As we were about to part company in front of the Court House, Red remembered that I was supposed to be in Europe that summer, and seemed very much disappointed when I said I didn't know whether I could go after all. "Oh, that's too bad," he said. "I like to think that I know somebody who is feeling the sea under his feet."

I felt I owed him a promise that I would go soon, and I promised him I would. Perhaps I really would.

I continued my early walks, but I intentionally avoided meeting Red. I saw him a couple of times but managed to change my route before he saw me. The last time I saw him was the very day he died. He was standing under the highway at the foot of Fulton Street, where we had met for the second time in one morning only a couple of months before, and he was staring at the masts of the Scotland, which had just been repainted.

The next day, I saw Red's picture—actually, one of a series of four pictures—in the *Times*, against the background of the Brooklyn Bridge, as he jumped from the mast. He looked like a long flying fish, crossing that beautiful network of wires against the sky. Someone had sold Red's suicide. And this exceptional picture must surely have won a photography contest somewhere.

---

1. This account consists almost entirely of facts: facts of physical description, conversation, and action. There are a few inferences stated by the author. What are some of them?
2. Though the author states only these few inferences, he presents the facts in such a way that the reader is led to make a number of inferences. What general ideas do you infer about Red? About the author? What are the facts that lead you to each inference?
3. What particular facts or impressions concerning Red does the author emphasize? What techniques of emphasis does he use?
4. What does the author emphasize about the background—the city itself? How does he achieve this emphasis, and what is its purpose?
5. What general idea does the author express by means of this emphasis and the facts he offers in the account? What does he seem to want the reader to think about?

Pigeon Woman

MAY SWENSON

Slate, or dirty-marble-colored,
or rusty-iron-colored, the pigeons
on the flagstones in front of the
Public Library make a sharp lake

into which the pigeon woman wades
at exactly 1:30. She wears a
plastic pink raincoat with a round
collar (looking like a little

girl, so gay) and flat gym shoes,
her hair square-cut, orange.
Wide-apart feet carefully enter
the spinning, crooning waves

(as if she'd just learned how
to walk, each step conscious,
an accomplishment); blue knots in the
calves of her bare legs (uglied marble),

age in angled cords of jaw
and neck, her pimento-colored hair,
hanging in thin tassels, is gray
around a balding crown.

The day-old bread drops down
from her veined hand dipping out
of a paper sack. Choppy, shadowy ripples,
the pigeons strike around her legs.

Sack empty, she squats and seems to rinse
her hands in them—the rainy greens and
oily purples of their necks. Almost
they let her wet her thirsty fingertips—

but drain away in an untouchable tide.
A make-believe trade
she has come to, in her lostness
or illness or age—to treat the motley

city pigeons at 1:30 every day, in all
weathers. It is for them she colors
her own feathers. Ruddy-footed
on the lime-stained paving,

purling to meet her when she comes,
they are a lake of love. Retreating
from her hands as soon as empty,
they are the flints of love.

---

1. Separate the facts about the woman from inference and imagery. What does each fact tell us about her?
2. What inferences does the poet make? From the facts offered in the poem, would you arrive at the same ones? If not, how would yours differ?
3. One image is emphasized by being placed both at the beginning and at the end of the poem. What is the image? What does it imply? Where else in the poem does it appear?
4. What general idea does the poet express?

---

1. *Mrs. Gamley* is painted simply, with little detail; yet it communicates a good deal about its subject. What are some facts about Mrs. Gamley that you can deduce from the character of her kitchen?
2. What can you infer about her way of life from the chicken she is holding?
3. What can you tell about her from her clothing? From her shoes? From the way she wears her hair?
4. What is communicated by the way she stands?
5. If you were a visitor in Mrs. Gamley's home, what would you expect your visit to be like? Describe what some of its details would be, and support each detail that occurs to you with direct or indirect evidence from the picture.
6. By simplifying, the artist has been able to give emphasis to qualities he wants us to notice. What has the artist emphasized about Mrs. Gamley, her clothing, and her kitchen?

PLATE VI

MRS. GAMLEY: George Luks. 1930. Oil on canvas. 66″ × 48″. Collection of Whitney Museum of American Art.

BEWARE

7

perceiving
emotional
attitudes

No one is completely rational. Everyone has some emotional attitudes, feelings about certain subjects or things or people that are not based on facts or good sense. A man who expresses the most calm and measured views on politics may turn into a spastic windmill when a bee flies near him. In a few minutes you could name a hundred subjects about which various people hold emotional attitudes.

Some of these attitudes are the result of stereotyping, the failure to discriminate among individual members of a large class. Stereotyping causes some people to fear all insects because a few bite or to judge whole groups of people by a few members. Other attitudes are the result of conditioning: a man who, as a child, failed in his first arithmetic lessons may hold a lifelong conviction that he can never understand figures. Still other attitudes take the form of a fixed outlook on life as a whole, such as incurable optimism or pessimism.

Emotional attitudes are at the root of most human conflicts, from private quarrels to world wars. Conflict arises from two sources: failure to examine our own emotional attitudes and failure to perceive those of others.

class discussion

Identify and describe a dislike of yours that you suspect may be a prejudice, an attitude that is emotional rather than reasonable. If you dislike oranges because they make you break out, this is probably not a prejudice;

but if you simply dislike them, it may be because of some association or conditioning in your past. Try to identify the source of your dislike. Let others in your class suggest possible sources.

alternate class discussion

Think of a person you know who maintains an attitude you find unreasonable. Describe the person, and make clear how the attitude shows itself in speech and action. Then open a discussion about how the person might have acquired the attitude and how it might be possible to change it.

writing assignment

At some time during your life you have no doubt changed or abandoned an emotional attitude. This attitude may have been in relation to a person, a group, an activity, a belief, a place, or even your own ability to do something or understand something.
1. Define clearly what the attitude was.
2. Determine as accurately as you can where, when, and how you acquired it, and write down the sequence of events.
3. Relate in some detail the events that led you to change the attitude.
4. Define your present attitude.

alternate writing assignment

It is likely that at some time in the past another person's emotional attitude has caused you trouble or pain or you have observed how someone caused distress to others.
1. Write a description of this person, contrasting the good and bad qualities, with specific examples of how these qualities show themselves in the person's words and actions.
2. Make clear what your relationship with this person was and how, when, and where you came to know each other.
3. Tell the story of how you discovered this person's emotional attitude and how it affected you or others. Be specific—include all relevant detail.

narration

Narration is storytelling. Most of us take to it naturally, since we have all listened to stories and told them. Whenever you tell a friend what happened at the drive-in last night, you are narrating. When you write narration, there are a few easy rules to observe. First, you should keep your story unified; it should be about one event or a series of closely related events. Second, it should follow a time sequence and not jump back and forth; you don't want to be one of those storytellers who is always saying, "Oh, I forgot to tell you. . . ." Third, it should begin at the beginning of the action and end with its end. A story about the night the dinner table collapsed needn't begin with your getting up in the morning.

"Primitive" or nonliterate people are often the best tellers of stories. The following Ethiopian folk tale is a perfect example of a story that begins at the beginning, marches forward economically until it gets to the point, and there ends.

Justice

A woman one day went out to look for her goats that had wandered away from the herd. She walked back and forth over the fields for a long time without finding them. She came at last to a place by the side of the road where a deaf man sat before a fire brewing himself a cup of coffee. Not realizing he was deaf, the woman asked:

"Have you seen my herd of goats come this way?"

The deaf man thought she was asking for the water hole, so he pointed vaguely toward the river.

The woman thanked him and went to the river. And there, by coincidence, she found the goats. But a young kid had fallen among the rocks and broken its foot.

She picked it up to carry it home. As she passed the place where the deaf man sat drinking his coffee, she stopped to thank him for his help. And in gratitude she offered him the kid.

JUSTICE from *The Fire on the Mountain and Other Ethiopian Stories* by Harold Courlander and Wolf Leslau. Copyright 1950 by Holt, Rinehart and Winston. Copyright © 1978 by Harold Courlander and Wolf Lesau. Reprinted by permission of Holt, Rinehart and Winston, Publishers.

But the deaf man didn't understand a word she was saying. When she held the kid toward him he thought she was accusing him of the animal's misfortune, and he became very angry.

"I had nothing to do with it!" he shouted.

"But you pointed the way," the woman said.

"It happens all the time with goats!" the man shouted.

"I found them right where you said they would be," the woman replied.

"Go away and leave me alone, I never saw him before in my life!" the man shouted.

People who came along the road stopped to hear the argument.

The woman explained to them:

"I was looking for the goats and he pointed toward the river. Now I wish to give him this kid."

"Do not insult me in this way!" the man shouted loudly. "I am not a leg breaker!" And in his anger he struck the woman with his hand.

"Ah! did you see? He struck me with his hand!" the woman said to the people. "I will take him before the judge!"

So the woman with the kid in her arms, the deaf man, and the spectators went to the house of the judge. The judge came out before his house to listen to their complaint. First, the woman talked, then the man talked, then people in the crowd talked. The judge sat nodding his head. But that meant very little, for the judge, like the man before him, was very deaf. Moreover, he was also very nearsighted.

At last, he put up his hand and the talking stopped. He gave them his judgment.

"Such family rows are a disgrace to the Emperor and an affront to the Church," he said solemnly. He turned to the man.

"From this time forward, stop mistreating your wife," he said.

He turned to the woman with the young goat in her arms.

"As for you, do not be so lazy. Hereafter do not be late with your husband's meals."

He looked at the baby goat tenderly.

"And as for the beautiful infant, may she have a long life and grow to be a joy to you both!"

The crowd broke up and the people went their various ways.

"Ah, how good it is!" they said to each other. "How did we ever get along before justice was given us?"

class writing assignment

Using whichever writing assignment you chose, reorganize the material into a story or narration. All you need to do is arrange the descriptions and incidents into the time sequence in which they occurred. If you can, use dialogue here and there, as Richard Wilbur does in "A Game of Catch." Keep coherence in mind: orient your reader with expressions like, "The next day, at my friend's house," and so on.

A Game of Catch

RICHARD WILBUR

Monk and Glennie were playing catch on the side lawn of the firehouse when Scho caught sight of them. They were good at it, for seventh-graders, as anyone could see right away. Monk, wearing a catcher's mitt, would lean easily sidewise and back, with one leg lifted and his throwing hand almost down to the grass, and then lob the white ball straight up into the sunlight. Glennie would shield his eyes with his left hand and, just as the ball fell past him, snag it with a little dart of his glove. Then he would burn the ball straight toward Monk, and it would spank into the round mitt and sit, like a still-life apple on a plate, until Monk flipped it over into his right hand and, with a negligent flick of his hanging arm, gave Glennie a fast grounder.

They were going on and on like that, in a kind of slow, mannered, luxurious dance in the sun, their faces perfectly blank and entranced, when Glennie noticed Scho dawdling along the other side of the street and called hello to him. Scho crossed over and stood at the front edge of the lawn, near an apple tree, watching.

"Got your glove?" asked Glennie after a time. Scho obviously hadn't.

"You could give me some easy grounders," said Scho. "But don't burn 'em."

"All right," Glennie said. He moved off a little, so the three of them formed a triangle, and they passed the ball around for about five minutes, Monk tossing easy grounders to Scho, Scho throwing to Glennie, and Glennie burning them in to Monk. After a while, Monk began to throw them back to Glennie once or twice before he let Scho have his grounder, and finally Monk gave Scho a fast, bumpy grounder that hopped over his shoulder and went in to the brake on the other side of the street.

"Not so hard," called Scho as he ran across to get it.

"You should've had it," Monk shouted.

It took Scho a little while to find the ball among the ferns and dead leaves, and when he saw it, he grabbed it up and threw it toward Glennie. It struck the trunk of the apple tree, bounced back at an angle, and rolled steadily and stupidly onto the cement apron in front of the firehouse, where one of the trucks was parked. Scho ran hard and stopped it just before it rolled under the truck, and this time he carried it back to his former position on the lawn and threw it carefully to Glennie.

"I got an idea," said Glennie. "Why don't Monk and I catch for five minutes more, and then you can borrow one of our gloves?"

"That's all right with me," said Monk. He socked his fist into his mitt, and Glennie burned one in.

"All right," Scho said, and went over and sat under the tree. There in the shade he watched them resume their skillful play. They threw lazily fast or lazily slow—high, low, or wide—and always handsomely, their expressions serene, changeless, and forgetful. When Monk missed a low backhand catch, he walked indolently after the ball and, hardly even looking flung it sidearm for an imaginary put-out. After a good while of this, Scho said, "Isn't it five minutes yet?"

"One minute to go," said Monk, with a fraction of a grin.

Scho stood up and watched the ball slap back and forth for several minutes more, and then he turned and pulled himself up into the crotch of the tree.

"Where you going?" Monk asked.

"Just up the tree," Scho said.

"I guess he doesn't want to catch," said Monk.

Scho went up and up through the fat light-gray branches until they grew slender and bright and gave under him. He found a place where several supple branches were knit to make a dangerous chair, and sat there with his head coming out of the leaves into the sunlight. He could see the two other boys down below, the ball going back and forth between them as if they were bowling on the grass, and Glennie's crew-cut head looking like a sea urchin.

"I found a wonderful seat up here," Scho said loudly. "If I don't fall out." Monk and Glennie didn't look up or comment and so he began jouncing gently in his chair of branches and singing "Yo-ho, heave ho" in an exaggerated way.

"Do you know what, Monk?" he announced in a few moments. "I can make you two guys do anything I want. Catch that ball, Monk! Now you catch it, Glennie!"

"I was going to catch it anyway," Monk suddenly said. "You're not making anybody do anything when they're already going to do it anyway."

"I made you say what you just said," Scho replied joyfully.

"No, you didn't," said Monk, still throwing and catching but now less serenely absorbed in the game.

"That's what I wanted you to say," Scho said.

The ball bounded off the rim of Monk's mitt and plowed into a gladiolus bed beside the firehouse, and Monk ran to get it while Scho jounced in his treetop and sang, "I wanted you to miss that. Anything you do is what I wanted you to do."

"Let's quit for a minute," Glennie suggested.

"We might as well, until the peanut gallery shuts up," Monk said.

They went over and sat crosslegged in the shade of the tree. Scho looked down between his legs and saw them on the dim, spotty ground, saying nothing to one another. Glennie soon began abstractedly spinning his glove between his palms; Monk pulled his nose and stared out across the lawn.

"I want you to mess around with your nose, Monk," said Scho, giggling. Monk withdrew his hand from his face.

"Do that with your glove, Glennie," Scho persisted. "Monk, I want you to pull up hunks of grass and chew on it."

Glennie looked up and saw a self-delighted, intense face staring down at him through the leaves. "Stop being a dope and come down and we'll catch for a few minutes," he said.

Scho hesitated, and then said, in a tentatively mocking voice, "That's what I wanted you to say."

"All right, then, nuts to you," said Glennie.

"Why don't you keep quiet and stop bothering people?" Monk asked.

"I made you say that," Scho replied, softly.

"Shut up," Monk said.

"I made you say that, and I want you to be standing there looking sore. And I want you to climb up the tree. I'm making you do it!"

Monk was scrambling up through the branches, awkward in his haste, and getting snagged on twigs. His face was furious and foolish, and he kept telling Scho to shut up, shut up, shut up, while the other's exuberant and panicky voice poured down upon his head.

"Now you shut up or you'll be sorry," Monk said, breathing hard as he reached up and threatened to shake the cradle of slight branches in which Scho was sitting.

"I *want*——" Scho screamed as he fell. Two lower branches broke his rustling, crackling fall, but he landed on his back with a deep thud and lay still, with a strangled look on his face and his eyes clenched. Glennie knelt down and asked breathlessly, "Are you O.K., Scho? Are you O.K.?"

while Monk swung down through the leaves crying that honestly he hadn't even touched him, the crazy guy just let go. Scho doubled up and turned over on his right side, and now both the other boys knelt beside him, pawing at his shoulder and begging to know how he was.

Then Scho rolled away from them and sat partly up, still struggling to get his wind but forcing a species of smile onto his face.

"I'm sorry, Scho," Monk said. "I didn't mean to make you fall."

Scho's voice came out weak and gravelly, in gasps. "I meant—you to do it. You—had to. You can't do—anything—unless I want—you to."

Glennie and Monk looked helplessly at him as he sat there, breathing a bit more easily and smiling fixedly, with tears in his eyes. Then they picked up their gloves and the ball, walked over to the street, and went slowly away down the sidewalk, Monk punching his fist into the mitt, Glennie juggling the ball between glove and hand.

From under the apple tree, Scho, still bent over a little for lack of breath, croaked after them in triumph and misery, "I want you to do whatever you're going to do for the whole rest of your life!"

---

1. "A Game of Catch" is told with great economy. Point out some sentences in which the feel of action is conveyed efficiently.
2. Why does the author begin the story at a particular point in the action? Why does he end it where he does?
3. How does he show us the differences in character between Monk and Glennie? What seems to be the emotional attitude of each? Who is the leader, and why? How is this shown?
4. What is Scho's attitude at the beginning? At the end?
5. How does Monk's attitude change? Why is the game spoiled for him?
6. In the physical contest, who wins? Who wins the battle for emotional domination? Consider this question carefully. You may want to give a qualified answer.
7. Deceptively simple, "A Game of Catch" is disturbing because it reflects some uncomfortable facts about the way human beings relate, or fail to relate, to each other. Translated into adult life, what kind of person does Monk represent? Glennie? Scho?
8. What kinds of experiences do you think make each of these "types" the way they are?
9. Some people who fail in the practical world turn to the occult, where they can manipulate illusions unchallenged. Is this the nature of Scho's retreat? Suggest some alternative interpretations.
10. Is life a contest?

The U.S. Sailor
with the Japanese Skull

WINFIELD TOWNLEY SCOTT

Bald-bare, bone-bare, and ivory yellow: skull
Carried by a thus two-headed U.S. sailor
Who got it from a Japanese soldier killed
At Guadalcanal in the ever-present war: our

Bluejacket, I mean, aged 20, in August strolled
Among the little bodies on the sand and hunted
Souvenirs: teeth, tags, diaries, boots; but bolder still
Hacked off this head and under a leopard tree skinned it:

Peeled with a lifting knife the jaw and cheeks, bared
The nose, ripped off the black-haired scalp and gutted
The dead eyes to these thoughtful hollows: a scarred
But bloodless job, unless it be said brains bleed.

Then, his ship underway, dragged this aft in a net
Many days and nights—the cold bone tumbling
Beneath the foaming wake, weed-worn and salt-cut
Rolling safe among fish and washed with Pacific;

Till on a warm and level-keeled day hauled in
Held to the sun and the sailor, back to a gun-rest,
Scrubbed the cured skull with lye, perfecting this:
Not foreign as he saw it first: death's familiar cast.

Bodiless, fleshless, nameless, it and the sun
Offend each other in strange fascination
As though one of the two were mocked; but nothing is in
This head, or it fills with what another imagines

THE U.S. SAILOR WITH THE JAPANESE SKULL Reprinted with permission of Macmillan Publishing Co., Inc., from *Collected Poems* by Winfield Townley Scott. Copyright 1945 by Winfield Townley Scott, renewed 1973 by Eleanor M. Scott.

As: here were love and hate and the will to deal
Death or to kneel before it, death emperor,
Recorded orders without reasons, bomb-blast, still
A child's morning, remembered moonlight on Fujiyama:

All scoured out now by the keeper of this skull
Made elemental, historic, parentless by our
Sailor boy who thinks of home, voyages laden, will
Not say, "Alas! I did not know him at all."

---

1. The action of the poem is presented in narrative form, in normal time sequence. At what point does it begin? With what action does it end? In what ways is narration more effective than a static picture?
2. The power of the poem is not only in its subject, but in the poet's choice of words and images. What are some words that strongly evoke the kinesthetic sense? Some strong action verbs?
3. The poet rubs his reader's nose, so to speak, in the unpleasant realities of his subject. What is his purpose in doing this? What are some of the images he uses to make sure we are aware of these realities?
4. What is the emotional attitude of the sailor? Of the poet?
5. Which of the three boys in "A Game of Catch" is most like the sailor? In what way?
6. The poet is saying something about the nature of evil. Try to formulate a definition of evil that he might agree with.
7. Have you ever known anyone who was like the sailor in some respect? What are this person's effects on other people?

---

1. This is a narrative picture, one that tells a story. The scene is Christmas Eve; the small girl has received presents, while her oldest brother, no doubt because he has not been good, has been given only a stick for his father to beat him with. (The younger brother holds the stick and points at him.) How do the positions of the figures' bodies, heads, and hands help to make the story clear?
2. What do their facial expressions tell us?
3. What is the parents' attitude toward the little girl? What may be a result of this attitude in terms of her developing character? What kind of adult do you feel she is likely to become?
4. Answer question 3 in respect to the oldest brother.
5. Do you find the picture funny, or serious, or both at once? Explain.
6. What connections can you perceive between this picture and "A Game of Catch" or "The U.S. Sailor with the Japanese Skull"?

PLATE VII

THE FEAST OF ST. NICHOLAS: Jan Steen. By courtesy of the Rijksmuseum, Amsterdam

Drawing by Chas. Addams; © 1975 The New Yorker Magazine, Inc.

8

estimating
a person

Many of our troubles arise from underestimating or overestimating people or failing to understand what to expect from them. Sometimes we come up against a strong prejudice we did not suspect was there; at other times we reject a person who might otherwise have been a good friend because we do not understand something he or she does or says. In such cases, we often realize later that the evidence we needed was there and we overlooked it. Like the reader of a detective story, we were taken by surprise because we failed to see the clues.

Many of the clues are inside ourselves. People are basically alike, but they differ in the experiences they have had and in the situations in which they find themselves. One way of estimating a person is to try to put yourself in that person's place, to imagine how you might act if you were in the same situation with the same background. Or, to put it another way, ask yourself, "If I did that, why would I be doing it?" By making an effort to understand others, we may make our own world more pleasant to live in.

class discussion

Think of a person you prefer to avoid because of a quality or habit that annoys you. Describe this quality or habit to the class and let others suggest possible reasons or motives behind it.

writing assignment

1. Of all the people around you, choose the one you have the least liking for.
2. Write a full paragraph, giving as many concrete examples as you can of the qualities that make you dislike this person. Exaggerate a little if you wish.
3. Write a second paragraph in which you suggest possible motives for each of these qualities. If you had these qualities, why would you have them?
4. Now write a third paragraph about all the good qualities of this person. Don't make them up; find them. Write about the person as though you felt affection. This may be difficult, but give it a good try.

contrast

When you are going to *contrast* two things, such as the good and bad qualities of the person you are writing about, you have a choice of two ways to organize your essay. If you prefer, you can put all the bad qualities into one paragraph and all the good ones into a second, being sure that each time you bring up one of the good ones, you relate it to one of the bad ones. Or you can deal with the good and bad qualities sentence by sentence, something like this: "Joe is slovenly in his personal habits; he chews tobacco, seldom shaves, and almost never combs his hair. On the other hand, he keeps his shop neat, with everything always in its place." If you choose the latter method, your overall organization will be determined by categories, such as personal habits, social behavior, and business ethics, with a paragraph devoted to each. Whatever organization and categories you use, remember that they should grow naturally out of your material. Don't impose too fixed an organization and then try to force your material into it. Be conscious of the need for organization, but don't be rigid.

class writing assignment

Look over the material you have from the writing assignment.
1. Decide which form of contrast organization will suit your material best.
2. Decide how you want to fit in the comments you have made about the person's motives. You may want to discuss these motives as you go along, or you may want to collect the comments in one paragraph; if so, decide where that paragraph should be.
3. Plan an introductory paragraph explaining who the person is and what your relationship with him or her is and a concluding paragraph summing up your qualified opinion of the person. Then write your essay.

The Catbird Seat

JAMES THURBER

Mr. Martin bought the pack of Camels on Monday night in the most crowded cigar store on Broadway. It was theater time and seven or eight men were buying cigarettes. The clerk didn't even glance at Mr. Martin, who put the pack in his overcoat pocket and went out. If any of the staff at F & S had seen him buy the cigarettes, they would have been astonished, for it was generally known that Mr. Martin did not smoke, and never had. No one saw him.

It was just a week to the day since Mr. Martin had decided to rub out Mrs. Ulgine Barrows. The term "rub out" pleased him because it suggested nothing more than the correction of an error—in this case an error of Mr. Fitweiler. Mr. Martin had spent each night of the past week working out his plan and examining it. As he walked home now he went over it again. For the hundredth time he resented the element of imprecision, the margin of guesswork that entered into the business. The project as he had worked it out was casual and bold, the risks were considerable. Something might go wrong anywhere along the line. And therein lay the cunning of his scheme. No one would ever see in it the cautious, painstaking hand of Erwin Martin, head of the filing department at F & S, of whom Mr. Fitweiler had once said, "Man is fallible but Martin isn't." No one would see his hand, that is, unless it were caught in the act.

Sitting in his apartment, drinking a glass of milk, Mr. Martin reviewed his case against Mrs. Ulgine Barrows, as he had every night for seven nights. He began at the beginning. Her quacking voice and braying laugh had first profaned the halls of F & S on March 7, 1941 (Mr. Martin had a head for dates). Old Roberts, the personnel chief, had introduced her as the newly appointed special adviser to the president of the firm, Mr. Fitweiler. The woman had appalled Mr. Martin instantly, but he hadn't shown it. He had given her his dry hand, a look of studious concentration, and a faint smile. "Well," she had said, looking at the papers on his desk, "are you lifting the oxcart out of the ditch?" As Mr. Martin recalled that moment, over his milk, he squirmed slightly. He must keep his mind on her crimes as a special adviser, not on her peccadillos as a personality. This he found difficult to do, in spite of entering an objection and sustaining it. The faults of the woman as a woman kept chattering on in his mind like an unruly witness. She had, for almost two years now, baited him. In the halls, in the elevator, even in his own office, into which she romped now and then like a circus horse, she was constantly shouting these silly questions at him. "Are you lifting the oxcart out of the ditch? Are you tearing up the pea patch? Are you hollering down the rain barrel? Are you scraping around the bottom of the pickle barrel? Are you sitting in the catbird seat?"

It was Joey Hart, one of Mr. Martin's two assistants, who had explained what the gibberish meant. "She must be a Dodger fan," he had said. "Red Barber announces the Dodger games over the radio and he uses those expressions—picked 'em up down South." Joey had gone on to explain one or two. "Tearing up the pea patch" meant going on a rampage; "sitting in the catbird seat" meant sitting pretty, like a batter with three balls and no strikes on him. Mr. Martin dismissed all this with an effort. It had been annoying, it had driven him near to distraction, but he was too solid a man to be moved to murder by anything so childish. It was fortunate, he reflected as he passed on to the important charges against Mrs. Barrows, that he had stood up under it so well. He had maintained always an outward appearance of polite tolerance. "Why, I even believe you like the woman," Miss Paird, his other assistant, had once said to him. He had simply smiled.

A gavel rapped in Mr. Martin's mind and the case proper was resumed. Mrs. Ulgine Barrows stood charged with willful, blatant, and persistent attempts to destroy the efficiency and system of F & S. It was competent, material, and relevant to review her advent and rise to power. Mr. Martin had got the story from Miss Paird, who seemed always able to find things out. According to her, Mrs. Barrows had met Mr. Fitweiler at a party, where she had rescued him from the embraces of a powerfully built drunken man who had mistaken the president of F & S for a famous retired Middle Western football coach. She had led him to a sofa and somehow worked upon him a monstrous magic. The aging gentleman had jumped to the conclusion there and then that this was a woman of singular attainments, equipped to bring out the best in him and in the firm. A week later he had introduced her into F & S as his special adviser. On that day confusion got its foot in the door. After Miss Tyson, Mr. Brundage, and Mr. Bartlett had been fired and Mr. Munson had taken his hat and stalked out, mailing in his resignation later, old Roberts had been emboldened to speak to Mr. Fitweiler. He mentioned that Mr. Munson's department had been "a little disrupted" and hadn't they perhaps better resume the old system there? Mr. Fitweiler had said certainly not. He had the greatest faith in Mrs. Barrows' ideas. "They require a little seasoning, a little seasoning, is all," he had added. Mr. Roberts had given it up. Mr. Martin reviewed in detail all the changes wrought by Mrs. Barrows. She had begun chipping at the cornices of the firm's edifice and now she was swinging at the foundation stones with a pickaxe.

Mr. Martin came now, in his summing up, to the afternoon of Monday, November 2, 1942—just one week ago. On that day, at 3 P.M., Mrs. Barrows had bounced into his office. "Boo!" she had yelled. "Are you scraping around the bottom of the pickle barrel?" Mr. Martin had looked at her from under his green eyeshade, saying nothing. She had begun to wander about the office, taking it in with her great, popping eyes. "Do you really need *all* these filing cabinets?" she had demanded suddenly. Mr. Martin's heart had jumped. "Each of these files," he had said, keeping his voice even, "plays an indispensable part in the system of F & S." She had brayed at him, "Well, don't tear up the pea patch!" and gone to the door. From there she had bawled, "But you sure have got a lot of fine scrap in here!" Mr. Martin could no longer doubt that the finger was on his beloved department. Her pickaxe was on the upswing, poised for the first blow. It had not come yet; he had received no blue memo from the enchanted Mr. Fitweiler bearing nonsensical instructions deriving from the obscene woman. But there was no doubt in Mr. Martin's mind that one would be forthcoming. He must act quickly. Already a precious week had gone by. Mr. Martin stood up in his living room, still holding his milk glass. "Gentlemen of the jury," he said to himself, "I demand the death penalty for this horrible person."

The next day Mr. Martin followed his routine, as usual. He polished his glasses more often and once sharpened an already sharp pencil, but not even Miss Paird noticed. Only once did he catch sight of his victim; she swept past him in the hall with a patronizing "Hi!" At five-thirty he walked home, as usual, and had a glass of milk, as usual. He had never drunk anything stronger in his life—unless you could count ginger ale. The late Sam Schlosser, the S of F & S, had praised Mr. Martin at a staff meeting several years before for his temperate habits. "Our most efficient worker neither drinks nor smokes," he had said. "The results speak for themselves." Mr. Fitweiler had sat by, nodding approval.

Mr. Martin was still thinking about that red-letter day as he walked over to the Schrafft's on Fifth Avenue near Forty-sixth Street. He got there, as he always did, at eight o'clock. He finished his dinner and the financial page of the *Sun* at a quarter to nine, as he always did. It was his custom after dinner to take a walk. This time he walked down Fifth Avenue at a casual pace. His gloved hands felt moist and warm, his forehead cold. He transferred the Camels from his overcoat to a jacket pocket. He wondered, as he did so, if they did not represent an unnecessary note of strain. Mrs. Barrows smoked only Luckies. It was his idea to puff a few puffs on a Camel (after the rubbing-out), stub it out in the ashtray holding her lipstick-stained Luckies, and thus drag a small red herring across the trail. Perhaps it was not a good idea. It would take time. He might even choke, too loudly.

Mr. Martin had never seen the house on West Twelfth Street where Mrs. Barrows lived, but he had a clear enough picture of it. Fortunately, she had bragged to everybody about her ducky first-floor apartment in the perfectly darling three-story red-brick. There would be no doorman or other attendants; just the tenants of the second and third floors. As he walked along, Mr. Martin realized that he would get there before nine-thirty. He had considered walking north on Fifth Avenue from Schrafft's to a point from which it would take him until ten o'clock to reach the house. At that hour people were less likely to be coming in or going out. But the procedure would have made an awkward loop in the straight thread of his casualness, and he had abandoned it. It was impossible to figure when people would be entering or leaving the house, anyway. There was a great risk at any hour. If he ran into anybody, he would simply have to place the rubbing-out of Ulgine Barrows in the inactive file forever. The same thing would hold true if there were someone in her apartment. In that case he would just say that he had been passing by, recognized her charming house and thought to drop in.

It was eighteen minutes after nine when Mr. Martin turned into Twelfth Street. A man passed him, and a man and a woman, talking. There was no one within fifty paces when he came to the house, halfway down the block. He was up the steps and in the small vestibule in no time, pressing the bell under the card that said "Mrs. Ulgine Barrows." When the clicking in the lock started, he jumped forward against the door. He got inside fast, closing the door behind him. A bulb in a lantern hung from the hall ceiling on a chain seemed to give a monstrously bright light. There was nobody on the stair, which went up ahead of him along the left wall. A door opened down the hall in the wall on the right. He went toward it swiftly, on tiptoe.

"Well, for God's sake, look who's here!" bawled Mrs. Barrows, and her braying laugh rang out like the report of a shotgun. He rushed past her like a football tackle, bumping her. "Hey, quit shoving!" she said, closing the door behind them. They were in her living room, which seemed to Mr. Martin to be lighted by a hundred lamps. "What's after you?" she said. "You're as jumpy as a goat." He found he was unable to speak. His heart was wheezing in his throat. "I—yes," he finally brought out. She was jabbering and laughing as she started to help him off with his coat. "No, no," he said. "I'll put it here." He took it off and put it on a chair near the door. "Your hat and gloves, too," she said. "You're in a lady's house." He put his hat on top of the coat. Mrs. Barrows seemed larger than he had thought. He kept his gloves on. "I was passing by," he said. "I recognized—is there anyone here?" She laughed louder than ever. "No," she said, "we're all alone. You're as white as a sheet, you funny man. Whatever *has* come over you? I'll mix you a toddy." She started toward a door across the room. "Scotch-and-soda be all right? But say, you don't drink, do you?" She turned and gave him her amused look. Mr. Martin pulled himself together. "Scotch-and-soda will be all right," he heard himself say. He could hear her laughing in the kitchen.

Mr. Martin looked quickly around the living room for the weapon. He had counted on finding one there. There were andirons and a poker and something in a corner that looked like an Indian club. None of them would do. It couldn't be that way. He began to pace around. He came to a desk. On it lay a metal paper knife with an ornate handle. Would it be sharp enough? He reached for it and knocked over a small brass jar. Stamps spilled out of it and it fell to the floor with a clatter. "Hey," Mrs. Barrows yelled from the kitchen, "are you tearing up the pea patch?" Mr. Martin gave a strange laugh. Picking up the knife, he tried its point against his left wrist. It was blunt. It wouldn't do.

When Mrs. Barrows reappeared, carrying two highballs, Mr. Martin, standing there with his gloves on, became acutely conscious of the fantasy he had wrought. Cigarettes in his pocket, a drink prepared for him—it was all too grossly improbable. It was more than that; it was impossible. Somewhere in the back of his mind a vague idea stirred, sprouted. "For heaven's sake, take off those gloves," said Mrs. Barrows. "I always wear them in the house," said Mr. Martin. The idea began to bloom, strange and wonderful. She put the glasses on a coffee table in front of a sofa and sat on the sofa. "Come over here, you odd little man," she said. Mr. Martin went over and sat beside her. It was difficult getting a cigarette out of the pack of Camels but he managed it. She held a match for him, laughing. "Well," she said, handing him his drink, "this is perfectly marvelous. You with a drink and a cigarette."

Mr. Martin puffed, not too awkwardly, and took a gulp of the highball. "I drink and smoke all the time," he said. He clinked his glass against hers. "Here's nuts to that old windbag, Fitweiler," he said, and gulped again. The stuff tasted awful, but he made no grimace. "Really, Mr. Martin," she said, her voice and posture changing, "you are insulting our employer." Mrs. Barrows was now all special adviser to the president. "I am preparing a bomb," said Mr. Martin, "which will blow the old goat higher than hell." He had only had a little of the drink, which was not strong. It couldn't be that. "Do you take dope or something?" Mrs. Barrows asked coldly. "Heroin," said Mr. Martin. "I'll be coked to the gills when I bump that old buzzard off." "Mr. Martin!" she shouted, getting to her feet. "That will be all of that. You must go at once." Mr. Martin took another swallow of his drink. He tapped his cigarette out in the ashtray and put the pack of Camels on the coffee table. Then he got up. She stood glaring at him. He walked over and put on his hat and coat. "Not a word about this," he said, and laid an index finger against his lips. All Mrs. Barrows could bring out was "Really!" Mr. Martin put his hand on the doorknob. "I'm sitting in the catbird seat," he said. He stuck his tongue out at her and left. Nobody saw him go.

Mr. Martin got to his apartment, walking, well before eleven. No one saw him go in. He had two glasses of milk after brushing his teeth, and he felt elated. It wasn't tipsiness, because he hadn't been tipsy. Anyway, the walk had worn off all effects of the whisky. He got in bed and read a magazine for a while. He was asleep before midnight.

Mr. Martin got to the office at eight-thirty the next morning, as usual. At a quarter to nine, Ulgine Barrows, who had never before arrived at work before ten, swept into his office. "I'm reporting to Mr. Fitweiler now!" she shouted. "If he turns you over to the police, it's no more than you deserve!" Mr. Martin gave her a look of shocked surprise. "I beg your pardon?" he said. Mrs. Barrows snorted and bounced out of the room, leaving Miss Paird and Joey Hart staring after her. "What's the matter with that old devil now?" asked Miss Paird. "I have no idea," said Mr. Martin, resuming his work. The other two looked at him and then at each other. Miss Paird got up and went out. She walked slowly past the closed door of Mr. Fitweiler's office. Mrs. Barrows was yelling inside, but she was not braying. Miss Paird could not hear what the woman was saying. She went back to her desk.

Forty-five minutes later, Mrs. Barrows left the president's office and went into her own, shutting the door. It wasn't until half an hour later that Mr. Fitweiler sent for Mr. Martin. The head of the filing department, neat, quiet, attentive, stood in front of the old man's desk. Mr. Fitweiler was pale and nervous. He took his glasses off and twiddled them. He made a small, bruffing sound in his throat. "Martin," he said, "you have been with us more than twenty years." "Twenty-two, sir," said Mr. Martin. "In that time," pursued the president, "your work and your—uh—manner have been exemplary." "I trust so, sir," said Mr. Martin. "Ah, yes." Mr. Fitweiler polished his glasses. "You may describe what you did after leaving the office yesterday, Martin," he said. Mr. Martin allowed less than a second for his bewildered pause. "Certainly, sir," he said. "I walked home. Then I went to Schrafft's for dinner. Afterward I walked home again. I went to bed early, sir, and read a magazine for a while. I was asleep before eleven." "Ah, yes," said Mr. Fitweiler again. He was silent for a moment, searching for the proper words to say to the head of the filing department. "Mrs. Barrows," he said finally, "Mrs. Barrows has worked hard, Martin, very hard. It grieves me to report that she has suffered a severe breakdown. It has taken the form of a persecution complex accompanied by distressing hallucinations." "I am very sorry, sir," said Mr. Martin. "Mrs. Barrows is under the delusion," continued Mr. Fitweiler, "that you visited her last evening and behaved yourself in an—uh—unseemly manner." He raised his hand to silence Mr. Martin's pained outcry. "It is the nature of these psychological diseases," Mr. Fitweiler said, "to fix upon the least likely and most innocent party as the—uh—source of persecution. These matters are not for the lay mind to grasp, Martin. I've just had my psychiatrist, Dr. Fitch, on the phone. He would not, of course, commit himself, but he made enough generalizations to substantiate my suspicions. I suggested to Mrs. Barrows when she had completed her—uh—story to me this morning, that she visit Dr. Fitch, for I suspected a condition at once. She flew, I regret to say, into a rage, and demanded—uh—requested that I call you on the carpet. You may not know, Martin, but Mrs. Barrows had planned a reorganization of your department—subject to my approval, of course, subject to my approval. This brought you, rather than anyone else, to her mind—but again that is a phenomenon for Dr. Fitch and not for us. So, Martin, I am afraid Mrs. Barrows' usefulness here is at an end." "I am dreadfully sorry, sir," said Mr. Martin.

It was at this point that the door to the office blew open with the suddenness of a gas-main explosion and Mrs. Barrows catapulted through it. "Is the little rat denying it?" she screamed. "He can't get away with that!" Mr. Martin got up and moved discreetly to a point beside Mr. Fitweiler's chair. "You drank and smoked at my apartment," she bawled at Mr. Martin, "and you know it! You called Mr. Fitweiler an old windbag and said you were going to blow him up when you got coked to the gills on your heroin!" She stopped yelling to catch her breath and a new glint came into her popping eyes. "If you weren't such a drab, ordinary little man," she said, "I'd think you'd planned it all. Sticking your tongue out, saying you were sitting in the catbird seat, because you thought no one would believe me when I told it! My God, it's really too perfect!" She brayed loudly and hysterically, and the fury was on her again. She glared at Mr. Fitweiler. "Can't you see how he has tricked us, you old fool? Can't you see his little game?" But Mr. Fitweiler had been surreptitiously pressing all the buttons under the top of his desk and employees of F & S began pouring into the room. "Stockton," said Mr. Fitweiler, "you and Fishbein will take Mrs. Barrows to her home. Mrs. Powell, you will go with them." Stockton, who had played a little football in high school, blocked Mrs. Barrows as she made for Mr. Martin. It took him and Fishbein together to force her out of the door and into the hall, crowded with stenographers and office boys. She was still screaming imprecations at Mr. Martin, tangled and contradictory imprecations. The hubbub finally died out down the corridor.

"I regret that this has happened," said Mr. Fitweiler. "I shall ask you to dismiss it from your mind, Martin." "Yes, sir," said Mr. Martin, anticipating his chief's "That will be all" by moving to the door. "I will dismiss it." He went out and shut the door, and his step was light and quick in the hall. When he entered his department he had slowed down to his customary gait, and he walked quietly across the room to the W20 file, wearing a look of studious concentration.

1. Contrasts in "The Catbird Seat" are exaggerated to make the story funny and to emphasize the point. What are some of these contrasts?
2. How are the contrasts made clear?
3. What is the point of the story? Try to state it in a one-sentence generalization.
4. What are Ulgine Barrows' assumptions about Mr. Martin? What are his about her? Who is nearer the truth, and why?
5. If Ulgine Barrows had been more perceptive, what clues might she have noticed in Mr. Martin?
6. What does this story have in common with "Red" (in Unit 6)? With "A Game of Catch" (in Unit 7)?

Richard Cory

EDWIN ARLINGTON ROBINSON

Whenever Richard Cory went down town,
We people on the pavement looked at him:
He was a gentleman from sole to crown,
Clean favored, and imperially slim.

And he was always quietly arrayed,
And he was always human when he talked;
But still he fluttered pulses when he said,
"Good-morning," and he glittered when he walked.

And he was rich—yes, richer than a king—
And admirably schooled in every grace:
In fine, we thought that he was everything
To make us wish that we were in his place.

So on we worked, and waited for the light,
And went without the meat, and cursed the bread;
And Richard Cory, one calm summer night,
Went home and put a bullet through his head.

---

1. What contrast is the poem based on?
2. What did people assume about Richard Cory? What would cause them to make such an assumption?
3. Is their assumption in any way similar to Ulgine Barrows' assumption in "The Catbird Seat"? If so, in what way is it similar?
4. Apparently Cory's fellow townspeople knew little about him. What are some possible reasons why they knew so little?
5. Have you ever been surprised—as the townspeople were—by someone's completely unexpected action? If so, why was the action unexpected? Explain the situation and its meaning.

RICHARD CORY from *Children of the Night* (1897) by Edwin Arlington Robinson. Reprinted by permission of Charles Scribner's Sons.

---

1. If you were standing before the man in this painting, how do you think you would evaluate him? What are your clues?
2. What contrasts, if any, do you find in this picture? What is their significance?
3. Most people believe they have good reasons for doing the things they do. Cardinal Niño was Grand Inquisitor toward the end of the sixteenth century and must have condemned people to torture and death because they did not conform to Church beliefs. How do you think he may have felt about his role? Why do you think so?
4. In the painting, Cardinal Niño is wearing red vestments, white lace, and four rings. Do you get the impression that he is vain? Why, or why not?
5. What do you think the painter's evaluation of Cardinal Niño was? Are there any clues in the way El Greco has represented him?
6. Cardinal Niño commissioned the portrait and must have approved of it, since it still exists. Does this fact incline you to revise any part of your estimate of his character?
7. How do you think Cardinal Niño saw himself?
8. Can you perceive any relationships between Cardinal Niño and any of the characters in the previous readings? If so, which character? Explain what the relationship is.

PLATE VIII

CARDINAL DON FERNANDO NIÑO DE GUEVARA: El Greco. The Metropolitan
Museum of Art, Bequest of Mrs. H. O. Havemeyer, 1929. The H. O. Havemeyer
Collection

UNKNOWN
CITIZEN

9

identifying
with
a person

One important way of using your imagination is in identifying with another person, imagining for a time that you are that person. This is only a step beyond estimating, but it is a big step and requires some effort. Of course it is impossible to identify entirely with another person: you have not had the same background, and the images in his or her mind are not yours. Nevertheless you can use things you know about yourself, combined with clues from that person's behavior, to gain a little insight into what it is like to be in another's shoes. When you know something about the things someone is interested in, you know something about the person.

class discussion

Turn to *Peasant Resting*, the drawing at the end of this unit. Put yourself in the place of the man pictured. How do you feel? (Use *I*, not *he* in your description.) Go beyond simply saying, "I feel tired." Be specific. Describe the feelings in your body and mind. What do you want most? What is your attitude toward the passing of time? Toward your own future? What do you remember from the past? What is your home life like? Discuss any thoughts or feelings you have.

writing assignment

1. Return to the person you used for the writing assignment in Unit 8—the person you like least among those around you. Write a full account—several pages—of ten or fifteen minutes in the life of that person, as though you were that person. Look for clues in speech, action, dress, and appearance. Imagining yourself as that person, what would you talk about most? What do you think your obsessions would be? How would you move about? What would you do with your hands, eyes, or mouth? Would you dress to impress others? If so, what impression would you try to make? What would you do with your hair? What facial expressions would you adopt when meeting others? Most important, ask yourself, "What would my motive be if I did that?"
2. Use *I* throughout, but do not insert your personality; try to figure out what your subject's thoughts and feelings are.
3. Focus especially on the thoughts of the person as he or she appears in the situations where you are together. What does he or she think about others, including yourself? How does your subject justify his or her own attitudes? Get inside your subject's skin and mind.

qualification

People who are looking for a fight or who just want to express their own emotions tend to make blanket statements in strong language like, "Women are lousy drivers." People who are searching for truth or who want to find a common ground for constructive action *qualify* their statements of opinion. A man who impartially reviewed his own experience might say, "While I have seen some women drivers do foolish things, I also know several who are very skillful." Or a man who took the trouble to inform himself of insurance company statistics might say, "Women drivers tend to have more minor accidents than men, but not nearly as many serious ones; and their insurance rates are lower." These are *qualified* statements closely reflecting the facts on which they are based. They are expressed in such a way as to be useful rather than inflammatory.

To state an unqualified opinion is, in many situations, to commit an act of aggression which can only incite others to behave aggressively. The first step toward peace and constructive social action is to learn to qualify opinion.

class exercise

Now that you have tried to estimate a person fairly and have tried to identify with this same person, see if you can formulate a qualified opinion about this person, one that will reflect objectively both his or her virtues and shortcomings. Take a few minutes to work out such a statement and write it down; then submit it to the class for comments and suggestions.

Sonny's Blues

JAMES BALDWIN

I read about it in the paper, in the subway, on my way to work. I read it, and I couldn't believe it, and I read it again. Then perhaps I just stared at it, at the newsprint spelling out his name, spelling out the story. I stared at it in the swinging lights of the subway car, and in the faces and bodies of the people, and in my own face, trapped in the darkness which roared outside.

It was not to be believed and I kept telling myself that, as I walked from the subway station to the high school. And at the same time I couldn't doubt it. I was scared, scared for Sonny. He became real to me again. A great block of ice got settled in my belly and kept melting there slowly all day long, while I taught my classes algebra. It was a special kind of ice. It kept melting, sending trickles of ice water all up and down my veins, but it never got less. Sometimes it hardened and seemed to expand until I felt my guts were going to come spilling out or that I was going to choke or scream. This would always be at a moment when I was remembering some specific thing Sonny had once said or done.

When he was about as old as the boys in my classes his face had been bright and open, there was a lot of copper in it; and he'd had wonderfully direct brown eyes, and great gentleness and privacy. I wondered what he looked like now. He had been picked up, the evening before, in a raid on an apartment downtown, for peddling and using heroin.

I couldn't believe it: but what I mean by this is that I couldn't find any room for it anywhere inside me. I had kept it outside me for a long time. I hadn't wanted to know. I had had suspicions, but I didn't name them, I kept putting them away. I told myself that Sonny was wild, but he wasn't crazy. And he'd always been a good boy, he hadn't ever turned hard or evil or disrespectful, the way kids can, so quick, so quick, especially in Harlem. I didn't want to believe that I'd ever see my brother going down, coming to nothing, all that light in his face gone out, in the condition I'd already seen so many others. Yet it had happened and here I was, talking about algebra to a lot of boys who might, every one of them for all I knew, be popping off needles every time they went to the head. Maybe it did more for them than algebra could.

I was sure that the first time Sonny had ever had horse, he couldn't have been much older than these boys were now. These boys, now, were living as we'd been living then, they were growing up with a rush and their heads bumped abruptly against the low ceiling of their actual possibilities. They were filled with rage. All they really knew were two darknesses, the darkness of their lives, which was now closing in on them, and the darkness of the movies, which had blinded them to that other darkness, and in which they now, vindictively, dreamed, at once more together than they were at any other time, and more alone.

When the last bell rang, the last class ended, I let out my breath. It seemed I'd been holding it for all that time. My clothes were wet—I may have looked as though I'd been sitting in a steam bath, all dressed up, all afternoon. I sat alone in the classroom a long time. I listened to the boys outside, downstairs, shouting and cursing and laughing. Their laughter struck me for perhaps the first time. It was not the joyous laughter which— God knows why—one associates with children. It was mocking and insular, its intent was to denigrate. It was disenchanted, and in this, also, lay the authority of their curses. Perhaps I was listening to them because I was thinking about my brother and in them I heard my brother. And myself.

One boy was whistling a tune, at once very complicated and very simple, it seemed to be pouring out of him as though he were a bird, and it sounded very cool and moving through all that harsh, bright air, only just holding its own through all those other sounds.

I stood up and walked over to the window and looked down into the courtyard. It was the beginning of the spring and the sap was rising in the boys. A teacher passed through them every now and again, quickly, as though he or she couldn't wait to get out of that courtyard, to get those boys out of their sight and off their minds. I started collecting my stuff. I thought I'd better get home and talk to Isabel.

The courtyard was almost deserted by the time I got downstairs. I saw this boy standing in the shadow of a doorway, looking just like Sonny. I almost called his name. Then I saw that it wan't Sonny, but somebody we used to know, a boy from around our block. He'd been Sonny's friend. He'd never been mine, having been too young for me, and, anyway, I'd never liked him. And now, even though he was a grown-up man, he still hung around that block, still spent hours on the street corners, was always high and raggy. I used to run into him from time to time and he'd often work around to asking me for a quarter or fifty cents. He always had some real good excuse, too, and I always gave it to him, I don't know why.

But now, abruptly, I hated him. I couldn't stand the way he looked at me, partly like a dog, partly like a cunning child. I wanted to ask him what the hell he was doing in the school courtyard.

He sort of shuffled over to me, and he said, "I see you got the papers. So you already know about it."

"You mean about Sonny? Yes, I already know about it. How come they didn't get you?"

He grinned. It made him repulsive and it also brought to mind what he'd looked like as a kid. "I wasn't there. I stay away from them people."

"Good for you." I offered him a cigarette and I watched him through the smoke. "You come all the way down here just to tell me about Sonny?"

"That's right." He was sort of shaking his head and his eyes looked strange, as though they were about to cross. The bright sun deadened his damp dark brown skin and it made his eyes look yellow and showed up the dirt in his kinked hair. He smelled funky. I moved a little away from him and I said, "Well, thanks. But I already know about it and I got to get home."

"I'll walk you a little ways," he said. We started walking. There were a couple of kids still loitering in the courtyard and one of them said goodnight to me and looked strangely at the boy beside me.

"What're you going to do?" he asked me. "I mean, about Sonny?"

"Look. I haven't seen Sonny for over a year, I'm not sure I'm going to do anything. Anyway, what the hell *can* I do?"

"That's right," he said quickly, "ain't nothing you can do. Can't much help old Sonny no more, I guess."

It was what I was thinking and so it seemed to me he had no right to say it.

"I'm surprised at Sonny, though," he went on—he had a funny way of talking, he looked straight ahead as though he were talking to himself— "I thought Sonny was a smart boy, I thought he was too smart to get hung."

"I guess he thought so too," I said sharply, "and that's how he got hung. And now about you? You're pretty goddamn smart, I bet."

Then he looked directly at me, just for a minute. "I ain't smart," he said. "If I was smart, I'd have reached for a pistol a long time ago."

"Look. Don't tell *me* your sad story, if it was up to me, I'd give you one." Then I felt guilty—guilty, probably, for never having supposed that the poor bastard *had* a story of his own, much less a sad one, and I asked, quickly, "What's going to happen to him now?"

He didn't answer this. He was off by himself some place. "Funny thing," he said, and from his tone we might have been discussing the quickest way to get to Brooklyn, "when I saw the papers this morning, the first thing I asked myself was if I had anything to do with it. I felt sort of responsible. "

I began to listen more carefully. The subway station was on the corner, just before us, and I stopped. He stopped too. We were in front of a bar and he ducked slightly, peering in, but whoever he was looking for didn't seem to be there. The juke box was blasting away with something black and bouncy and I half watched the barmaid as she danced her way from the juke box to her place behind the bar. And I watched her face as she laughingly responded to something someone said to her, still keeping time to the music. When she smiled one saw the little girl, one sensed the doomed, still-struggling woman beneath the battered face of the semi-whore.

"I never *give* Sonny nothing," the boy said finally, "but a long time ago I come to school high and Sonny asked me how it felt." He paused, I couldn't bear to watch him, I watched the barmaid, and I listened to the music which seemed to be causing the pavement to shake. "I told him it felt great." The music stopped, the barmaid paused and watched the juke box until the music began again. "It did."

All this was carrying me some place I didn't want to go. I certainly didn't want to know how it felt. It filled everything, the people, the houses, the music, the dark, quicksilver barmaid, with menace; and this menace was their reality.

"What's going to happen to him now?" I asked again.

"They'll send him away some place and they'll try to cure him." He shook his head. "Maybe he'll even think he's kicked the habit. Then they'll let him loose"—he gestured, throwing his cigarette into the gutter. "That's all."

"What do you mean, that's *all?*"

But I knew what he meant.

"I *mean*, that's *all*." He turned his head and looked at me, pulling down the corners of his mouth. "Don't you know what I mean?" he asked, softly.

"How the hell *would* I know what you mean?" I almost whispered it, I don't know why.

"That's right," he said to the air, "how would *he* know what I mean?" He turned toward me again, patient and calm, and yet I somehow felt him shaking, shaking as though he were going to fall apart. I felt that ice in my guts again, the dread I'd felt all afternoon; and again I watched the barmaid, moving about the bar, washing glasses, and singing. "Listen. They'll let him out and then it'll just start all over again. That's what I mean."

"You mean—they'll let him out. And then he'll just start working his way back in again. You mean he'll never kick the habit. Is that what you mean?"

"That's right," he said cheerfully. "*You* see what I mean."

"Tell me," I said at last, "why does he want to die? He must want to die, he's killing himself, why does he want to die?"

He looked at me in surprise. He licked his lips. "He don't want to die. He wants to live. Don't nobody want to die, ever."

Then I wanted to ask him—too many things. He could not have answered, or if he had, I could not have borne the answers. I started walking. "Well, I guess it's none of my business."

"It's going to be rough on old Sonny," he said. We reached the subway station. "This is your station?" he asked. I nodded. I took one step down. "Damn!" he said, suddenly. I looked up at him. He grinned again. "Damn it if I didn't leave all my money home. You ain't got a dollar on you, have you? Just for a couple of days, is all."

All at once something inside gave and threatened to come pouring out of me. I didn't hate him any more. I felt that in another moment I'd start crying like a child.

"Sure," I said. "Don't sweat." I looked in my wallet and didn't have a dollar, I only had a five. "Here," I said. "That hold you?"

He didn't look at it—he didn't want to look at it. A terrible, closed look came over his face, as though he were keeping the number on the bill a secret from him and me. "Thanks," he said, and now he was dying to see me go. "Don't worry about Sonny. Maybe I'll write him or something."

"Sure," I said. "You do that. So long."

"Be seeing you," he said. I went on down the steps.

And I didn't write Sonny or send him anything for a long time. When I finally did, it was just after my little girl died, he wrote me back a letter which made me feel like a bastard.

Here's what he said:

Dear brother,

You don't know how much I needed to hear from you. I wanted to write you many a time but I dug how much I must have hurt you and so I didn't write. But now I feel like a man who's been trying to climb up out of some deep, real deep and funky hole and just saw the sun up there, outside. I got to get outside.

I can't tell you much about how I got here. I mean I don't know how to tell you. I guess I was afraid of something or I was trying to escape from something and you know I have never been very strong in the head (smile). I'm glad Mama and Daddy are dead and can't see what's happened to their son and I swear if I'd known what I was doing I would never have hurt you so, you and a lot of other fine people who were nice to me and who believed in me.

I don't want you to think it had anything to do with me being a musician. It's more than that. Or maybe less than that. I can't get anything straight in my head down here and I try not to think about what's going to happen to me when I get outside again. Sometime I think I'm going to flip and *never* get outside and sometime I think I'll come straight back. I tell you one thing, though, I'd rather blow my brains out than go through this again. But that's what they all say, so they tell me. If I tell you when I'm coming to New York and if you could meet me, I sure would appreciate it. Give my love to Isabel and the kids and I was sure sorry to hear about little Gracie. I wish I could be like Mama and say the Lord's will be done, but I don't know it seems to me that trouble is the one thing that never does get stopped and I don't know what good it does to blame it on the Lord. But maybe it does some good if you believe it.

Your brother,
Sonny

Then I kept in constant touch with him and I sent him whatever I could and I went to meet him when he came back to New York. When I saw him many things I thought I had forgotten came flooding back to me. This was because I had begun, finally, to wonder about Sonny, about the life that Sonny lived inside. This life, whatever it was, had made him older and thinner and it had deepened the distant stillness in which he had always moved. He looked very unlike my baby brother. Yet, when he smiled, when we shook hands, the baby brother I'd never known looked out from the depths of his private life, like an animal waiting to be coaxed into the light.

"How you been keeping?" he asked me.

"All right. And you?"

"Just fine." He was smiling all over his face. "It's good to see you again."

"It's good to see you."

The seven years' difference in our ages lay between us like a chasm: I wondered if these years would ever operate between us as a bridge. I was remembering, and it made it hard to catch my breath, that I had been there when he was born; and I had heard the first words he had ever spoken. When he started to walk, he walked from our mother straight to me. I caught him just before he fell when he took the first steps he ever took in this world.

"How's Isabel?"

"Just fine. She's dying to see you."

"And the boys?"

"They're fine, too. They're anxious to see their uncle."

"Oh, come on. You know they don't remember me."

"Are you kidding? Of course they remember you."

He grinned again. We got into a taxi. We had a lot to say to each other, far too much to know how to begin.

As the taxi began to move, I asked, "You still want to go to India?"

He laughed. "You still remember that. Hell, no. This place is Indian enough for me."

"It used to belong to them," I said.

And he laughed again. "They damn sure knew what they were doing when they got rid of it."

Years ago, when he was around fourteen, he'd been all hipped on the idea of going to India. He read books about people sitting on rocks, naked, in all kinds of weather, but mostly bad, naturally, and walking barefoot through hot coals and arriving at wisdom. I used to say that it sounded to me as though they were getting away from wisdom as fast as they could. I think he sort of looked down on me for that.

"Do you mind," he asked, "if we have the driver drive alongside the park? On the west side—I haven't seen the city in so long."

"Of course not," I said. I was afraid that I might sound as though I were humoring him, but I hoped he wouldn't take it that way.

So we drove along, between the green of the park and the stony, lifeless elegance of hotels and apartment buildings, toward the vivid, killing streets of our childhood. These streets hadn't changed, though housing projects jutted up out of them now like rocks in the middle of a boiling sea. Most of the houses in which we had grown up had vanished, as had the stores from which we had stolen, the basements in which we had first tried sex, the rooftops from which we had hurled tin cans and bricks. But houses exactly like the houses of our past yet dominated the landscape, boys exactly like the boys we once had been found themselves smothering in these houses, came down into the streets for light and air and found themselves encircled by disaster. Some escaped the trap, most didn't. Those who got out always left something of themselves behind, as some animals amputate a leg and leave it in the trap. It might be said, perhaps, that I had escaped, after all, I was a school teacher; or that Sonny had, he hadn't lived in Harlem for years. Yet, as the cab moved uptown through streets which seemed, with a rush, to darken with dark people, and as I covertly studied Sonny's face, it came to me that what we both were seeking through our separate cab windows was that part of ourselves which had been left behind. It's always at the hour of trouble and confrontation that the missing member aches.

We hit 110th Street and started rolling up Lenox Avenue. And I'd known this avenue all my life, but it seemed to me again, as it had seemed on the day I'd first heard about Sonny's trouble, filled with a hidden menace which was its very breath of life.

"We almost there," said Sonny.

"Almost." We were both too nervous to say anything more.

We live in a housing project. It hasn't been up long. A few days after it was up it seemed uninhabitably new, now, of course, it's already rundown. It looks like a parody of the good, clean, faceless life—God knows the people who live in it do their best to make it a parody. The beat-looking grass lying around isn't enough to make their lives green, the hedges will never hold out the streets, and they know it. The big windows fool no one, they aren't big enough to make space out of no space. They don't bother with the windows, they watch the TV screen instead. The playground is most popular with the children who don't play at jacks, or skip rope, or roller skate, or swing, and they can be found in it after dark. We moved in partly because it's not too far from where I teach, and partly for the kids; but it's really just like the houses in which Sonny and I grew up. The same things happen, they'll have the same things to remember. The moment Sonny and I started into the house I had the feeling that I was simply bringing him back into the danger he had almost died trying to escape.

Sonny has never been talkative. So I don't know why I was sure he'd be dying to talk to me when supper was over the first night. Everything went fine, the oldest boy remembered him, and the youngest boy liked him, and Sonny had remembered to bring something for each of them; and Isabel, who is really much nicer than I am, more open and giving, had gone to a lot of trouble about dinner and was genuinely glad to see him. And she's always been able to tease Sonny in a way that I haven't. It was nice to see her face so vivid again and to hear her laugh and watch her make Sonny laugh. She wasn't, or anyway, she didn't seem to be, at all uneasy or embarrassed. She chatted as though there were no subject which had to be avoided and she got Sonny past his first, faint stiffness. And thank God she was there, for I was filled with that icy dread again. Everything I did seemed awkward to me, and everything I said sounded freighted with hidden meaning. I was trying to remember everything I'd heard about dope addiction and I couldn't help watching Sonny for signs. I wasn't doing it out of malice. I was trying to find out something about my brother. I was dying to hear him tell me he was safe.

"Safe!" my father grunted, whenever Mama suggested trying to move to a neighborhood which might be safer for children. "Safe, hell! Ain't no place safe for kids, nor nobody."

He always went on like this, but he wasn't, ever, really as bad as he sounded, not even on weekends, when he got drunk. As a matter of fact, he was always on the lookout for "something a little better," but he died before he found it. He died suddenly, during a drunken weekend in the middle of the war, when Sonny was fifteen. He and Sonny hadn't ever got on too well. And this was partly because Sonny was the apple of his father's eye. It was because he loved Sonny so much and was frightened for him, and he was always fighting with him. It doesn't do any good to fight with Sonny. Sonny just moves back, inside himself, where he can't be reached. But the principal reason that they never hit it off is that they were so much alike. Daddy was big and rough and loudtalking, just the opposite of Sonny, but they both had—the same privacy.

Mama tried to tell me something about this, just after Daddy died. I was home on leave from the army.

This was the last time I ever saw my mother alive. Just the same, this picture gets all mixed up in my mind with pictures I had of her when she was younger. The way I always see her is the way she used to be on a Sunday afternoon, say, when the old folks were talking after the big Sunday dinner. I always see her wearing pale blue. She'd be sitting on the sofa. And my father would be sitting in the easy chair, not far from her. And the living room would be full of church folks and relatives. There they sit, in chairs all around the living room, and the night is creeping up outside, but nobody knows it yet. You can see the darkness growing against the windowpanes and you hear the street noises every now and again, or maybe the jangling beat of a tambourine from one of the churches close by, but it's real quiet in the room. For a moment nobody's talking, but every face looks darkening, like the sky outside. And my mother rocks a little from the waist, and my father's eyes are closed. Everyone is looking at something a child can't see. For a minute they've forgotten the children. Maybe a kid is lying on the rug, half asleep. Maybe somebody's got a kid in his lap and is absent-mindedly stroking the kid's head. Maybe there's a kid, quiet and big-eyed, curled up in a big chair in the corner. The silence, the darkness coming, and the darkness in the faces frighten the child obscurely. He hopes that the hand which strokes his forehead will never stop—will never die. He hopes that there will never come a time when the old folks won't be sitting around the living room, talking about where they've come from, and what they've seen, and what's happened to them and their kinfolk.

But something deep and watchful in the child knows that this is bound to end, is already ending. In a moment someone will get up and turn on the light. Then the old folks will remember the children and they won't talk any more that day. And when light fills the room, the child is filled with darkness. He knows that every time this happens he's moved just a little closer to that darkness outside. The darkness outside is what the old folks have been talking about. It's what they've come from. It's what they endure. The child knows that they won't talk any more because if he knows too much about what's happened to *them*, he'll know too much too soon, about what's going to happen to *him*.

The last time I talked to my mother, I remember I was restless. I wanted to get out and see Isabel. We weren't married then and we had a lot to straighten out between us.

There Mama sat, in black, by the window. She was humming an old church song, *Lord, you brought me from a long ways off*. Sonny was out somewhere. Mama kept watching the streets.

"I don't know," she said, "if I'll ever see you again, after you go off from here. But I hope you'll remember the things I tried to teach you."

"Don't talk like that," I said, and smiled. "You'll be here a long time yet."

She smiled, too, but said nothing. She was quiet for a long time. And I said, "Mama, don't you worry about nothing. I'll be writing all the time, and you be getting the checks. . . ."

"I want to talk to you about your brother," she said, suddenly. "If anything happens to me he ain't going to have nobody to look out for him."

"Mama," I said, "ain't nothing going to happen to you *or* Sonny. Sonny's all right. He's a good boy and he's got good sense."

"It ain't a question of his being a good boy," Mama said, "nor of his having good sense. It ain't only the bad ones, nor yet the dumb ones that gets sucked under." She stopped, looking at me. "Your Daddy once had a brother," she said, and she smiled in a way that made me feel she was in pain. "You didn't never know that, did you?"

"No," I said, "I never knew that," and I watched her face.

"Oh, yes," she said, "your Daddy had a brother." She looked out of the window again. "I know you never saw your Daddy cry. But *I* did— many a time, through all these years."

I asked her, "What happened to his brother? How come nobody's ever talked about him?"

This was the first time I ever saw my mother look old.

"His brother got killed," she said, "when he was just a little younger than you are now. I knew him. He was a fine boy. He was maybe a little full of the devil, but he didn't mean nobody no harm."

Then she stopped and the room was silent, exactly as it had sometimes been on those Sunday afternoons. Mama kept looking out into the streets.

"He used to have a job in the mill," she said, "and, like all young folks, he just liked to perform on Saturday nights. Saturday nights, him and your father would drift around to different places, go to dances and things like that, or just sit around with people they knew, and your father's brother would sing, he had a fine voice, and play along with himself on his guitar. Well, this particular Saturday night, him and your father was coming home from some place, and they were both a little drunk and there was a moon that night, it was bright like day. Your father's brother was feeling kind of good, and he was whistling to himself, and he had his guitar slung over his shoulder. They was coming down a hill and beneath them was a road that turned off from the highway. Well, your father's brother, being always kind of frisky, decided to run down this hill, and he did, with that guitar banging and clanging behind him, and he ran across the road, and he was making water behind a tree. And your father was sort of amused at him and he was still coming down the hill, kind of slow. Then he heard a car motor and that same minute his brother stepped from behind the tree, into the road, in the moonlight. And he started to cross the road. And your father started to run down the hill, he says he don't know why. This car was full of white men. They was all drunk, and when they seen your father's brother they let out a great whoop and holler and they aimed the car straight at him. They was having fun, they just wanted to scare him, the way they do sometimes, you know. But they was drunk. And I guess the boy, being drunk, too, and scared, kind of lost his head. By the time he jumped it was too late. Your father says he heard his brother scream when the car rolled over him, and he heard the wood of that guitar when it give, and he heard them strings go flying, and he heard them white men shouting, and the car kept on a-going and it ain't stopped till this day. And, time your father got down the hill, his brother weren't nothing but blood and pulp."

Tears were gleaming on my mother's face. There wasn't anything I could say.

"He never mentioned it," she said, "because I never let him mention it before you children. Your Daddy was like a crazy man that night and for many a night thereafter. He says he never in his life seen anything as dark as that road after the lights of that car had gone away. Weren't nothing, weren't nobody on that road, just your Daddy and his brother and that busted guitar. Oh, yes. Your Daddy never did really get right again. Till the day he died he weren't sure but that every white man he saw was the man that killed his brother."

She stopped and took out her handkerchief and dried her eyes and looked at me.

"I ain't telling you all this," she said, "to make you scared or bitter or to make you hate nobody. I'm telling you this because you got a brother. And the world ain't changed."

I guess I didn't want to believe this. I guess she saw this in my face. She turned away from me, toward the window again, searching those streets.

"But I praise my Redeemer," she said at last, "that He called your Daddy home before me. I ain't saying it to throw no flowers at myself, but, I declare, it keeps me from feeling too cast down to know I helped your father get safely through this world. Your father always acted like he was the roughest, strongest man on earth. And everybody took him to be like that. But if he hadn't had *me* there—to see his tears!"

She was crying again. Still, I couldn't move. I said, "Lord, Lord, Mama, I didn't know it was like that."

"Oh, honey," she said, "there's a lot that you don't know. But you are going to find it out." She stood up from the window and came over to me. "You got to hold on to your brother," she said, "and don't let him fall, no matter what it looks like is happening to him and no matter how evil you gets with him. You going to be evil with him many a time. But don't you forget what I told you, you hear?"

"I won't forget," I said. "Don't you worry, I won't forget. I won't let nothing happen to Sonny."

My mother smiled as though she were amused at something she saw in my face. Then, "You may not be able to stop nothing from happening. But you got to let him know you's *there*."

Two days later I was married, and then I was gone. And I had a lot of things on my mind and I pretty well forgot my promise to Mama until I got shipped home on a special furlough for her funeral.

And, after the funeral, with just Sonny and me alone in the empty kitchen, I tried to find out something about him.

"What do you want to do?" I asked him.

"I'm going to be a musician," he said.

For he had graduated, in the time I had been away, from dancing to the juke box to finding out who was playing what, and what they were doing with it, and he had bought himself a set of drums.

"You mean, you want to be a drummer?" I somehow had the feeling that being a drummer might be all right for other people but not for my brother Sonny.

"I don't think," he said, looking at me very gravely, "that I'll ever be a good drummer. But I think I can play a piano."

I frowned. I'd never played the role of the older brother quite so seriously before, had scarcely ever, in fact, *asked* Sonny a damn thing. I sensed myself in the presence of something I didn't really know how to handle, didn't understand. So I made my frown a little deeper as I asked: "What kind of musician do you want to be?"

He grinned. "How many kinds do you think there are?"

"Be *serious*," I said.

He laughed, throwing his head back, and then looked at me. "I *am* serious."

"Well, then, for Christ's sake, stop kidding around and answer a serious question. I mean, do you want to be a concert pianist, you want to play classical music and all that, or—or what?" Long before I finished he was laughing again. "For Christ's *sake*, Sonny!"

He sobered, but with difficulty. "I'm sorry. But you sound so— *scared!*" and he was off again.

"Well, you may think it's funny now, baby, but it's not going to be so funny when you have to make your living at it, let me tell you *that*." I was furious because I knew he was laughing at me and I didn't know why.

"No," he said, very sober now, and afraid, perhaps, that he'd hurt me, "I don't want to be a classical pianist. That isn't what interests me. I mean"—he paused, looking hard at me, as though his eyes would help me to understand, and then gestured helplessly, as though perhaps his hand would help—"I mean, I'll have a lot of studying to do, and I'll have to study *everything*, but, I mean, I want to play *with*—jazz musicians." He stopped. "I want to play jazz," he said.

Well, the word had never before sounded as heavy, as real as it sounded that afternoon in Sonny's mouth. I just looked at him and I was probably frowning a real frown by this time. I simply couldn't see why on earth he'd want to spend his time hanging around nightclubs, clowning around on bandstands, while people pushed each other around a dance floor. It seemed—beneath him, somehow. I had never thought about it before, had never been forced to, but I suppose I had always put jazz musicians in a class with what Daddy called "good-time people."

"Are you *serious?*"

"Hell, *yes*, I'm serious."

He looked more helpless than ever, and annoyed, and deeply hurt.

I suggested, helpfully: "You mean—like Louis Armstrong?"

His face closed as though I'd struck him. "No. I'm not talking about none of that old-time, down home crap."

"Well, look, Sonny, I'm sorry, don't get mad. I just don't altogether get it, that's all. Name somebody—you know, a jazz musician you admire."

"Bird."

"Who?"

"Bird! Charlie Parker! Don't they teach you nothing in the goddamn army?"

I lit a cigarette. I was surprised and then a little amused to discover that I was trembling. "I've been out of touch," I said. "You'll have to be patient with me. Now. Who's this Parker character?"

"He's just one of the greatest jazz musicians alive," said Sonny, sullenly, his hands in his pockets, his back to me. "Maybe *the* greatest," he added, bitterly, "that's probably why *you* never heard of him."

"All right," I said, "I'm ignorant. I'm sorry. I'll go out and buy all the cat's records right away, all right?"

"It don't," said Sonny, with dignity, "make any difference to me. I don't care what you listen to. Don't do me no favors."

I was beginning to realize that I'd never seen him so upset before. With another part of my mind I was thinking that this would probably turn out to be one of those things kids go through and that I shouldn't make it seem important by pushing it too hard. Still, I didn't think it would do any harm to ask: "Doesn't all this take a lot of time? Can you make a living at it?"

He turned back to me and half leaned, half sat, on the kitchen table. "Everything takes time," he said, "and—well, yes, sure, I can make a living at it. But what I don't seem to be able to make you understand is that it's the only thing I want to do."

"Well, Sonny," I said, gently, "you know people can't always do exactly what they *want* to do—"

"*No*, I don't know that," said Sonny, surprising me. "I think people *ought* to do what they want to do, what else are they alive for?"

"You getting to be a big boy," I said desperately, "it's time you started thinking about your future."

"I'm thinking about my future," said Sonny, grimly. "I think about it all the time."

I gave up. I decided, if he didn't change his mind, that we could always talk about it later. "In the meantime," I said, "you got to finish school." We had already decided that he'd have to move in with Isabel and her folks. I knew this wasn't the ideal arrangement because Isabel's folks are inclined to be dicty and they hadn't especially wanted Isabel to marry me. But I didn't know what else to do. "And we have to get you fixed up at Isabel's."

There was a long silence. He moved from the kitchen table to the window. "That's a terrible idea. You know it yourself."

"Do you have a *better* idea?"

He just walked up and down the kitchen for a minute. He was as tall as I was. He had started to shave. I suddenly had the feeling that I didn't know him at all.

He stopped at the kitchen table and picked up my cigarettes. Looking at me with a kind of mocking, amused defiance, he put one between his lips. "You mind?"

"You smoking already?"

He lit the cigarette and nodded, watching me through the smoke. "I just wanted to see if I'd have the courage to smoke in front of you." He grinned and blew a great cloud of smoke to the ceiling. "It was easy." He looked at my face. "Come on, now. I bet you was smoking at my age, tell the truth."

I didn't say anything but the truth was on my face, and he laughed. But now there was something very strained in his laugh. "Sure. And I bet that ain't all you was doing."

He was frightening me a little. "Cut the crap," I said, "We already decided that you was going to go and live at Isabel's. Now what's got into you all of a sudden?"

"*You* decided it," he pointed out. "*I* didn't decide nothing." He stopped in front of me, leaning against the stove, arms loosely folded. "Look, brother. I don't want to stay in Harlem no more, I really don't." He was very earnest. He looked at me, then over toward the kitchen window. There was something in his eyes I'd never seen before, some thoughtfulness, some worry all his own. He rubbed the muscle of one arm. "It's time I was getting out of here."

"Where do you want to *go*, Sonny?"

"I want to join the army. Or the navy, I don't care. If I say I'm old enough, they'll believe me."

Then I got mad. It was because I was so scared. "You must be crazy. You goddamn fool, what the hell do you want to go and join the *army* for?"

"I just told you. To get out of Harlem."

"Sonny, you haven't even finished *school*. And if you really want to be a musician, how do you expect to study if you're in the *army?*"

He looked at me, trapped, and in anguish. "There's ways. I might be able to work out some kind of deal. Anyway, I'll have the G.I. Bill when I come out."

"*If* you come out." We stared at each other. "Sonny, please. Be reasonable. I know the setup is far from perfect. But we got to do the best we can."

"I ain't learning nothing in school," he said. "Even when I go." He turned away from me and opened the window and threw his cigarette out into the narrow alley. I watched his back. "At least, I ain't learning nothing you'd want me to learn." He slammed the window so hard I thought the glass would fly out, and turned back to me. "And I'm sick of the stink of these garbage cans!"

"Sonny," I said, "I know how you feel. But if you don't finish school now, you're going to be sorry later that you didn't." I grabbed him by the shoulders. "And you only got another year. It ain't so bad. And I'll come back and I swear I'll help you do *whatever* you want to do. Just try to put up with it till I come back. Will you please do that? For me?"

He didn't answer and he wouldn't look at me.

"Sonny. You hear me?"

He pulled away. "I hear you. But you never hear anything *I* say."

I didn't know what to say to that. He looked out of the window and then back at me. "OK," he said, and sighed. "I'll try."

Then I said, trying to cheer him up a little, "They got a piano at Isabel's. You can practice on it."

And as a matter of fact, it did cheer him up for a minute. "That's right," he said to himself. "I forgot that." His face relaxed a little. But the worry, the thoughtfulness, played on it still, the way shadows play on a face which is staring into the fire.

But I thought I'd never hear the end of that piano. At first, Isabel would write me, saying how nice it was that Sonny was so serious about his music and how, as soon as he came in from school, or wherever he had been when he was supposed to be at school, he went straight to that piano and stayed there until suppertime. And, after supper, he went back to that piano and stayed there until everybody went to bed. He was at the piano all day Saturday and all day Sunday. Then he bought a record player and started playing records. He'd play one record over and over again, all day long sometimes, and he'd improvise along with it on the piano. Or he'd play one section of the record, one chord, one change, one progression, then he'd do it on the piano. Then back to the record. Then back to the piano.

Well, I really don't know how they stood it. Isabel finally confessed that it wasn't like living with a person at all, it was like living with sound. And the sound didn't make any sense to her, didn't make any sense to any of them—naturally. They began, in a way, to be afflicted by this presence that was living in their home. It was as though Sonny were some sort of god, or monster. He moved in an atmosphere which wasn't like theirs at all. They fed him and he ate, he washed himself, he walked in and out of their door; he certainly wasn't nasty or unpleasant or rude, Sonny isn't any of those things; but it was as though he were all wrapped up in some cloud, some fire, some vision all his own; and there wasn't any way to reach him.

At the same time, he wasn't really a man yet, he was still a child, and they had to watch out for him in all kinds of ways. They certainly couldn't throw him out. Neither did they dare to make a great scene about that piano because even they dimly sensed, as I sensed, from so many thousands of miles away, that Sonny was at that piano playing for his life.

But he hadn't been going to school. One day a letter came from the school board and Isabel's mother got it—there had, apparently, been other letters but Sonny had torn them up. This day, when Sonny came in, Isabel's mother showed him the letter and asked where he'd been spending his time. And she finally got it out of him that he'd been down in Greenwich Village, with musicians and other characters, in a white girl's apartment. And this scared her and she started to scream at him and what came up, once she began—though she denies it to this day—was what sacrifices they were making to give Sonny a decent home and how little he appreciated it.

Sonny didn't play the piano that day. By evening, Isabel's mother had calmed down and then there was the old man to deal with, and Isabel herself. Isabel says she did her best to be calm but she broke down and started crying. She says she just watched Sonny's face. She could tell, by watching him, what was happening with him. And what was happening was that they penetrated his cloud, they had reached him. Even if their fingers had been a thousand times more gentle than human fingers ever are, he could hardly help feeling that they had stripped him naked and were spitting on that nakedness. For he also had to see that his presence, that music, which was life or death to him, had been torture for them and that they had endured it, not at all for his sake, but only for mine. And Sonny couldn't take that. He can take it a little better today than he could then but he's still not very good at it and, frankly, I don't know anybody who is.

The silence of the next few days must have been louder than the sound of all the music ever played since time began. One morning, before she went to work, Isabel was in his room for something and she suddenly realized that all of his records were gone. And she knew for certain that he was gone. And he was. He went as far as the navy would carry him. He finally sent me a postcard from some place in Greece and that was the first I knew that Sonny was still alive. I didn't see him any more until we were both back in New York and the war had long been over.

He was a man by then, of course, but I wasn't willing to see it. He came by the house from time to time, but we fought almost every time we met. I didn't like the way he carried himself, loose and dreamlike all the time, and I didn't like his friends, and his music seemed to be merely an excuse for the life he led. It sounded just that weird and disordered.

Then we had a fight, a pretty awful fight, and I didn't see him for months. By and by I looked him up, where he was living, in a furnished room in the Village, and I tried to make it up. But there were lots of other people in the room and Sonny just lay on his bed, and he wouldn't come downstairs with me, and he treated these other people as though they were his family and I weren't. So I got mad and then he got mad, and then I told him that he might just as well be dead as live the way he was living. Then he stood up and he told me not to worry about him any more in life, and he *was* dead as far as I was concerned. Then he pushed me to the door and the other people looked on as though nothing were happening, and he slammed the door behind me. I stood in the hallway, staring at the door. I heard somebody laugh in the room and then tears came to my eyes. I started down the steps, whistling to keep from crying, I kept whistling to myself, *You going to need me, baby, one of these cold, rainy days.*

I read about Sonny's troubles in the spring. Little Grace died in the fall. She was a beautiful little girl. But she only lived a little over two years. She died of polio and she suffered. She had a slight fever for a couple of days, but it didn't seem like anything and we just kept her in bed. And we would certainly have called the doctor, but the fever dropped, she seemed to be all right. So we thought it had just been a cold. Then, one day, she was up, playing, Isabel was in the kitchen fixing lunch for the two boys when they'd come in from school, and she heard Grace fall down in the living room. When you have a lot of children you don't always start running when one of them falls, unless they start screaming or something. And, this time, Grace was quiet. Yet, Isabel says that when she heard that *thump* and then that silence, something happened in her to make her afraid. And she ran to the living room and there was little Grace on the floor, all twisted up, and the reason she hadn't screamed was that she couldn't get her breath. And when she did scream, it was the worst sound, Isabel says, that she'd ever heard in all her life, and she still hears it sometimes in her dreams.

Isabel will sometimes wake me up with a low, moaning, strangled sound and I have to be quick to awaken her and hold her to me and where Isabel is weeping against me seems a mortal wound.

I think I may have written Sonny the very day that little Grace was buried. I was sitting in the living room in the dark, by myself, and I suddenly thought of Sonny. My trouble made his real.

One Saturday afternoon, when Sonny had been living with us, or, anyway, been in our house, for nearly two weeks, I found myself wandering aimlessly about the living room, drinking from a can of beer, and trying to work up the courage to search Sonny's room. He was out, he was usually out whenever I was home, and Isabel had taken the children to see their grandparents. Suddenly I was standing still in front of the living room window, watching Seventh Avenue. The idea of searching Sonny's room made me still. I scarcely dared to admit to myself what I'd be searching for. I didn't know what I'd do if I found it. Of if I didn't.

On the sidewalk across from me, near the entrance to a barbecue joint, some people were holding an old-fashioned revival meeting. The barbecue cook, wearing a dirty white apron, his conked hair reddish and metallic in the pale sun, and a cigarette between his lips, stood in the doorway, watching them. Kids and older people paused in their errands and stood there, along with some older men and a couple of very tough-looking women who watched everything that happened on the avenue, as though they owned it, or were maybe owned by it. Well, they were watching this, too. The revival was being carried on by three sisters in black, and a brother. All they had were their voices and their Bibles and a tambourine. The brother was testifying and while he testified two of the sisters stood together, seeming to say, amen, and the third sister walked around with the tambourine outstretched and a couple of people dropped coins into it. Then the brother's testimony ended and the sister who had been taking up the collection dumped the coins into her palm and transferred them to the pocket of her long black robe. Then she raised both hands, striking the tambourine against the air, and then against one hand, and she started to sing. And the two other sisters and the brother joined in.

It was strange, suddenly, to watch, though I had been seeing these street meetings all my life. So, of course, had everybody else down there. Yet, they paused and watched and listened and I stood still at the window. "Tis the old ship of Zion," they sang, and the sister with the tambourine kept a steady, jangling beat, "it has rescued many a thousand!" Not a soul under the sound of their voices was hearing this song for the first time, not one of them had been rescued. Nor had they seen much in the way of rescue work being done around them. Neither did they especially believe in the holiness of the three sisters and the brother, they knew too much about them, knew where they lived and how. The woman with the tambourine, whose voice dominated the air, whose face was bright with joy,

was divided by very little from the woman who stood watching her, a cigarette between her heavy, chapped lips, her hair a cuckoo's nest, her face
scarred and swollen from many beatings, and her black eyes glittering like
coal. Perhaps they both knew this, which was why, when, as rarely, they
addressed each other, they addressed each other as Sister. As the singing
filled the air the watching, listening faces underwent a change, the eyes
focusing on something within; the music seemed to soothe a poison out of
them; and time seemed, nearly, to fall away from the sullen, belligerent,
battered faces, as though they were fleeing back to their first condition,
while dreaming of their last. The barbecue cook half shook his head and
smiled, and dropped his cigarette and disappeared into his joint. A man
fumbled in his pockets for change and stood holding it in his hand impatiently, as though he had just remembered a pressing appointment further
up the avenue. He looked furious. Then I saw Sonny, standing on the edge
of the crowd. He was carrying a wide, flat notebook with a green cover, and
it made him look, from where I was standing, almost like a schoolboy. The
coppery sun brought out the copper in his skin, he was very faintly smiling,
standing very still. Then the singing stopped, the tambourine turned into
a collection plate again. The furious man dropped in his coins and vanished,
so did a couple of the women, and Sonny dropped some change in the plate,
looking directly at the woman with a little smile. He started across the
avenue, toward the house. He has a slow, loping walk, something like the
way Harlem hipsters walk, only he's imposed on this his own half-beat. I
had never really noticed it before.

I stayed at the window, both relieved and apprehensive. As Sonny
disappeared from my sight, they began singing again. And they were still
singing when his key turned in the lock.

"Hey," he said.

"Hey, yourself. You want some beer?"

"No. Well, maybe." But he came up to the window and stood beside
me, looking out. "What a warm voice," he said.

They were singing *If I could only hear my mother pray again!*

"Yes," I said, "and she can sure beat that tambourine."

"But what a terrible song," he said, and laughed. He dropped his
notebook on the sofa and disappeared into the kitchen. "Where's Isabel and
the kids?"

"I think they went to see their grandparents. You hungry?"

"No." He came back into the living room with his can of beer. "You
want to come some place with me tonight?"

I sensed, I don't know how, that I couldn't possibly say no. "Sure.
Where?"

He sat down on the sofa and picked up his notebook and started
leafing through it. "I'm going to sit in with some fellows in a joint in the
Village."

"You mean, you're going to play, tonight?"

"That's right." He took a swallow of his beer and moved back to the window. He gave me a sidelong look. "If you can stand it."

"I'll try," I said.

He smiled to himself and we both watched as the meeting across the way broke up. The three sisters and the brother, heads bowed, were singing *God be with you till we meet again*. The faces around them were very quiet. Then the song ended. The small crowd dispersed. We watched the three women and the lone man walk slowly up the avenue.

"When she was singing before," said Sonny, abruptly, "her voice reminded me for a minute of what heroin feels like sometimes—when it's in your veins. It makes you feel sort of warm and cool at the same time. And distant. And—and sure." He sipped his beer, very deliberately not looking at me. I watched his face. "It makes you feel—in control. Sometimes you've got to have that feeling."

"Do you?" I sat down slowly in the easy chair.

"Sometimes." He went to the sofa and picked up his notebook again. "Some people do."

"In order," I asked, "to play?" And my voice was very ugly, full of contempt and anger.

"Well"—he looked at me with great, troubled eyes, as though, in fact, he hoped his eyes would tell me things he could never otherwise say—"they *think* so. And *if* they think so—!"

"And what do *you* think?" I asked.

He sat on the sofa and put his can of beer on the floor. "I don't know," he said, and I couldn't be sure if he were answering my question or pursuing his thoughts. His face didn't tell me. "It's not so much to *play*. It's to *stand* it, to be able to make it at all. On any level." He frowned and smiled: "In order to keep from shaking to pieces."

"But these friends of yours," I said, "they seem to shake themselves to pieces pretty goddamn fast."

"Maybe." He played with the notebook. And something told me that I should curb my tongue, that Sonny was doing his best to talk, that I should listen. "But of course you only know the ones that've gone to pieces. Some don't—or at least they haven't *yet* and that's just about all *any* of us can say." He paused. "And then there are some who just live, really, in hell, and they know it and they see what's happening and they go right on. I don't know." He sighed, dropped the notebook, folded his arms. "Some guys, you can tell from the way they play, they on something *all* the time. And you can see that, well, it makes something real for them. But of course," he picked up his beer from the floor and sipped it and put the can down again, "they *want* to, too, you've got to see that. Even some of them that say they don't—*some*, not all."

"And what about you?" I asked—I couldn't help it. "What about you? Do *you* want to?"

He stood up and walked to the window and remained silent for a long time. Then he sighed. "Me," he said. Then: "While I was downstairs before, on my way here, listening to that woman sing, it struck me all of a sudden how much suffering she must have had to go through—to sing like that. It's *repulsive* to think you have to suffer that much."

I said: "But there's no way not to suffer—is there, Sonny?"

"I believe not," he said and smiled, "but that's never stopped anyone from trying." He looked at me. "Has it?" I realized, with this mocking look, that there stood between us, forever, beyond the power of time or forgiveness, the fact that I had held silence—so long!—when he had needed human speech to help him. He turned back to the window. "No, there's no way not to suffer. But you try all kinds of ways to keep from drowning in it, to keep on top of it, and to make it seem—well, like *you*. Like you did something, all right, and now you're suffering for it. You know?" I said nothing. "Well you know," he said, impatiently, "why *do* people suffer? Maybe it's better to do something to give it a reason, *any* reason."

"But we just agreed," I said, "that there's no way not to suffer. Isn't it better, then, just to—take it?"

"But nobody just takes it," Sonny cried, "that's what I'm telling you! *Everybody* tries not to. You're just hung up on the *way* some people try—it's not *your* way!"

The hair on my face began to itch, my face felt wet. "That's not true," I said, "that's not true. I don't give a damn what other people do, I don't even care how they suffer. I just care how *you* suffer." And he looked at me. "Please believe me," I said, "I don't want to see you—die—trying not to suffer."

"I won't," he said, flatly, "die trying not to suffer. At least, not any faster than anybody else."

"But there's no need," I said, trying to laugh, "is there? in killing yourself."

I wanted to say more, but I couldn't. I wanted to talk about will power and how life could be—well, beautiful. I wanted to say that it was all within; but was it? or, rather, wasn't that exactly the trouble? And I wanted to promise that I would never fail him again. But it would all have sounded—empty words and lies.

So I made the promise to myself and prayed that I would keep it.

"It's terrible sometimes, inside," he said, "that's what's the trouble. You walk these streets, black and funky and cold, and there's not really a living ass to talk to, and there's nothing shaking, and there's no way of getting it out—that storm inside. You can't talk it and you can't make love with it, and when you finally try to get with it and play it, you realize *nobody's* listening. So *you've* got to listen. You got to find a way to listen."

And then he walked away from the window and sat on the sofa again, as though all the wind had suddenly been knocked out of him. "Sometimes you'll do *anything* to play, even cut your mother's throat." He laughed and looked at me. "Or your brother's." Then he sobered. "Or your own." Then: "Don't worry. I'm all right now and I think I'll *be* all right. But I can't forget—where I've been. I don't mean just the physical place I've been, I mean where I've *been*. And *what* I've been."

"What have you been, Sonny?" I asked.

He smiled—but sat sideways on the sofa, his elbow resting on the back, his fingers playing with his mouth and chin, not looking at me. "I've been something I didn't recognize, didn't know I could be. Didn't know anybody could be." He stopped, looking inward, looking helplessly young, looking old. "I'm not talking about it now because I feel *guilty* or anything like that—maybe it would be better if I did, I don't know. Anyway, I can't really talk about it. Not to you, not to anybody," and now he turned and faced me. "Sometimes, you know, and it was actually when I was most *out* of the world, I felt that I was in it, and that I was *with* it, really, and I could play or I didn't really have to *play*, it just came out of me, it was there. And I don't know how I played, thinking about it now, but I know I did awful things, those times, sometimes, to people. Or it wasn't that I *did* anything to them—it was that they weren't real." He picked up the beer can; it was empty, he rolled it between his palms: "And other times—well, I needed a fix, I needed to find a place to lean, I needed to clear a space to *listen*—and I couldn't find it, and I—went crazy, I did terrible things to *me*, I was terrible *for* me." He began pressing the beer can between his hands, I watched the metal begin to give. It glittered, as he played with it, like a knife, and I was afraid he would cut himself, but I said nothing. "Oh well. I can never tell you. I was all by myself at the bottom of something, stinking and sweating and crying and shaking, and I smelled it, you know? *my* stink, and I thought I'd die if I couldn't get away from it and yet, all the same, I knew that everything I was doing was just locking me in with it. And I didn't know," he paused, still flattening the beer can, "I didn't know, I still *don't* know, something kept telling me that maybe it was good to smell your stink, but I didn't think that *that* was what I'd been trying to do—and—who can stand it?" and he abruptly dropped the ruined beer can, looking at me with a small, still smile, and then rose, walking to the window as though it were the lodestone rock. I watched his face, he watched the avenue. "I couldn't tell you when Mama died—but the reason I wanted to leave Harlem so bad was to get away from drugs. And then, when I ran away, that's what I was running from—really. When I came back, nothing had changed. *I* hadn't changed, I was just—older." And he stopped, drumming with his fingers on the windowpane. The sun had vanished, soon darkness would fall. I watched his face. "It can come again," he said, almost as though speaking to himself. Then he turned to me. "It can come again," he repeated. "I just want you to know that."

"All right," I said, at last. "So it can come again. All right."

He smiled, but the smile was sorrowful. "I had to try to tell you," he said.

"Yes," I said. "I understand that."

"You're my brother," he said, looking straight at me, and not smiling at all.

"Yes," I repeated, "yes. I understand that."

He turned back to the window, looking out. "All that hatred down there," he said, "all that hatred and misery and love. It's a wonder it doesn't blow the avenue apart."

We went to the only nightclub on a short, dark street, downtown. We squeezed through the narrow, chattering, jam-packed bar to the entrance of the room, where the bandstand was. And we stood there for a moment, for the lights were very dim in this room and we couldn't see. Then, "Hello, boy," said a voice and an enormous black man, much older than Sonny or myself, erupted out of all that atmospheric lighting and put an arm around Sonny's shoulder. "I been sitting right here," he said, "waiting for you."

He had a big voice, too, and heads in the darkness turned towards us.

Sonny grinned and pulled away, and said, "Creole, this is my brother. I told you about him."

Creole shook my hand. "I'm glad to meet you, son," he said, and it was clear that he was glad to meet me *there*, for Sonny's sake. And he smiled, "You got a real musician in *your* family," and he took his arm from Sonny's shoulder and slapped him, lightly, affectionately, with the back of his hand.

"Well. Now I've heard it all," said a voice behind us. This was another musician, and a friend of Sonny's, a coal-black, cheerful-looking man, built close to the ground. He immediately began confiding to me, at the top of his lungs, the most terrible things about Sonny, his teeth gleaming like a lighthouse and his laugh coming up out of him like the beginning of an earthquake. And it turned out that everyone at the bar knew Sonny, or almost everyone; some were musicians, working there, or nearby, or not working, some were simply hangers-on, and some were there to hear Sonny play. I was introduced to all of them and they were all very polite to me. Yet, it was clear that, for them, I was only Sonny's brother. Here, I was in Sonny's world. Or, rather: his kingdom. Here, it was not even a question that his veins bore royal blood.

They were going to play soon and Creole installed me, by myself, at a table in a dark corner. Then I watched them, Creole, and the little black man, and Sonny, and the others, while they horsed around, standing just below the bandstand. The light from the bandstand spilled just a little short of them and, watching them laughing and gesturing and moving about, I had the feeling that they, nevertheless, were being most careful not to step into that circle of light too suddenly: that if they moved into the light too suddenly, without thinking, they would perish in flame. Then, while I watched, one of them, the small, black man, moved into the light and crossed the bandstand and started fooling around with his drums. Then— being funny and being, also, extremely ceremonious—Creole took Sonny by the arm and led him to the piano. A woman's voice called Sonny's name and a few hands started clapping. And Sonny, also being funny and being ceremonious, and so touched, I think, that he could have cried, but neither hiding it nor showing it, riding it like a man, grinned, and put both hands to his heart and bowed from the waist.

Creole then went to the bass fiddle and a lean, very bright-skinned brown man jumped up on the bandstand and picked up his horn. So there they were, and the atmosphere on the bandstand and in the room began to change and tighten. Someone stepped up to the microphone and announced them. Then there were all kinds of murmurs. Some people at the bar shushed others. The waitress ran around, frantically getting the last orders, guys and chicks got closer to each other, and the lights on the bandstand, on the quartet, turned to a kind of indigo. Then they all looked different there. Creole looked about him for the last time, as though he were making certain that all his chickens were in the coop, and then he—jumped and struck the fiddle. And there they were.

All I know about music is that not many people ever really hear it. And even then, on the rare occasions when something opens within, and the music enters, what we mainly hear, or hear corroborated, are personal, private, vanishing evocations. But the man who creates the music is hearing something else, is dealing with the roar rising from the void and imposing order on it as it hits the air. What is evoked in him, then, is of another order, more terrible because it has no words, and triumphant, too, for that same reason. And his triumph, when he triumphs, is ours. I just watched Sonny's face. His face was troubled, he was working hard, but he wasn't with it. And I had the feeling that, in a way, everyone on the bandstand was waiting for him, both waiting for him and pushing him along. But as I began to watch Creole, I realized that it was Creole who held them all back. He had them on a short rein. Up there, keeping the beat with his whole body, wailing on the fiddle, with his eyes half closed, he was listening to everything, but he was listening to Sonny. He was having a dialogue with Sonny. He wanted Sonny to leave the shoreline and strike out for the deep water. He was Sonny's witness that deep water and drowning were not the same thing—he had been there, and he knew. And he wanted Sonny to know. He was waiting for Sonny to do the things on the keys which would let Creole know that Sonny was in the water.

And, while Creole listened, Sonny moved, deep within, exactly like someone in torment. I had never before thought of how awful the relation-ship must be between the musician and his instrument. He has to fill it, this instrument, with the breath of life, his own. He has to make it do what he wants it to do. And a piano is just a piano. It's made out of so much wood and wires and little hammers and big ones, and ivory. While there's only so much you can do with it, the only way to find this out is to try; to try and make it do everything.

And Sonny hadn't been near a piano for over a year. And he wasn't on much better terms with his life, not the life that stretched before him now. He and the piano stammered, started one way, got scared, stopped; started another way, panicked, marked time, started again; then seemed to have found a direction, panicked again, got stuck. And the face I saw on Sonny I'd never seen before. Everything had been burned out of it, and, at the same time, things usually hidden were being burned in, by the fire and fury of the battle which was occurring in him up there.

Yet, watching Creole's face as they neared the end of the first set, I had the feeling that something had happened, something I hadn't heard. Then they finished, there was scattered applause, and then, without an instant's warning, Creole started into something else, it was almost sardonic, it was *Am I Blue*. And, as though he commanded, Sonny began to play. Something began to happen. And Creole let out the reins. The dry, low, black man said something awful on the drums. Creole answered, and the drums talked back. Then the horn insisted, sweet and high, slightly de-tached perhaps, and Creole listened, commenting now and then, dry, and driving, beautiful and calm and old. Then they all came together again, and Sonny was part of the family again. I could tell this from his face. He seemed to have found, right there beneath his fingers, a damn brand-new piano. It seemed that he couldn't get over it. Then, for awhile, just being happy with Sonny, they seemed to be agreeing with him that brand-new pianos cer-tainly were a gas.

Then Creole stepped forward to remind them that what they were playing was the blues. He hit something in all of them, he hit something in me, myself, and the music tightened and deepened, apprehension began to beat the air. Creole began to tell us what the blues were all about. They were not about anything very new. He and his boys up there were keeping it new, at the risk of ruin, destruction, madness, and death, in order to find new ways to make us listen. For, while the tale of how we suffer, and how we are delighted, and how we may triumph is never new, it always must be heard. There isn't any other tale to tell, it's the only light we've got in all this darkness.

And this tale, according to that face, that body, those strong hands on those strings, has another aspect in every country, and a new depth in every generation. Listen, Creole seemed to be saying, listen. Now these are Sonny's blues. He made the little black man on the drums know it, and the bright, brown man on the horn. Creole wasn't trying any longer to get Sonny in the water. He was wishing him Godspeed. Then he stepped back, very slowly, filling the air with the immense suggestion that Sonny speak for himself.

Then they all gathered around Sonny and Sonny played. Every now and again one of them seemed to say, amen. Sonny's fingers filled the air with life, his life. But that life contained so many others. And Sonny went all the way back, he really began with the spare, flat statement of the opening phrase of the song. Then he began to make it his. It was very beautiful because it wasn't hurried and it was no longer a lament. I seemed to hear with what burning he had made it his, with what burning we had yet to make it ours, how we could cease lamenting. Freedom lurked around us and I understood, at last, that he could help us to be free if we would listen, that he would never be free until we did. Yet, there was no battle in his face now. I heard what he had gone through, and would continue to go through until he came to rest in earth. He had made it his: that long line, of which we knew only Mama and Daddy. And he was giving it back, as everything must be given back, so that, passing through death, it can live forever. I saw my mother's face again, and felt, for the first time, how the stones of the road she had walked on must have bruised her feet. I saw the moonlit road where my father's brother died. And it brought something else back to me, and carried me past it, I saw my little girl again and felt Isabel's tears again, and I felt my own tears begin to rise. And I was yet aware that this was only a moment, that the world waited outside, as hungry as a tiger, and that trouble stretched above us, longer than the sky.

Then it was over. Creole and Sonny let out their breath, both soaking wet, and grinning. There was a lot of applause and some of it was real. In the dark, the girl came by and I asked her to take drinks to the bandstand. There was a long pause, while they talked up there in the indigo light and after awhile I saw the girl put a Scotch and milk on top of the piano for Sonny. He didn't seem to notice it, but just before they started playing again, he sipped from it and looked toward me, and nodded. Then he put it back on top of the piano. For me, then, as they began to play again, it glowed and shook above my brother's head like the very cup of trembling.

1. The narrator of "Sonny's Blues" wants to establish contact with his younger brother, but he finds it difficult to do so. Why? Is the fault his, or Sonny's, or both?

2. When the narrator is telling Sonny to stay in school, Sonny says, "I hear you. But you never hear anything *I* say." What things has the narrator failed to hear? Why doesn't he hear them?

3. What are some of the events that finally bring him closer to identifying with Sonny?

4. After telling about what happend to his father's brother, the narrator's mother says, "You may not be able to stop nothing from happening. But you got to let him know you's *there*." What does she mean? What does this have to do with the death of his little daughter?

5. Would the narrator be able to identify more completely with Sonny if he took drugs himself? How could he be of most value to Sonny?

6. Does the author succeed in identifying with the narrator of the story? What are some of the ways in which he helps you to stand in the narrator's shoes?

7. What stereotype would most people apply to Sonny? How does this stereotype affect the narrator's relationship with Sonny?

8. The narrator overcomes, or changes, an emotional attitude. What is that attitude, and why is it changed?

9. Emotional attitudes involve fear. What is the nature of the narrator's fear?

10. Try to sum up the meaning of "Sonny's Blues" in a carefully *qualified* generalization. This may require more than one sentence.

Mr. Flood's Party

EDWIN ARLINGTON ROBINSON

Old Eben Flood, climbing alone one night
Over the hill between the town below
And the forsaken upland hermitage
That held as much as he should ever know
On earth again of home, paused warily.
The road was his with not a native near;
And Eben, having leisure, said aloud,
For no man else in Tilbury Town to hear:

"Well, Mr. Flood, we have the harvest moon
Again, and we may not have many more;
The bird is on the wing, the poet says,
And you and I have said it here before.
Drink to the bird." He raised up to the light
The jug that he had gone so far to fill,
And answered huskily: "Well, Mr. Flood,
Since you propose it, I believe I will."

Alone, as if enduring to the end
A valiant armor of scarred hopes outworn,
He stood there in the middle of the road
Like Roland's ghost winding a silent horn.
Below him, in the town among the trees,
Where friends of other days had honored him,
A phantom salutation of the dead
Rang thinly till old Eben's eyes were dim.

Then, as a mother lays her sleeping child
Down tenderly, fearing it may awake,
He set the jug down slowly at his feet
With trembling care, knowing that most things break;

MR. FLOOD'S PARTY Reprinted with permission of Macmillan Publishing Co., Inc., from *Collected Poems* by Edwin Arlington Robinson. Copyright 1921 by Edwin Arlington Robinson, renewed 1949 by Ruth Nivison.

And only when assured that on firm earth
It stood, as the uncertain lives of men
Assuredly did not, he paced away,
And with his hand extended paused again:

"Well, Mr. Flood, we have not met like this
In a long time; and many a change has come
To both of us, I fear, since last it was
We had a drop together. Welcome home!"
Convivially returning with himself,
Again he raised the jug up to the light;
And with an acquiescent quaver said:
"Well, Mr. Flood, if you insist, I might.

"Only a very little, Mr. Flood—
For auld lang syne. No more, sir; that will do."
So, for the time, apparently it did,
And Eben evidently thought so too;
For soon amid the silver loneliness
Of night he lifted up his voice and sang,
Secure, with only two moons listening,
Until the whole harmonious landscape rang—

"For auld lang syne." The weary throat gave out.
The last word wavered, and the song was done.
He raised again the jug regretfully
And shook his head, and was again alone.
There was not much that was ahead of him,
And there was nothing in the town below—
Where strangers would have shut the many doors
That many friends had opened long ago.

1. Like Sonny, Eben Flood is a victim of stereotyping. What is the stereotype in this case?
2. Describe clearly and vividly how Eben Flood would look to a person who did not identify with him.
3. What are some facts about Eben Flood that we know only because the poet told us? Could the poet, if he wished, help us even more in identifying with him? If so, how?
4. What parts of his environment has Eben lost contact with? How do you guess this has come about? Have his experiences been in any way similar to Sonny's?
5. If you lived in Tilbury Town, what is the best thing you could do in relation to Eben Flood? (Notice that the question is not what you could do *for* him; maybe he doesn't want your help.)

1. What is the first feeling you get when you look at *Peasant Resting*? What communicates this feeling to you?
2. What can you infer from the picture about what it is like to be such a peasant? What does he think about? What is his home life like? What hopes does he have?
3. What feelings enable you to identify with the peasant?
4. The drawing is done with little detail. Why?
5. The few details that are shown are emphasized. What are they? What do they mean?
6. The title uses the word *peasant*. Is this likely to lead to stereotyped thinking? Discuss.

PLATE IX

PEASANT RESTING: Jean François Millet. Ashmolean Museum, Oxford, England

10

perceiving
a relationship

As a human being, you exist only in relation to other human beings. If you had been raised by wolves or in an isolation cell, you would not know what it is to be human. If you were turned loose naked on a deserted island, you could survive only by using knowledge you have learned from others; without that knowledge, you could not build a fire or even figure out what was safe to eat.

Human relations are necessary, but they are also difficult and confusing. Often they are not what they seem to be. You have probably observed couples who use loving expressions as weapons to hurt each other and other couples who express genuine love by yelling at each other; or you have seen parents who spoil their children to hide real indifference and other parents who are strict with their children because they are deeply concerned about their welfare.

Human relationships are the subject of most books, plays, movies, television dramas, and even news items. Perhaps we are fascinated with crime and war because they're the last stages of failure in human relationships. (This final breakdown is the subject of the poem "The U.S. Sailor and the Japanese Skull" in Unit 7.) Your own happiness depends a great deal on how your relations with others are going.

You need to perceive human relationships, your own and others', as sharply as you can. And if you write about them well, you are guaranteed interested readers.

class discussion

Call to mind a relationship you have observed that is not what it seems on the surface. Describe the surface impression, if possible giving specific examples of language and behavior; then explain how the reality is different from the appearance. Such a relationship might be between any two members of a family, two friends, an employer and employee, a student and teacher, business partners, or any other close combination.

alternate class discussion

Tell about an experience of your own involving a change in your relationship to another person. This need not be an extremely personal experience. Perhaps you found there was more to an acquaintance than you thought at first, or mutual understanding might have ended a long-standing quarrel, or you might have drifted away from a childhood friend because your interests diverged. The important thing is to recall the specifics and bring out the contrasts. Make clear what happened.

paragraphing

Like coherence, good *paragraphing* helps your readers know what you are doing. When they reach a sentence whose beginning is indented, they know that you are changing your subject or your approach, or that there is some sort of division in your thought. A paragraph is usually a unit of several sentences about the same thing. In Unit 5, the description of how Lucretia carries her purse forms a paragraph; if we went on to tell what kinds of shoes she wears, readers would expect a new paragraph. A paragraph break is like a pause in speaking before you go on to the next subject.

writing assignment

Taking your cue from either of the preceding class discussions, write an account in three paragraphs of a contrast in a human relationship you have experienced or observed. There are two possible approaches to this essay:

1. Write about a relationship between two people that is not what it appears to be on the surface, with one paragraph about each of the following:

a. the appearance of the relationship as the casual observer sees it;
with specific evidence

b. the real feelings that exist between the two people, with specific
evidence

c. the meaning of the contrast, answering the question, "Why don't
these people act the way they feel?"

2. Write about a relationship of your own that changed, with one paragraph
for each of the following:

a. a description with some concrete detail of what the relationship
was like before it changed

b. a narration of the episode or series of actions that brought about
the change

c. a description of the relationship as it was (or is) after the change,
making clear what the change means to you.

Discovery of a Father

SHERWOOD ANDERSON

One of the strangest relationships in the world is that between father and
son. I know it now from having sons of my own.

A boy wants something very special from his father. You hear it said
that fathers want their sons to be what they feel they cannot themselves be,
but I tell you it also works the other way. I know that as a small boy I
wanted my father to be a certain thing he was not. I wanted him to be a
proud, silent, dignified father. When I was with other boys and he passed
along the street, I wanted to feel a glow of pride: 'There he is. That is my
father.'

But he wasn't such a one. He couldn't be. It seemed to me then that
he was always showing off. Let's say someone in our town had got up a
show. They were always doing it. The druggist would be in it, the shoe-
store clerk, the horse-doctor, and a lot of women and girls. My father would
manage to get the chief comedy part. It was, let's say, a Civil War play and
he was a comic Irish soldier. He had to do the most absurd things. They
thought he was funny, but I didn't.

I thought he was terrible. I didn't see how Mother could stand it.
She even laughed with the others. Maybe I would have laughed if it hadn't
been my father.

DISCOVERY OF A FATHER   adapted from *Sherwood Anderson's Memoirs: A Critical Edition*, edited by Ray Lewis
White, © 1969 The University of North Carolina Press, by permission of the publisher.

Or there was a parade, the Fourth of July or Decoration Day. He'd be in that, too, right at the front of it, as Grand Marshal or something, on a white horse hired from a livery stable.

He couldn't ride for shucks. He fell off the horse and everyone hooted with laughter, but he didn't care. He even seemed to like it. I remember once when he had done something ridiculous, and right out on Main Street, too. I was with some other boys and they were laughing and shouting at him and he was shouting back and having as good a time as they were. I ran down an alley back of some stores and there in the Presbyterian Church sheds I had a good long cry.

Or I would be in bed at night and Father would come home a little lit up and bring some men with him. He was a man who was never alone. Before he went broke, running a harness shop, there were always a lot of men loafing in the shop. He went broke, of course, because he gave too much credit. He couldn't refuse it and I thought he was a fool. I had got to hating him.

There'd be men I didn't think would want to be fooling around with him. There might even be the superintendent of our schools and a quiet man who ran the hardware store. Once I remember there was a white-haired man who was a cashier of the bank. It was a wonder to me they'd want to be seen with such a windbag. That's what I thought he was. I know now what it was that attracted them. It was because life in our town, as in all small towns, was at times pretty dull and he livened it up. He made them laugh. He could tell stories. He'd even get them to singing.

If they didn't come to our house, they'd go off, say, at night, to where there was a grassy place by a creek. They'd cook food there and drink beer and sit about listening to his stories.

He was always telling stories about himself. He'd say this or that wonderful thing had happened to him. It might be something that made him look like a fool. He didn't care.

If an Irishman came to our house, right away Father would say he was Irish. He'd tell what county in Ireland he was born in. He'd tell things that happened there when he was a boy. He'd make it seem so real that, if I hadn't known he was born in southern Ohio, I'd have believed him myself.

If it was a Scotchman the same thing happened. He'd get a burr into his speech. Or he was a German or a Swede. He'd be anything the other man was. I think they all knew he was lying, but they seemed to like him just the same. As a boy that was what I couldn't understand.

And there was Mother. How could she stand it? I wanted to ask, but never did. She was not the kind you asked such questions.

I'd be upstairs in my bed, in my room above the porch, and Father would be telling some of his tales. A lot of Father's stories were about the Civil War. To hear him tell it he'd been in about every battle. He'd known

Grant, Sherman, Sheridan, and I don't know how many others. He'd been particularly intimate with General Grant so that when Grant went East, to take charge of all the armies, he took Father along.

'I was an orderly at headquarters and Sam Grant said to me, "Irve," he said, "I'm going to take you along with me." '

It seems he and Grant used to slip off sometimes and have a quiet drink together. That's what my father said. He'd tell about the day Lee surrendered, and how, when the great moment came, they couldn't find Grant.

'You know,' my father said, 'about General Grant's book, his memoirs. You've read of how he said he had a headache and how, when he got word that Lee was ready to call it quits, he was suddenly and miraculously cured.

'Huh,' said Father. 'He was in the woods with me.

'I was in there with my back against a tree. I was pretty well corned. I had got hold of a bottle of pretty good stuff.

'They were looking for Grant. He had got off his horse and come into the woods. He found me. He was covered with mud.

'I had the bottle in my hand. What'd I care? The war was over. I knew we had them licked.'

My father said that he was the one who told Grant about Lee. An orderly riding by had told him, because the orderly knew how thick he was with Grant. Grant was embarrassed.

'But, Irve, look at me. I'm all covered with mud,' he said to Father.

And then, my father said, he and Grant decided to have a drink together. They took a couple of shots and then, because he didn't want Grant to show up potted before the immaculate Lee, he smashed the bottle against the tree.

'Sam Grant's dead now and I wouldn't want it to get out on him,' my father said.

That's just one of the kind of things he'd tell. Of course the men knew he was lying, but they seemed to like it just the same.

When we got broke, down and out, do you think he ever brought anything home? Not he. If there wasn't anything to eat in the house, he'd go off visiting around at farmhouses. They all wanted him. Sometimes he'd stay away for weeks, Mother working to keep us fed, and then home he'd come bringing, let's say, a ham. He'd got it from some farmer friend. He'd slap it on the table in the kitchen. 'You bet I'm going to see that my kids have something to eat,' he'd say, and Mother would just stand smiling at him. She'd never say a word about all the weeks and months he'd been away, not leaving us a cent for food. Once I heard her speaking to a woman in our street. Maybe the woman had dared to sympathize with her. 'Oh,' she said, 'it's all right. He isn't ever dull like most of the men in this street. Life is never dull when my man is about.'

But often I was filled with bitterness, and sometimes I wished he wasn't my father. I'd even invent another man as my father. To protect my mother I'd make up stories of a secret marriage that for some strange reason never got known. As though some man, say, the president of a railroad company or maybe a Congressman, had married my mother, thinking his wife was dead and then it turned out she wasn't.

Now they had to hush it up, but I got born just the same. I wasn't really the son of my father. Somewhere in the world there was a very dignified, quite wonderful man who was really my father. I even made myself half-believe these fancies.

And then there came a certain night. Mother was away from home. Maybe there was a church that night. Father came in. He'd been off somewhere for two or three weeks. He found me alone in the house, reading by the kitchen table.

It had been raining and he was very wet. He sat and looked at me for a long time, not saying a word. I was startled, for there was on his face the saddest look I had ever seen. He sat for a time, his clothes dripping. Then he got up.

'Come on with me,' he said.

I got up and went with him out of the house. I was filled with wonder, but I wasn't afraid. We went along a dirt road that led down into a valley, about a mile out of town, where there was a pond. We walked in silence. The man who was always talking had stopped his talking.

I didn't know what was up and had the queer feeling that I was with a stranger. I don't know whether my father intended it so. I don't think he did.

The pond was quite large. It was still raining hard and there were flashes of lightning followed by thunder. We were on a grassy bank at the pond's edge when my father spoke, and in the darkness and rain his voice sounded strange.

'Take off your clothes,' he said. Still filled with wonder, I began to undress. There was a flash of lightning and I saw that he was already naked.

Naked, we went into the pond. Taking my hand he pulled me in. It may be that I was too frightened, too full of a feeling of strangeness, to speak. Before that night my father had never seemed to pay any attention to me.

'And what is he up to now?' I kept asking myself. I did not swim very well, but he put my hand on his shoulder and struck out into the darkness.

He was a man with big shoulders, a powerful swimmer. In the darkness I could feel the movement of his muscles. We swam to the far edge of the pond and then back to where we had left our clothes. The rain continued and the wind blew. Sometimes my father swam on his back and when he did, he took my hand in his large powerful one and moved it over so that it rested always on his shoulder. Sometimes there would be a flash of lightning and I could see his face quite clearly.

It was as it was earlier, in the kitchen, a face filled with sadness. There would be the momentary glimpse of his face and then again the darkness, the wind and the rain. In me there was a feeling I had never known before.

It was a feeling of closeness. It was something strange. It was as though there were only we two in the world. It was as though I had been jerked suddenly out of myself, out of my world of the schoolboy, out of a world in which I was ashamed of my father.

He had become blood of my blood; the strong swimmer and I the boy clinging to him in the darkness. We swam in silence and in silence we dressed in our wet clothes, and went home.

There was a lamp lighted in the kitchen, and when we came in, the water dripping from us, there was my mother. She smiled at us. I remember that she called us 'boys.' 'What have you boys been up to?' she asked, but my father did not answer. As he had begun the evening's experience with me in silence, so he ended it. He turned and looked at me. Then he went, I thought, with a new and strange dignity, out of the room.

I climbed the stairs to my own room, undressed in darkness and got into bed. I couldn't sleep and did not want to sleep. For the first time I knew that I was the son of my father. He was a story-teller as I was to be. It may be that I even laughed a little softly there in the darkness. If I did, I laughed knowing that I would never again be wanting another father.

1. "Discovery of a Father" was prepared for a popular magazine and, unlike most of Sherwood Anderson's writing, is broken up into short, choppy paragraphs for the hasty or inattentive reader. Point out places where two or three of these short paragraphs are about the same subject and should be joined into a single paragraph.
2. What are some concrete examples of the father's behavior that made the writer ashamed of him?
3. What was the basis for this feeling of shame? Whose standards was the boy accepting as best? What kinds of standards were they?
4. What was the mother's attitude toward the father? Give a qualified answer, with evidence.
5. What pivotal action of the father's changed the boy's attitude? What is the significance of that action—that is, what does it stand for? What lesson about life does it illustrate?
6. The writer finds in the end that his father has his own kind of dignity. What is the foundation of this dignity?
7. Sherwood Anderson became a famous writer and teller of tales, and here he gives his father credit. But his father gave him something more important that is implied without being stated. What was it?

My Papa's Waltz

THEODORE ROETHKE

The whiskey on your breath
Could make a small boy dizzy;
But I hung on like death:
Such waltzing was not easy.

We romped until the pans
Slid from the kitchen shelf;
My mother's countenance
Could not unfrown itself.

The hand that held my wrist
Was battered on one knuckle;
At every step you missed
My right ear scraped a buckle.

You beat time on my head
With a palm caked hard by dirt,
Then waltzed me off to bed
Still clinging to your shirt.

---

1. Describe from beginning to end the scene that is implied in the poem so that you have it clearly in mind. What are the actual events?
2. What kind of man was the poet's father, according to the evidence? Qualify your answer. What evidence of the father's character is offered?
3. What is the significance of the last line?
4. What is the nature of the relationship between the boy and his father? How do you think each feels about the other?

---

1. Though the subject of the painting is Joseph and the child Jesus, its essential meaning is not changed if we regard it as any father and his child. What has made Joseph look up from his work? What does he see?
2. What might the sudden flaring of the candle and the translucency of the child's hand suggest to Joseph's imagination?
3. The flaring candle and the child's hand are used as *symbols,* objects that stand for general ideas. What do they stand for?
4. Joseph is caught in a moment of sudden awareness. What is he aware of?
5. Interpreting only the evidence in the picture, how would you describe the relationship between father and son?

PLATE X

JOSEPH THE CARPENTER: Georges de la Tour. Louvre/Giraudon

11

identifying
with
an animal

When you read stories, often you identify with the leading characters, seeing through their eyes and feeling as they do. When you read "Contents of the Dead Man's Pockets" (in Unit 5) you were out on the ledge with Tom Benecke, feeling his terror, and when you read "Discovery of a Father" (in Unit 10) you felt, with the boy, some of the joy of plunging into the adventure of life. Reading is sharing others' knowledge or experience, seeing from their points of view, adding parts of their lives to your own. Writing, on the other hand, can be an exploration of your own experience, an expansion of your imagination.

Identifying with an animal is an exercise of the imagination. It is not to be taken seriously, of course, but at the same time, the more you get into it the more you will get out of it. If you identify with a dog, for example, you will find yourself in a different world, a world where smells and sounds are more important than appearances, where television sets tell you nothing but telephone poles a great deal, where garbage collectors are criminals stealing good things to eat.

class exercise

Most of us have had more opportunities to observe dogs than any other kind of animal. Discuss the ways a dog perceives its world that are different from human perceptions. What is a dog most aware of in houses, yards, and streets? How does it view people? Other animals? Various objects? Be careful to base your conjectures on observation. Don't project your own feelings into the dog unless you have evidence that those feelings are there.

definition

We think of *definition* as the explanation of a word using other words, the way a dictionary does it. But dictionary definitions are substitutes that we fall back on only when we have no experience of the thing defined. You don't need a dictionary to tell you what sandpaper or soup is; you've used sandpaper and eaten soup. The best kind of definition is experience. The next best is a full description of experience. If you've never experienced terror, you will have an idea of what it is from reading "Contents of the Dead Man's Pockets."

To define something is to make clear what it is like and what it is different from. Jack Finney defines Tom Benecke's terror and discomfort by placing him only the thickness of a pane of glass from the security and comfort of his apartment. This sharp and homely contrast with what terror is *not* is what makes the definition more effective than does, say, a Frankenstein movie.

If you want to put across a good experiential definition of "a dog's life," then, keep your dog close to the areas of *your* experience, so that the differences will be heightened by contrast.

writing assignment

1. If possible, observe for some time an animal around you—a dog, cat, parakeet, goldfish, or other pet if you live in the city, or, if you live in the country, a horse, cow, or wild bird; or go to a zoo if one is nearby. If you don't have an animal around, recall your past observations of one.
2. Project your consciousness into the animal as completely as you can. Try to *become* the animal for a while, perceiving things as it does.
3. Take notes on the animal's experiences. Use *I* as the subject of all your sentences, and identify with these experiences. As the animal, what are you most keenly aware of at each moment? What are your motives and desires, here and now? What sensations do you feel—kinesthetic, touch, taste, smell, hearing, seeing?
4. Organize your material into a narrative of a few minutes or an hour in the life of your subject, using *I* all the way through. Don't name the kind of animal you are—after all, you don't know what you are, do you?— but make your description vivid enough so that the reader will know.

alternate class exercise

Choose an animal that is very different from a human being—a fish, bird, snake, or an insect. Try to define what it is, not in terms of classification or structure, but in terms of experience. What can it do that you can't, and what can you do that it can't do? What can it perceive that you can't, and vice versa?

Hook

WALTER VAN TILBURG CLARK

Hook, the hawks' child, was hatched in a dry spring among the oaks beside the seasonal river, and was struck from the nest early. In the drouth his single-willed parents had to extend their hunting ground by more than twice, for the ground creatures upon which they fed died and dried by the hundreds. The range became too great for them to wish to return and feed Hook, and when they had lost interest in each other they drove Hook down into the sand and brush and went back to solitary courses over the bleaching hills.

Unable to fly yet, Hook crept over the ground, challenging all large movements with recoiled head, erected rudimentary wings and the small rasp of his clattering beak. It was during this time of abysmal ignorance and continual fear that his eyes took on the first quality of hawk, that of being wide, alert, and challenging. He dwelt, because of his helplessness, among the rattling brush which grew between the oaks and the river. Even in his thickets, and near the water, the white sun was the dominant presence. Except in the dawn, when the land wind stirred, or in the late afternoon, when the sea wind became strong enough to penetrate the half-mile inland to this turn in the river, the sun was the major force, and everything was dry and motionless under it. The brush, small plants and trees alike, husbanded the little moisture at their hearts; the moving creatures waited for dark, when sometimes the sea fog came over and made a fine, soundless rain which relieved them.

The two spacious sounds of his life environed Hook at this time. One was the great rustle of the slopes of yellowed wild wheat, with over it the chattering rustle of the leaves of the California oaks, already as harsh and individually tremulous as in autumn. The other was the distant whisper of the foaming edge of the Pacific, punctuated by the hollow shoring of the waves. But these Hook did not yet hear, for he was attuned by fear and hunger to the small, spasmodic rustlings of live things. Dry, shrunken, and nearly starved, and with his plumage delayed, he snatched at beetles, dragging in the sand to catch them. When swifter and stronger birds and animals did not reach them first, which was seldom, he ate the small silver fish left in the mud by the failing river. He watched, with nearly chattering beak, the quick, thin lizards pause, very alert, and raise and lower themselves, but could not catch them because he had to raise his wings to move rapidly, which startled them.

Only one sight and sound not of his world of microscopic necessity was forced upon Hook. That was the flight of the big gulls from the beaches, which sometimes, in quealing play, came spinning back over the foothills and the river bed. For some inherited reason the big, ship-bodied birds did not frighten Hook, but angered him. Small and chewed-looking, with his wide, already yellowing eyes glaring up at them, he would stand in an open place on the sand in the sun and spread his shaping wings and clatter his bill like shaken dice. Hook was furious about the swift, easy passage of gulls.

His first opportunity to leave off living like a ground owl came accidentally. He was standing in the late afternoon in the red light under the thicket, his eyes half-filmed with drowse and the stupefaction of starvation, when suddenly something beside him moved, and he struck, and killed a field mouse driven out of the wheat by thirst. It was a poor mouse, shriveled and lice-ridden, but in striking Hook had tasted blood, which raised nest memories and restored his nature. With started neck plumage and shining eyes he tore and fed. When the mouse was devoured Hook had entered hoarse adolescence. He began to seek with a conscious appetite, and move more readily out of shelter. Impelled by the blood appetite, so glorious after his long preservation upon the flaky and bitter stuff of bugs, he ventured even into the wheat in the open sun beyond the oaks, and discovered the small trails and holes among the roots. With his belly often partially filled with flesh he grew rapidly in strength and will. His eyes were taking on their final change, their yellow growing deeper and more opaque, their stare more constant, their challenge less desperate. Once during this transformation he surprised a ground squirrel, and although he was ripped and wing-bitten and could not hold his prey, he was not dismayed by the conflict, but exalted. Even while the wing was still drooping and the pinions not grown back he was excited by other ground squirrels and pursued them futilely, and was angered by their dusty escape. He realized that his world was a great arena for killing, and felt the magnificence of it.

The two major events of Hook's young life occurred in the same day. A little after dawn he made the customary essay and succeeded in flight. A little before sunset he made his first sustained flight of over two hundred yards, and at its termination struck and slew a great buck squirrel whose thrashing and terrified gnawing and squealing gave him a wild delight. When he had gorged on the strong meat, Hook stood upright, and in his eyes was the stare of the hawk, never flagging in intensity but never swelling beyond containment. After that the stare had only to grow more deeply challenging and more sternly controlled as his range and deadliness increased. There was no change in kind. Hook had mastered the first of the three hungers which are fused into the single flaming will of a hawk, and he had experienced the second.

The third and consummating hunger did not awaken in Hook until the following spring, when the exultation of space had grown slow and steady in him, so that he swept freely with the wind over the miles of the coastal foothills, circling, and ever in sight of the sea, and used without struggle the warm currents lifting from the slopes, and no longer desired to scream at the range of his vision, but intently sailed above his shadow swiftly climbing to meet him on the hillsides, sinking away and rippling across the brush-grown canyons.

That spring the rains were long, and Hook sat for hours, hunched and angry under their pelting, glaring into the fogs of the river valley, and killed only small, drenched things flooded up from their tunnels. But when the rains had dissipated, and there were sun and sea wind again, the game ran plentiful, the hills were thick and shining green, and the new river flooded about the boulders where battered turtles climbed up to shrink and sleep. Hook then was scorched by the third hunger. Ranging farther, often forgetting to kill and eat, he sailed for days with growing rage, and woke at night clattering on his dead tree limb, and struck and struck and struck at the porous wood of the trunk, tearing it away. After days, in the draft of a coastal canyon miles below his own hills, he came upon the acrid taint he did not know but had expected, and, sailing down it, felt his neck plumes rise and his wings quiver so that he swerved unsteadily. He saw the unmated female perched upon the tall and jagged stump of a tree that had been shorn by storm, and, as if upon game, he stooped. But she was older than he, and wary of the gripe of his importunity, and banked off screaming, and he screamed also at the intolerable delay.

At the head of the canyon the screaming pursuit was crossed by another male with a great wing spread and the light golden in the fringe of his plumage. But his more skillful opening played him false against the ferocity of the twice-balked Hook. His rising maneuver for position was cut short by Hook's wild upward stoop, and at the blow he raked wildly and tumbled off to the side. Dropping, Hook struck him again, struggled to clutch, but only raked and could not hold, and, diving, struck once more in passage, and then beat up, yelling triumph, and saw the crippled antagonist sideslip away, half-tumble once as the ripped wing failed to balance, then steady and glide obliquely into the cover of brush on the canyon side.

Beating hard and stationary in the wind above the bush that covered his competitor, Hook waited an instant, but, when the bush was still, screamed again, and let himself go off with the current, reseeking, infuriated by the burn of his own wounds, the thin choke-thread of the acrid taint.

On a hilltop projection of stone two miles inland he struck her down, gripping her rustling body with his talons, beating her wings down with his wings, belting her head when she whimpered or thrashed, and at last clutching her neck with his hook, and, when her coy struggles had given way to stillness, succeeded.

In the early summer Hook drove the three young ones from their nest and went back to lone circling above his own range. He was complete.

II

Throughout that summer and the cool, growthless weather of the winter, when the gales blew in the river canyon and the ocean piled upon the shore, Hook was master of the sky and the hills of his range. His flight became a lovely and certain thing, so that he played with the treacherous currents of the air with a delicate ease surpassing that of the gulls. He could sail for hours searching the blanched grasses below him with telescopic eyes, gaining height against the wind, descending in mile-long, gently declining swoops when he curved and rode back, and never beating either wing. At the swift passage of his shadow within their vision gophers, ground squirrels, and rabbits froze, or plunged gibbering into their tunnels beneath matted turf. Now, when he struck, he killed easily in one hard-knuckled blow. Occasionally, in sport, he soared up over the river and drove the heavy and weaponless gulls downstream again, until they would no longer venture inland.

There was nothing which Hook feared now, and his spirit was wholly belligerent, swift, and sharp, like his gaze. Only the mixed smells and incomprehensible activities of the people at the Japanese farmer's home, inland of the coastwise highway and south of the bridge across Hook's river, troubled him. The smells were strong, unsatisfactory, and never clear, and the people, though they behaved foolishly, constantly running in and out of their built-up holes, were large, and appeared capable, with fearless eyes looking up at him, so that he instinctively swerved aside from them. He cruised over their yard, their gardens, and their bean fields, but he would not alight close to their buildings.

But this one area of doubt did not interfere with his life. He ignored it, save to look upon it curiously as he crossed, his afternoon shadow sliding in an instant over the chicken- and crate-cluttered yard, up the side of the unpainted barn, and then out again smoothly, just faintly, liquidly rippling over the furrows and then the stubble of the grazing slopes. When the season was dry, and the dead earth blew on the fields, he extended his range to satisfy his great hunger, and again narrowed it when the fields were once more alive with the minute movements he could not only see but anticipate.

Four times in that year he was challenged by other hawks blowing up from behind the coastal hills to scud down his slopes, but two of these he slew in mid-air, and saw hurtle down to thump on the ground and lie still while he circled; and a third, whose wing he tore, he followed closely to earth and beat to death in the grass, making the crimson jet out from its breast and neck into the pale wheat. The fourth was a strong flier and experienced fighter, and theirs was a long, running battle, with brief, rising flurries of striking and screaming, from which down and plumage soared off.

Here, for the first time, Hook felt doubts, and at moments wanted to drop away from the scoring, burning talons and the twisted hammer strokes of the strong beak, drop away shrieking and take cover and be still. In the end, when Hook, having outmaneuvered his enemy and come above him, wholly in control and going with the wind, tilted and plunged for the death rap, the other, in desperation, threw over on his back and struck up. Talons locked, beaks raking, they dived earthward. The earth grew and spread under them amazingly, and they were not fifty feet above it when Hook, feeling himself turning toward the underside, tore free and beat up again on heavy, wrenched wings. The other, stroking swiftly, and so close to down that he lost wing plumes to a bush, righted himself and planed up, but flew on lumberingly between the hills and did not return. Hook screamed the triumph, and made a brief pretense of pursuit, but was glad to return, slow and victorious, to his dead tree.

In all of these encounters Hook was injured, but experienced only the fighter's pride and exultation from the sting of wounds received in successful combat. And in each of them he learned new skill. Each time the wounds healed quickly, and left him a more dangerous bird.

In the next spring, when the rains and the night chants of the little frogs were past, the third hunger returned upon Hook with a new violence. In this quest he came into the taint of a young hen. Others, too, were drawn by the unnerving perfume, but only one of them, the same with which Hook had fought his great battle, was a fit competitor. This hunter drove off two, while two others, game but neophytes, were glad enough that Hook's impatience would not permit him to follow and kill. Then the battle between the two champions fled inland and was a tactical marvel, but Hook lodged the neck-breaking blow, and struck again as they dropped past the treetops. The blood had already begun to pool on the gray, fallen foliage as Hook flapped up between branches, too spent to cry victory. Yet his hunger would not let him rest until, late in the second day, he drove the female to ground among the laurels of a strange river canyon.

When the two fledglings of this second brood had been driven from the nest, and Hook had returned to his own range, he was not only complete but supreme. He slept without concealment on his bare limb, and did not open his eyes when, in the night, the heavy-billed cranes coughed in the shallows below him.

III

The turning point of Hook's career came that autumn, when the brush in the canyons rustled dryly and the hills, mowed close by the cattle, smoked under the wind as if burning. One midafternoon, when the black clouds were torn on the rim of the sea and the surf flowered white and high on the rocks, raining in over the low cliffs, Hook rode the wind diagonally across the river mouth. His great eyes, focused for small things stirring in the dust and leaves, overlooked so large and slow a movement as that of the Japanese farmer rising from the brush and lifting the two black eyes of his shotgun. Too late Hook saw, and, startled, swerved, but wrongly. The surf muffled the reports, and nearly without sound Hook felt the minute whips of the first shot, and the astounding, breath-taking blow of the second.

Beating his good wing, tasting the blood that quickly swelled into his beak, he tumbled off with the wind and struck into the thickets on the far side of the river mouth. The branches tore him. Wild with rage, he thrust up, clattered his beak, challenging, but, when he had twice fallen over, knew that the trailing wing would not carry, and then heard the boots of the hunter among the stones in the river bed, and, seeing him loom at the edge of the bushes, crept back amid the thickest brush, and was still. When he saw the boots stand before him he reared back, lifting his good wing and cocking his head for the serpent-like blow, his beak open but soundless, his great eyes hard and very shining. The boots passed on. The Japanese farmer, who believed that he had lost chickens, and who had cunningly observed Hook's flight for many afternoons until he could plot it, did not greatly want a dead hawk.

When Hook could hear nothing but the surf and the wind in the thicket he let the sickness and shock overcome him. The fine film of the inner lid dropped over his big eyes. His heart beat frantically, so that it made the plumage of his shot-aching breast throb. His own blood throttled his breathing. But these things were nothing compared to the lightning of pain in his left shoulder where the shot had bunched, shattering the airy bones so the pinions trailed on the ground and could not be lifted. Yet when a sparrow lit in the bush over him Hook's eyes flew open again, hard and challenging, his good wing was lifted and his beak strained open. The startled sparrow darted piping out over the river.

Throughout that night, while the long clouds blew across the stars and the wind shook the bushes about him, and throughout the next day, while the clouds still blew and massed until there was no gleam of sunlight on the sand bar, Hook remained stationary, enduring his sickness. In the second evening, the rains began. First there was a long, running patter of drops upon the beach and over the dry trees and bushes. At dusk there came a heavier squall, which did not die entirely, but slacked off to a continual, spaced splashing of big drops, and then returned with the front of the storm. In long, misty curtains, gust by gust, the rain swept over the sea, beating down its heaving, and coursed up the beach. The little jets of dust ceased to rise about the drops in the fields, and the mud began to gleam. Among the boulders of the river bed darkling pools grew slowly.

Still Hook stood behind his tree from the wind, only gentle drops reaching him, falling from the upper branches and then again from the brush. His eyes remained closed, and he could still taste his own blood in his mouth though it had ceased to come up freshly. Out beyond him he heard the storm changing. As rain conquered the sea the heave of the surf became a hushed sound, often lost in the crying of the wind. Then gradually, as the night turned toward morning, the wind also was broken by the rain. The crying became fainter, the rain settled toward steadiness, and the creep of the waves could be heard again, quiet and regular upon the beach.

At dawn there was no wind and no sun, but everywhere the roaring of the vertical, relentless rain. Hook then crept among the rapid drippings of the bushes, dragging his torn sail, seeking better shelter. He stopped often, and stood with the shutters of film drawn over his eyes. At midmorning he found a little cave under a ledge at the base of the sea cliff. Here, lost without branches and leaves about him, he settled to await improvement.

When, at midday of the third day, the rain stopped altogether and the sky opened before a small, fresh wind, letting light through to glitter upon a tremulous sea, Hook was so weak that his good wing also trailed to prop him upright, and his open eyes were lusterless. But his wounds were hardened and he felt the return of hunger. Beyond his shelter he heard the gulls flying in great numbers and crying their joy at the cleared air. He could even hear, from the fringe of the river, the ecstatic and unstinted bubblings and chirpings of the small birds. The grassland, he felt, would be full of the stirring anew of the close-bound life, the undrowned insects clicking as they dried out, the snakes slithering down, heads half erect, into the grasses where the mice, gophers, and ground squirrels ran and stopped and chewed and licked themselves smoother and drier.

With the aid of this hunger, and on the crutches of his wings, Hook came down to stand in the sun beside his cave, whence he could watch the beach. Before him, in ellipses on tilting planes, the gulls flew. The surf was rearing again and beginning to shelve and hiss on the sand. Through the white foam-writing it left the long-billed pipers twinkled in bevies, escaping each wave, then racing down after it to plunge their fine drills into the minute double holes where the sand crabs bubbled. In the third row of breakers two seals lifted sleek, streaming heads and barked, and over them, trailing his spider legs, a great crane flew south. Among the stones at the foot of the cliff small red and green crabs made a little, continuous rattling and knocking. The cliff swallows glittered and twanged on aerial forays.

The afternoon began auspiciously for Hook also. One of the two gulls which came squabbling above him dropped a freshly caught fish to the sand. Quickly Hook was upon it; gripping it, he raised his good wing and cocked his head with open beak at the many gulls which had circled and come down at once toward the fall of the fish. The gulls sheered off, cursing raucously. Left alone on the sand, Hook devoured the fish, and, after resting in the sun, withdrew again to his shelter.

IV

In the succeeding days, between rains, he foraged on the beach. He learned to kill and crack the small green crabs. Along the edge of the river mouth he found the drowned bodies of mice and squirrels and even sparrows. Twice he managed to drive feeding gulls from their catch, charging upon them with buffeting wing and clattering beak. He grew stronger slowly, but the shot sail continued to drag. Often, at the choking thought of soaring and striking and the good, hot-blood kill, he strove to take off, but only the one wing came up, winnowing with a hiss, and drove him over on to his side in the sand. After these futile trials he would rage and clatter. But gradually he learned to believe that he could not fly, that his life must now be that of the discharged nestling again. Denied the joy of space, without which the joy of loneliness was lost, the joy of battle and killing, the blood lust, became his whole concentration. It was his hope, as he charged feeding gulls, that they would turn and offer battle, but they never did. The sandpipers at his approach fled peeping, or, like a quiver of arrows shot together, streamed out over the surf in a long curve. Once, pent beyond bearing, he disgraced himself by shrieking challenge at the businesslike heron which flew south every evening at the same time. The heron did not even turn his head, but flapped and glided on.

Hook's shame and anger became such that he stood awake at night. Hunger kept him awake also, for these little leavings of the gulls could not sustain his great body in its renewed violence. He became aware that the gulls slept at night in flocks on the sand, each with one leg tucked under him. He discovered also that the curlews and the pipers, often mingling, likewise slept, on the higher remnant of the bar. A sensation of evil delight filled him in the consideration of protracted striking among them.

There was only half of a sick moon in a sky of running but far-separated clouds on the night when he managed to stalk into the center of the sleeping gulls. This was light enough, but so great was his vengeful pleasure that there broke from him a shrill scream of challenge as he first struck. Without the power of flight behind it the blow was not murderous, and this newly discovered impotence made Hook crazy, so that he screamed again and again as he struck and tore at the felled gull. He slew the one, but was twice knocked over by its heavy flounderings, and all the others rose above him, weaving and screaming, protesting in the thin moonlight. Wakened by their clamor, the wading birds also took wing, startled and plaintive. When the beach was quiet again the flocks had settled elsewhere, beyond his pitiful range, and he was left alone beside the single kill. It was a disappointing victory. He fed with lowering spirit.

Thereafter he stalked silently. At sunset he would watch where the gulls settled along the miles of beach, and after dark he would come like a sharp shadow among them, and drive with his hook on all sides of him, till the beatings of a poorly struck victim sent the flock up. Then he would turn vindictively upon the fallen and finish them. In his best night he killed five from one flock. But he ate only a little from one, for the vigor resulting from occasional repletion strengthened only his ire, which became so great at such a time that food revolted him. It was not the joyous, swift, controlled hunting anger of a sane hawk, but something quite different, which made him dizzy if it continued too long, and left him unsatisfied with any kill.

Then one day, when he had very nearly struck a gull while driving it from a gasping yellowfin, the gull's wing rapped against him as it broke for its running start, and, the trailing wing failing to support him, he was knocked over. He flurried awkwardly in the sand to regain his feet, but his mastery of the beach was ended. Seeing him, in clear sunlight, struggling after the chance blow, the gulls returned about him in a flashing cloud, circling and pecking on the wing. Hook's plumage showed quick little jets of irregularity here and there. He reared back, clattering and erecting the good wing, spreading the great, rusty tail for balance. His eyes shone with a little of the old pleasure. But it died, for he could reach none of them. He was forced to turn and dance awkwardly on the sand, trying to clash bills with each tormentor. They banked up quealing and returned, weaving about him in concentric and overlapping circles. His scream was lost in their clamor, and he appeared merely to be hopping clumsily with his mouth open. Again he fell sidewards. Before he could right himself he was bowled over, and a second time, and lay on his side, twisting his neck to reach them and clappering in blind fury, and was struck three times by three successive gulls, shrieking their flock triumph.

Finally he managed to roll to his breast, and to crouch with his good wing spread wide and the other stretched nearly as far, so that he extended like a gigantic moth, only his snake head, with its now silent scimitar, erect. One great eye blazed under its level brow, but where the other had been was a shallow hole from which thin blood trickled to his russet gap.

In this crouch, by short stages, stopping to turn and drive the gulls up repeatedly, Hook dragged into the river canyon and under the stiff cover of the bitter-leafed laurel. There the gulls left him, soaring up with great clatter of their valor. Till nearly sunset Hook, broken-spirited and enduring his hardening eye socket, heard them celebrating over the waves.

When his will was somewhat replenished, and his empty eye socket had stopped the twitching and vague aching which had forced him often to roll ignominiously to rub it in the dust, Hook ventured from the protective lacings of his thicket. He knew fear again, and the challenge of his remaining eye was once more strident, as in adolescence. He dared not return to the beaches, and with a new, weak hunger, the home hunger, enticing him, made his way by short hunting journeys back to the wild wheat slopes and the crisp oaks. There was in Hook an unwonted sensation now, that of the ever-neighboring possibility of death. This sensation was beginning, after his period as a mad bird on the beach, to solidify him into his last stage of life. When, during his slow homeward passage, the gulls wafted inland over him, watching the earth with curious, miserish eyes, he did not cower, but neither did he challenge, either by opened beak or by raised shoulder. He merely watched carefully, learning his first lesson in observing the world with one eye.

At first the familiar surroundings of the bend in the river and the tree with the dead limb to which he could not ascend aggravated his humiliation, but in time, forced to live cunningly and half-starved, he lost much of his savage pride. At the first flight of a strange hawk over his realm he was wild at his helplessness, and kept twisting his head like an owl, or spinning in the grass like a small and feathered dervish, to keep the hateful beauty of the wind rider in sight. But in the succeeding weeks, as one after another coasted his beat, his resentment declined, and when one of the raiders, a haughty yearling, sighted his up-staring eye and plunged and struck him dreadfully, and only failed to kill him because he dragged under a thicket in time, the second of his great hungers was gone. He had no longer the true lust to kill, no joy of battle, but only the poor desire to fill his belly.

Then truly he lived in the wheat and the brush like a ground owl, ridden with ground lice, dusty or muddy, ever half-starved, forced to sit hours by small holes for petty and unsatisfying kills. Only once during the final months before his end did he make a kill where the breath of danger recalled his valor, and then the danger was such as a hawk with wings and eyes would scorn. Waiting beside a gopher hole, surrounded by the high yellow grass, he saw the head emerge and struck, and was amazed that there writhed in his clutch the neck and dusty coffin-skull of a rattlesnake. Holding his grip, Hook saw the great thick body slither up after, the tip an erect, strident blur, and writhe on the dirt of the gopher's mound. The weight of the snake pushed Hook about, and once threw him down, and the rising and falling whine of the rattles made the moment terrible, but the vaulted mouth, gaping from the closeness of Hook's gripe, so that the pale, envenomed sabers stood out free, could not reach him. When Hook replaced the grip of his beak with the grip of his talons, and was free to strike again and again at the base of the head, the struggle was over. Hook tore and fed on the fine, watery flesh and left the tattered armor and the long, jointed bone for the marching ants.

When the heavy rains returned he ate well during the period of the first escapes from flooded burrows, and then well enough, in a vulture's way, on the drowned creatures. But as the rains lingered, and the burrows hung full of water, and there were no insects in the grass and no small birds sleeping in the thickets, he was constantly hungry, and finally unbearably hungry. His sodden and ground-broken plumage stood out raggedly about him, so that he looked fat, even bloated, but underneath it his skin clung to his bones. Save for his great talons and clappers, and the rain in his down, he would have been like a handful of air. He often stood for a long time under some bush or ledge, heedless of the drip, his one eye filmed over, his mind neither asleep nor awake, but between. The gurgle and swirl of the brimming river, and the sound of chunks of the bank cut away to splash and dissolve in the already muddy flood, became familiar to him, and yet a torment, as if that great, ceaselessly working power of water ridiculed his frailty, within which only the faintest spark of valor still glimmered. The last two nights before the rain ended he huddled under the floor of the bridge on the coastal highway and heard the palpitant thunder of motors swell and roar over him. The trucks shook the bridge so that Hook, even in his famished lassitude, would sometimes open his one great eye wide and startled.

V

After the rains, when things became full again, bursting with growth and sound, the trees swelling, the thickets full of song and chatter, the fields, turning green in the sun, alive with rustling passages, and the moonlit nights strained with the song of the peepers all up and down the river and in pools in the fields, Hook had to bear the return of the one hunger left him. At times this made him so wild that he forgot himself and screamed challenge from the open ground. The fretfulness of it spoiled his hunting, which was now entirely a matter of patience. Once he was in despair, and lashed himself through the grass and thickets trying to rise, when that virgin scent drifted for a few moments above the current of his own river. Then, breathless, his beak agape, he saw the strong suitor ride swiftly down on the wind over him, and heard afar the screaming fuss of the harsh wooing in the alders. For that moment even the battle heart beat in him again. The rim of his good eye was scarlet, and a little bead of new blood stood in the socket of the other. With beak and talon he ripped at a fallen log, made loam and leaves fly from above it.

But the season of love passed over to the nesting season, and Hook's love hunger, unused, shriveled in him with the others, and there remained in him only one stern quality befitting a hawk, and that the negative one, the remnant, the will to endure. He resumed his patient, plotted hunting, now along a field on the land of the Japanese farmer, but ever within reach of the river thickets.

Growing tough and dry again as the summer advanced, inured to the family of the farmer, whom he saw daily stooping and scraping with sticks in the ugly, open rows of their fields, where no lovely grass rustled and no life stirred save the shameless gulls which walked at the heels of the workers, gobbling the worms and grubs they turned up, Hook became nearly content with his shard of life. The only longing or resentment to pierce him was that he suffered occasionally when forced to hide at the edge of the mile-long bean field from the wafted cruising and the restive, down-bent gaze of one of his own kind. For the rest he was without flame, a snappish, dust-colored creature, fading into the grasses he trailed through and suited to his petty way.

At the end of that summer, for the second time in his four years, Hook underwent a drouth. The equinoctial period passed without a rain. The laurel and the rabbit brush dropped dry leaves. The foliage of the oaks shriveled and curled. Even the night fogs in the river canyon failed. The farmer's red cattle on the hillside lowed constantly, and could not feed on the dusty stubble. Grass fires broke out along the highway and ate fast in the wind, filling the hollows with the smell of smoke, and died in the dirt of the shorn hills. The river made no sound; scum grew on its vestigial pools, and turtles died and stank among the rocks. The dust rode before the wind, and ascended and flowered to nothing between the hills, and every sunset was red with the dust in the air. The people in the farmer's house quarreled, and even struck one another. Birds were silent, and only the hawks flew much. The animals lay breathing hard for very long spells, and ran and crept jerkily. Their flanks were fallen in, and their eyes were red.

At first Hook gorged at the fringe of the grass fires on the multitudes of tiny things that came running and squeaking. But thereafter there were the blackened strips on the hills, and little more in the thin, crackling grass. He found mice and rats, gophers and ground squirrels and even rabbits, dead in the stubble and under the thickets, but so dry and fleshless that only a faint smell rose from them, even on the sunny days. He starved on them. By early December he had wearily stalked the length of the eastern foothills, hunting at night to escape the voracity of his own kind, resting often upon his wings. The queer trail of his short steps and great horned toes zigzagged in the dust and was erased by the wind at dawn. He was nearly dead, and could make no sound through the horn funnels of his clappers.

Then one night the dry wind brought him, with the familiar, lifeless dust, another familiar scent, troublesome, mingled, and unclear. In his vision-dominated brain he remembered the swift circle of his flight a year past, crossing in one segment, his shadow beneath him, a yard cluttered with crates and chickens, a gray barn, and then again the plowed land and the stubble. Traveling faster than he had for days, impatient of his shrunken sweep, Hook came down to the farm. In the dark, wisps of cloud blown among the stars over him, but no moon, he stood outside the wire of the chicken run. The scent of fat and blooded birds reached him from the shelter, and also within the enclosure was water. At the breath of the water Hook's gorge contracted and his tongue quivered and clove in its groove of horn. But there was the wire. He stalked its perimeter and found no opening. He beat it with his good wing, and felt it cut but not give. He wrenched at it with his beak in many places, but could not tear it. Finally, in a fury which drove the thin blood through him, he leaped repeatedly against it, beating and clawing. He was thrown back from the last leap as from the first, but in it he had risen so high as to clutch with his beak at the top wire. While he lay on his breast on the ground the significance of this came upon him.

Again he leapt, clawed up the wire, and as he would have fallen, made even the dead wing bear a little. He grasped the top and tumbled within. There again he rested flat, searching the dark with quick-turning head. There was no sound or motion but the throb of his own body. First he drank at the chill metal trough hung for the chickens. The water was cold, and loosened his tongue and his tight throat, but it also made him drunk and dizzy, so that he had to rest again, his claws spread wide to brace him. Then he walked stiffly, to stalk down the scent. He trailed it up the runway. Then there was the stuffy, body-warm air, acrid with droppings, full of soft rustlings as his talons clicked on the board floor. The thick white shapes showed faintly in the darkness. Hook struck quickly, driving a hen to the floor with one blow, its neck broken and stretched out stringily. He leaped on the still pulsing body and tore it. The rich, streaming blood was overpowering to his dried senses, his starved, leathery body. After a few swallows the flesh choked him. In his rage he struck down another hen. The urge to kill took him again, insanely, as in those nights on the beach. He could let nothing go; balked of feeding, he was compelled to slaughter. Clattering, he struck again and again. The henhouse was suddenly filled with the squawking and helpless rushing and buffeting of the terrified, brainless fowls.

Hook reveled in mastery. Here was game big enough to offer weight against a strike, and yet unable to soar away from his blows. Turning in the midst of the turmoil, cannily, his fury caught at the perfect pitch, he struck unceasingly. When the hens finally discovered the outlet and streamed into the yard to run around the fence, beating and squawking, Hook followed them, scraping down the incline, clumsy and joyous. In the yard the cock, a bird as large as he and much heavier, found him out and gave valiant battle. In the dark, and both earth-bound, there was little skill, but blow upon blow and only chance parry. The still squawking hens pressed into one corner of the yard. While the duel went on a dog, excited by the sustained scuffling, began to bark. He continued to bark, running back and forth along the fence on one side. A light flashed on in an uncurtained window of the farmhouse and streamed whitely over the crates littering the ground.

Enthralled by his old battle joy, Hook knew only the burly cock before him. Now in the farthest reach of the window light they could see each other dimly. The Japanese farmer, with his gun and his lantern, was already at the gate when the finish came. The great cock leapt to jab with his spurs, and, toppling forward with extended neck as he fell, was struck and extinguished. Blood had loosened Hook's throat. Shrilly he cried his triumph. It was a thin and exhausted cry, but within him as good as when he shrilled in mid-air over the plummeting descent of a fine foe in his best spring.

The light from the lantern partially blinded Hook. He first turned and ran directly from it, into the corner where the hens were huddled. They fled apart before his charge. He essayed the fence, and on the second try, in his desperation, was out. But in the open dust the dog was on him, circling, dashing in, snapping. The farmer, who at first had not fired because of the chickens, now did not fire because of the dog, and, when he saw that the hawk was unable to fly, relinquished the sport to the dog, holding the lantern up in order to see better. The light showed his own flat, broad, dark face as sunken also, the cheekbones very prominent, and showed the torn-off sleeves of his shirt and the holes in the knees of his overalls. His wife, in a stained wrapper and barefooted, heavy black hair hanging around a young, passionless face, joined him hesitantly, but watched, fascinated and a little horrified. His son joined them, too, encouraging the dog, but quickly grew silent. Courageous and cruel death, however it may afterward sicken the one who has watched it, is impossible to look away from.

In the circle of the light Hook turned to keep the dog in front of him. His one eye gleamed with malevolence. The dog was an Airedale, and large. Each time he pounced Hook stood ground, raising his good wing, the pinions torn by the fence, opening his beak soundlessly, and at the closest approach hissed furiously and at once struck. Hit and ripped twice by the whetted horn, the dog recoiled more quickly on several subsequent jumps, and, infuriated by his own cowardice, began to bark wildly. Hook maneuvered to watch him, keeping his head turned to avoid losing the foe on the blind side. When the dog paused, safely away, Hook watched him quietly, wing partially lowered, beak closed, but at the first move again lifted the wing and gaped. The dog whined, and the man spoke to him encouragingly. The awful sound of his voice made Hook for an instant twist his head to stare up at the immense figures behind the light. The dog again sallied, barking, and Hook's head spun back. His wing was bitten this time, and with a furious side blow he caught the dog's nose. The dog dropped him with a yelp, then, smarting, came on more warily as Hook propped himself up from the ground again between his wings. Hook's artificial strength was waning, but his heart still stood to the battle, sustained by a fear of such dimension as he had never known before, but only anticipated when the arrogant young hawk had driven him to cover. The dog, unable to find any point at which the merciless, unwinking eye was not watching him, the parted beak waiting, paused and whimpered again.

"Oh, kill the poor thing," the woman begged.

The man, though, encouraged the dog again, saying, "Sick him, sick him."

The dog rushed bodily. Unable to avoid him, Hook was bowled down, snapping and raking. He left long slashes, as from the blade of a knife, on the dog's flank, but before he could right himself and assume guard again was caught by the good wing and dragged, clattering and seeking to make a good stroke from his back. The man followed them to keep the light on them, as the boy went with him, wetting his lips with his tongue and keeping his fists closed tightly. The woman remained behind, but could not help watching the diminished conclusion.

In the little palely shining arena the dog repeated his successful maneuver three times, growling but not barking, and when Hook thrashed up from the third blow both wings were trailing and dark, shining streams crept on his black-fretted breast from the shoulders. The great eye flashed more furiously than it ever had in victorious battle, and the beak still gaped, but there was no more clatter. He faltered when turning to keep front; the broken wings played him false even as props. He could not rise to use his talons.

The man had tired of holding the lantern up, and put it down to rub his arm. In the low, horizontal light the dog charged again, this time throwing the weight of his fore-paws against Hook's shoulder, so that Hook was crushed as he struck. With his talons up, Hook raked at the dog's belly, but the dog conceived the finish, and furiously worried the feathered bulk. Hook's neck went limp, and between his gaping clappers came only a faint chittering, as from some small kill of his own in the grasses.

In this last conflict there had been some minutes of the supreme fire of the hawk whose three hungers are perfectly fused in the one will; enough to burn off a year of shame.

Between the great sails the light body lay caved and perfectly still.

The dog, smarting from his cuts, came to the master and was praised. The woman, joining them slowly, looked at the great wingspread, her husband raising the lantern that she might see it better.

"Oh, the brave bird,"she said.

---

1. "Hook" is an interesting experiment. The writer has had to move back and forth between identifying with the hawk and looking at him from the outside. If he identified completely with the hawk, we would have a hard time following the complex story; if he merely described the hawk, we wouldn't care. Can you find sentences written strictly from Hook's point of view?

2. The writer attributes feelings to Hook that are certainly human but may not be hawk feelings. Do you think he is justified, for example, in supposing that a hawk feels shame? What kind of evidence could be found to support such an idea?

3. Facts are referred to that a hawk could not know—for example, that the man who shot him is a Japanese farmer. What are some others?

4. Since Hook is shown in a setting that makes more human sense than hawk sense, what do you conclude was Clark's purpose in writing the story?

5. What aspects of Hook's experience are you able to identify with? What aspects remain alien to you?

6. On the basis of the story, attempt a partial definition of a hawk in terms of experience: "A hawk is a being that experiences . . . and does not experience. . . ."

Hawk Roosting

TED HUGHES

I sit in the top of the wood, my eyes closed.
Inaction, no falsifying dream
Between my hooked head and hooked feet:
Or in sleep rehearse perfect kills and eat.

The convenience of the high trees!
The air's buoyancy and the sun's ray
Are of advantage to me;
And the earth's face upward for my inspection.

My feet are locked upon the rough bark.
It took the whole of Creation
To produce my foot, my each feather:
Now I hold Creation in my foot

Or fly up, and revolve it all slowly—
I kill where I please because it is all mine.
There is no sophistry in my body:
My manners are tearing off heads—

The allotment of death.
For the one path of my flight is direct
Through the bones of the living.
No arguments assert my right:

The sun is behind me.
Nothing has changed since I began.
My eye has permitted no change.
I am going to keep things like this.

1. In part, this poem is an attempt to define a hawk in terms of its physical and emotional experience. What is at the heart of this experience?
2. Does the poet make you want to be a hawk? Why, or why not?
3. Does the poet project ideas into the hawk that a hawk could not have? If so, which ideas?
4. The final stanza hints that the poet may be using the hawk as a symbol of something else. If so, what?

1. A painting is a kind of definition of its subject. A picture of an eagle in a bird-watcher's manual would define an eagle differently from the way this picture does. What would the scientific illustration emphasize?
2. What aspects of the eagle does this painting emphasize?
3. What sensations are evoked?
4. One part of each eagle is represented in a startlingly unscientific way. What part? What do you think is the artist's purpose in this distortion?
5. What kind of definition of an eagle does the painting offer? Explain. Is it possible that the artist is not "talking" about eagles at all, but about something else?

PLATE XI

TWO EAGLES: Chu-ta. Anonymous

Drawing by W. Miller; © 1976 The New Yorker Magazine, Inc.

12

looking
at yourself

Through your sensory and emotional experiences, and through your observation and identification with others, you arrive at some kind of idea about your "self," about what kind of person you are. And then something happens to change that idea. The self is not an unchanging thing, but a process. You sometimes "surprise yourself" and ask, "Did I do that?" and then you deal with the new aspect, integrate it into a larger concept of what you are.

When you explore the world, or when you have new experiences, your self grows. In "The Supper" (Unit 2) James Agee experiences a part of the life of poor people and takes it into himself. In "Contents of the Dead Man's Pockets" (Unit 5), Tom Benecke, when facing death, changes his whole view of what is important in life. Talking with the bum in "Red" (Unit 6), Niccolo Tucci finds a new perspective, as does the narrator of "Sonny's Blues" (Unit 9) and the boy in "Discovery of a Father" (Unit 10). In each case the self deals with new experience and is changed by it.

There are several ways you can look at your self. Part of your self is the way you see the world, and part is the way you think the world sees you; part is changes that have taken place in the past, and part changes the future will bring. Part is what you learn and what you do with new knowledge; part is what you believe. All is process, event, change.

class discussion

Imagine that you have been put in a bare cell and know that you will remain there the rest of your life. There is no possibility of escape and no contact with living beings—food is conveyed to you mechanically. Under these circumstances, how do you define your self?

alternate class discussion

What kind of experience can change your concept of self, your idea of the kind of person you are? Think of an experience of your own, or of someone you know, that had this profound effect. What was the experience? What quality of it caused the change? Exactly what—if you can pin it down—was the nature of the change? How did the change express itself in action?

analysis

Analysis is examining part by part in order to understand. If we want to define a bicycle, we ride it; but if we want to know how it works, we examine each part in its relation to the others and perhaps even take it apart to see what goes on inside. We would use the same method to investigate or explain an atom or a government.

Not just physical objects can be analyzed; such things as emotions and experiences can be analyzed as well. To analyze them is to separate their component parts and observe how they are related to each other. Then, when you put the whole back together again you understand it better.

writing assignment

1. Narrate in some detail an experience that changed your view of life or that caused you to find out something new about yourself.
2. Analyze this experience. Find and separate the aspects that were most important in changing your view, and make clear why and how they were important.
3. Describe what practical effects this self-discovery has had, giving concrete examples.

class writing assignment

Write a paragraph describing yourself as you believe others see you. Begin with a physical description and progress to mannerisms and personality. Be objective. Avoid the silliness of false modesty, and avoid being coy. Just try to see yourself in the mirror of others. Do not write about your feelings; write as though you were a casual acquaintance who knows nothing about such matters. Use *he* or *she*, not *I*.

The Intruder

ROBERT HENDERSON

My name is Neil Wainwright, and I am a teacher. Professor of history. Sixteenth century. Married. Thirty-four years married. Wife's name: Elizabeth. One married daughter: Ann. I haven't seen Ann in nearly ten months. It seems too long. I live in a place I've loved for seventeen years, in a block off lower Fifth Avenue that has trees, and grace, and quiet people. This apartment is a rambling duplex, and I am writing not in my own workroom but in a small room upstairs.

Tonight Elizabeth is at a concert with friends and I am alone, searching for something that I have not yet been able to define. Something—well, faceless. I've said "panic" to myself all week, but that is just a dodge. I know it. What lies *back* of panic is the question.

I keep writing, running along, and I am reluctantly aware that behind me is the window through which someone entered this room one warm night last April. Is that what I am looking for? Perhaps. Yes, that night must be the starting place. And was it because of that intrusion, though it wasn't much in itself, that I came to the room tonight? I think so.

It really is rather a ridiculous little room. It makes no sense, has no coherence, though it can start memories up like rabbits. Ann is in it, so to speak. It was her room for three years before she went to college, and she left a few tokens. High-school texts; a clay model she made of her poodle which is quite good. She was only thirteen. The proportions are rough, maybe, but the thing is alive.

On the daybed is one of Elizabeth's handbags. She used to leave a row of them there—she often dresses in this room—but since that night in

---

THE INTRUDER   reprinted by permission of the author, first published in *The Saturday Evening Post,* March 13, 1975. © Copyright 1965 by the Curtis Publishing Co.

April she generally keeps them out of sight. The burglar went through them, and afterward they seemed unclean to her. She brushed and rubbed them half the next afternoon. Then there are filing cases and stacks of big envelopes, all full of work I finished long ago. Cards I made out in Gloucestershire and other places. On the table in front of me is a round smooth, honey-colored stone. I picked it up in a meadow in Greece. It's not a fragment of anything that I know of, though it could be. I just believed that it must have been there when the temples were. With some things you don't have to care too much about verification. They connect. Besides, the Greeks aren't my field, and I can imagine them to suit myself.

So, begin with the burglar—or at least with the burglary, for I never saw him. Elizabeth saw a shape. Our bedroom door is next to the door of this room. The night was warm. We had put on the air conditioner, which, of course, made a sound in the room. Opposite the bedroom door is another door giving on an outer stairway. Elizabeth heard someone moving and groping in the little hall between. She thought I had got up and was ill or confused, and she called to me, and I woke up and answered from the bed beside hers. The stair door opened, and a man slipped out, and it closed behind him. All I saw, half awake, was a burst of light and the return of the dark; and then Elizabeth screamed.

I jumped for the door—a hero—but listened before I opened it. There was no sound, and no one was outside. No one was on the staircase. I shut and locked the door and put on the hall light. Elizabeth was standing in the middle of the bedroom. She is almost as tall as I am, but she seemed quite small. I could see her shaking. So was I. We just looked at each other, and then, at the same moment, hurried into Ann's room—this room.

The window was open, though not very wide. He must have been agile; he had come in over a row of potted plants on the sill. The handbags on the bed had been thrown about. There had been money in only one of them—a few dollars. Nothing else seemed to be gone. We went downstairs and I called the police, who came quickly. They looked around, asked questions, and left, and we waited there awhile without saying that what we were waiting for was dawn. When it came, we went upstairs, and before going back to bed, looked into the room again. I closed the window, feeling an odd distaste at touching it. Elizabeth found a few nickels and dimes on the bed and table, and then a little red coin purse lying in a corner of the hall. I picked up a large number of burnt matches from the rug. He had been lighting matches—for how long?—a dozen feet away from us while we slept.

Now it suddenly seems strange that that was all there was to it. It happened half a year ago, and this room is still always *that* room. Worse things—terrible things—have happened to peaceful people. A man happens to jostle another man and is followed and stabbed to death with a broken bottle. A women rings for her elevator and finds her husband in it, shot through the heart. But this place is not the street, or some alien corner of town. It is where Elizabeth and I live—where we and Ann have lived, full of certainty—and it was entered by stealth, invaded in darkness by someone silent and faceless.

Certainty. I suppose that may be the word I am reaching for at the moment. How do you write down what the place you live in is to you? Seventeen years' worth of the growth of certainties. That's enough to lay a soft luster over the rooms and the furniture and us. It didn't always exist, either; there have been changes and storms—even here, at first. But this apartment lies at the physical heart of a kind of enclave, a haven. The Avenues at each end are busy, but our block is apart and knows it. When you turn into the block, you feel as if you had entered a private place, come through a gate. It has legends of ghosts in old town houses, and other minor traditions. It even has a tame beggar—a tall, watery, middle-aged man with a foolish smile, who turns up each spring and cruises the block once or twice a day during the good weather. He pets the dogs and picks up a few coins. People tolerate him. He isn't around *too* much, and he's part of the scene.

No one seems to move away. Some of the neighbors get up a caroling session at Christmas. We've never joined in, but it is extremely pleasant to hear. So yes, it is a scene where certainties develop. For instance, the certainty of things in balance—weatherproof, watertight. The certainty of safety.

Elizabeth and I didn't sleep any more that morning, and the rest of the day was out of kilter, though we pretended it wasn't. We would catch ourselves speaking low and listening to nothing. We weren't afraid. There was nothing to be afraid of. But I know I felt displaced, or somehow guilty of defilement, and I resented it. I gave two lectures. I wanted to cancel the second and get back home, but what for? To startle Elizabeth? I had bolts put on the doors, which did seem sensible. I fitted a two-by-four into the upper frame of that window—I told myself I did it to calm Elizabeth—and ordered a special window lock. And then, going through the room while she was cleaning handbags, I saw a smudge of black at the edge of the rug. It was sticky. We hadn't been talking much about the burglar, so I didn't point it out, but I knew that the roof next door was newly tarred, and I saw smears of black on our gutter. Later, I found a grimy empty match packet under this table. He was hard to exorcise. We had been asked out to dinner that night. When we got home and were preparing for bed, I saw Elizabeth absently look back of several doors. As I came out of the bathroom, she was closing the one to the staircase. "There's some of that tar on the landing," she said offhandedly, and we went to bed without turning on the air conditioner, though the night was warm again.

The window lock came in less than a week, and I put it on, myself. It seemed more than just a device to secure a window—more like a promise that the nights, and days, would be as they always had been. The window is a dormer, with triangles of wall on either side. I installed the lock to the left of the frame and tightened it, and as I turned away I saw a clear hand-print high on the right-hand wall. He was not gone yet. I scrubbed it off at once, and never told Elizabeth it had been there.

Perhaps, because of later events, I am dwelling too much on how upset we were—perhaps I am even magnifying it, but I think not. At any rate, this is what happened. We tried to forget the intruder, but for a long time untethered pronouns would keep slipping into the talk—just "he" or "him" or "his." "He must be small," Elizabeth would say, out of the blue; or, "I wish I could know who he is, or *what* he is." She seemed to need to give him a face and a definition. It bothered her that he might be someone she had passed on the street, and she began to scrutinize all grocers' boys and repairmen.

Between then and now, a secretary has been shot down at her desk in a college office, no one knows why—no one but the person who shot her. A quiet, elderly woman has been strangled for two dollars and thirty cents in a great hive of a building not far from here. A middle-aged teacher has been raped and killed in her own hallway. These are the incidents that happen to come to mind at the moment; there have been a hundred others, and, in a way, our burglar has been guilty of them all.

I used to walk everywhere on this island, sometimes with Elizabeth, sometimes alone, often at night. We would stay up prowling small bars or penny arcades, or the Washington Market. Once we waited all night to go out on the Brooklyn Bridge at dawn. "The whole thing belongs to you, doesn't it?" Elizabeth said, as we stood looking back at the skyline. I had just been given some sort of promotion, and that was why she said it. I like to recall how her face looked.

I love to be in strange sections of Manhattan, to turn a corner and come unexpectedly on trees, or a glimpse of a ship. I love the way darkness comes into the streets, while the sun still burns on the windows of a building that has, itself, turned dusty red. And such things as I am putting down here used to add up to a curious contentment. Lively but casual. Free. One recent winter, there was such a snow that no cars were allowed on the streets, and people poured outdoors and wandered in them. Neighbors became friends. The goodness of the city was boundless. I guess I did know better, but that was how it seemed.

Well, not now. For a while, Elizabeth gathered a small bouquet of suspects. I don't think she really believed in them herself, but she needed them. She remembered a skinny painter who had once worked in our building. She tried to believe that the block beggar was a burglar's lookout, though even she wouldn't argue that he could have made the climb to this window. Later, she recalled that when the man who picked up our laundry had been ill, a lithe little Puerto Rican had taken his place.

And as Elizabeth narrowed the field, I widened it. Before long, I had stopped thinking about one man. "He" has become "they," and I was conscious of all the stealthy and violent men. Facelessness became a multiplicity of faces. And now I think I am coming to one of the things I was afraid I would find out: All of the faces, or most of them, were dark. Black, or at least swarthy. I think I pretended they weren't. I tried to blur the picture or dismiss it. I had never yet confronted prejudice in myself; it was something I was not supposed to have. But the faces were dark. After a while, some of the faces changed. Pale ones crept in. Addicts. Sick boys. Crazy ones. Drifters from the Bowery, or from the South or West. "They" came from everywhere; they *are* everywhere, and they are of all complexions. But most of the faces were dark for quite a while. Eventually they blurred, and violence grew anonymous again. A climate. A component of the air. Every so often you read of a stone thrown through a window of a commuter train; a commuter has an eye put out on his way home. Done by the climate. A young girl, going home at night from a graduation party, is picked off by a sniper from some anonymous roof.

But even home is not always safe. One is aware of that in spite of new locks and bars. Elizabeth is not safe. I sometimes wonder what I would have done if I had wakened and found the man there in the bedroom with us. I don't know. I believe I would have tackled him somehow, but only out of confusion or shock, or because it would seem incumbent on me in Elizabeth's presence. That is the only way I do anything brave—under pressure or grimly. Something is expected of me, or expected by myself. Mostly I try to evade the need—and I am evading now. I am stalling. I do not want to face the fears I have for Elizabeth. Too explicit pictures come to the edge of vision sometimes, and I deny them, refuse them entry. One day when Ann was four, she was playing outside with a part-time maid, who left her for a short while. I went out, just by chance, and saw a squat, unshaven man with her. He scuttled away. I thought she had never looked so tiny. She said he was nice—he had promised to buy her candy and take her to a park, and I can feel again, now, the sensation in my belly. They would have been gone around the corner in a minute, and I have never let myself imagine beyond that.

Well, I am not going to imagine what harm could come to Elizabeth. I want no harm at all to come to her, and there must be other ways of thinking this through. For instance, start with the old stone, there, that came from Greece. There is more clinging to it than a doubtful antiquity. When I brought it home, it was also a kind of token, a private promise that wherever I went afterward, Elizabeth would go too. It has been a paper-weight in here for a dozen years, but that is how it got here. I've kept the promise. It has been easy.

That Greek meadow is a shallow green cup that tilts to the edge of a high cliff beside the Aegean Sea. I could see islands, I remember. I went there in search of presences. I was also there because I had ruined Eliza-beth's plans for a summer on Cape Cod by banging off to do research in Naples, and then going on to Greece just to show her that I could. Inde-pendence. Rubbing it in. We quarreled too much, in those days. I was always snatching at traveling grants and fellowships to get away. I liked to put on a bit of swagger, for one thing, and I could never enjoy it around home. I liked to wear jaunty old soft-brimmed hats and carry a blackthorn cane, and look appraisingly at people. I don't suppose they took much no-tice, but I thought they did.

Elizabeth and I were very far apart by that summer. We scarcely wrote, and I was miserable from June until late August. But I hung around there in that meadow all my last afternoon in Greece, turning this stone in my hand and feeling no presence except hers. I grew peculiarly happy, and somehow I made peace with myself and, in my mind, with her. I don't know how I managed it—effect of the pale-gold light, the sea; maybe, after all, the other presences. Or else I felt that I deserved a reward for having been so miserable. Now that I was going home, I calculated that I didn't even need to be forgiven. And I forgave Elizabeth for her part in all our wars. I meant it, and with love.

Yes, but there was so little to forgive. Even tonight, when there is nothing whatever left of those old quarrels, they seem immeasurably sad and wasteful. She would plunge into some needless piece of housework afterward. At midnight, her hair flying, she would passionately wax the kitchen floor. (Her hair is very fine and light, and it has always flown a little.) I thought then that she was showing me how put-upon she was, but now I know she was also setting her house in order against the time when order would come back to it. She has always longed for order.

She has found it. We have it. That was a turning-point summer. The battles stopped. They never were the large part of our life, only the worst part. We've traveled; the fellowships still come, and the college is generous with time. But getting back here, to Manhattan and to this smaller island of our own within it, has always been at least as good as going away. Cer-tainty and order. I haven't been to Greece again, but someday we will go there. We will try to find some presences. I think Elizabeth will feel at home with them, and they with her. *Nothing* must happen to her.

So, then—what does lie back of panic? What is the deep source? That is what I've told myself I was looking for, chiefly, and all these matters of fear and love may add up to part of the answer, but not to all of it. Now I had better set down quickly what happened that night last week.

I went to an evening meeting uptown. I sometimes carry my black-thorn cane at night, and I had it with me. Coming home, I wasn't able to get a cab, so I took the subway. I got off at Fourteenth Street, walked down Sixth Avenue, and turned into our block, and a man stepped out of the shadows around a tree directly in front of me and stood blocking my path. I was badly startled, and I swung and pushed at him with the cane in an awkward, womanish way, but he didn't speak, just loomed there. And then—and I assume this was panic—I hit him with the heavy end of it, and he went down. It happened fast. I will have to try to remember at what point I recognized him. This is crucial. It was our foolish beggar. For a minute or so I was sure that I had killed him. I felt as if I might be drowning.

It was panic and it wasn't. That day, some boys with knives had run loose on a subway platform, cutting two men and a girl selected at random. Nothing really untoward had happened on my own train, but a man—yes, a Negro; and yes, I do know now that this must have mattered to me, at least a little—had been across the car, talking to himself and swaying and lurching, and watching me, but he had stayed there. And the beggar is white.

I didn't want to touch him, though I thought I must. If Elizabeth had been there, of course I would have. Everything would have been dif-ferent. He moved and grunted and sat up. He was facing away from me, and I walked backward to the corner, where there is a police call box. The man got up. He went east slowly without looking around, staggering a good deal. I called the police and reported an injured derelict wandering in this block. By then, he was gone in the darkness, but a police car came and drove slowly down the block, and stopped near Fifth Avenue. I had waited just around the corner on Sixth, and now I followed at a distance. The car stood a while. I suppose they picked him up. They left, and when I walked down there, the block was empty.

There it is. A ludicrous affair with an unspeakably shabby ending. A nineteenth-century caning in the streets. A twentieth-century panic. But something besides panic swung the cane, for before I hit him hard, I rec-ognized him. And I hit him more than once. I don't say that I could have stopped my arm. But—I have to say—I *wanted* to hit him.

No—not *him*, I suppose. He is harmless. I never for a moment thought otherwise. He was only going to try to wheedle a small donation. He stands and simpers at you before he comes to the point. I knew him, but at the same time, he was—well, faceless. Irrelevant in himself, but suddenly one of *them*. I may have been defending myself, my ordered life, from them, but I know that just for a few seconds there, I joined them. I can't say what's fear and what's hate—they are all but synonymous. But I know you can get a lot said with a few swings of a blackthorn cane, and then you have to figure out what it was.

I will find some anonymous way to make amends to him. I would like to think I could face him, but this is an evening for at least approximate truth. I can find him. He has not been back, but I saw him from a taxi yesterday, in a seedy block of rooming houses and small stores, shambling along as usual, smiling his silly smile. He seemed all right. But why did I remain anonymous *then?* Cowardice? No. No, no—not really. I just didn't want to get mixed up in a mess. Well, I have *never* wanted to be mixed up with anyone but Elizabeth and Ann and a few friends, or anything but my work and selected pleasures. But for a long time now, Elizabeth and I have been caught up inescapably in the climate, the violent air. The intruder came, and in a sense, he stayed. In this room. In our lives. In me.

Yes. There it is, at last. In me. And in me all along. Sleeping, but there. Fear that had no call to stir out of doors, becoming hate, in all the good years. The faces were dark because of something in me. Something embedded. I have been thinking of that stealthy little man as a invader, but perhaps he is more of a resident, after all. Sometimes, when Elizabeth lies awake, I can guess that she is listening, more than half expecting him to come back. But now I know that he has been here all the while. We may never really exorcise him, but we must try.

1. At first this story seems to ramble, to be a long time getting to the point. But as you analyze the ramblings you will find they are full of clues. What are the three, or possibly four, central subjects of the narrator's thoughts?

2. How are these subjects connected? What common theme runs through them?

3. What does Wainwright value in his home and in the street where he lives? What does he value in his marriage?

4. What is the most disturbing thing that happens to him? Why is it so disturbing to him?

5. What does he find out about himself?

6. What do we find out about him that he does not find out about himself?

7. Can you point out a relationship, or theme, that connects this story with "The Catbird Seat" (in Unit 8), "Sonny's Blues" (in Unit 9), or "Discovery of a Father" (in Unit 10)?

The Heavy Bear

DELMORE SCHWARTZ

"The withness of the body"—WHITEHEAD

The heavy bear who goes with me,
A manifold honey to smear his face,
Clumsy and lumbering here and there,
The central ton of every place,
The hungry beating brutish one
In love with candy, anger, and sleep,
Crazy factotum, dishevelling all,
Climbs the building, kicks the football,
Boxes his brother in the hate-ridden city.

Breathing at my side, that heavy animal,
That heavy bear who sleeps with me,
Howls in his sleep for a world of sugar,
A sweetness intimate as the water's clasp,
Howls in his sleep because the tight-rope
Trembles and shows the darkness beneath.
—The strutting show-off is terrified,
Dressed in his dress-suit, bulging his pants,
Trembles to think that his quivering meat.
Must finally wince to nothing at all.

That inescapable animal walks with me,
Has followed me since the black womb held,
Moves where I move, distorting my gesture,
A caricature, a swollen shadow,
A stupid clown of the spirit's motive,
Perplexes and affronts with his own darkness,
The secret life of belly and bone,
Opaque, too near, my private, yet unknown,
Stretches to embrace the very dear

With whom I would walk without him near,
Touches her grossly, although a word
Would bare my heart and make me clear,
Stumbles, flounders, and strives to be fed
Dragging me with him in his mouthing care,
Amid the hundred million of his kind,
The scrimmage of appetite everywhere.

---

1. What is the subject of the poem?
2. What is the poet's attitude toward it?
3. What aspects of it does he emphasize? What aspects does he omit?
4. What do you find to be the poet's basic feeling about himself, as he expresses it here?
5. Would it be possible for one to assume a point of view opposite that of the poem? Make a few statements that would express such a point of view.
6. Like many good poems, this one is full of strong, sensual words and images. Point out some of these. How does each contribute to the total effect?
7. What is the emotional tone of the poem?

1. These are four of the many self-portraits van Gogh painted, but they are representative. Looking at them, what do you feel was the artist's motive in painting these self-portraits?

2. Try to put into words how van Gogh sees himself in each of the four portraits.

3. Which seems to have been painted when he felt the most self-confident? Which might have been done when he was most disturbed? Which seems to have an element of self-critical humor? In which does he seem to emphasize his peasant origins?

4. Analyze the differences that lead you to the above judgments. How has van Gogh expressed his attitude toward himself in each case?

a

b

c

d

PLATE XII Four self portraits: Vincent van Gogh.   (a) SELF PORTRAIT, 1887. National Museum
Kröller-Müller. Otterlo, Netherlands   (b) SELF PORTRAIT WITH FELT HAT, 1888. National
Museum, Vincent van Gogh, Amsterdam   (c) SELF PORTRAIT AT THE EASEL, 1888. Nation-
al Museum, Vincent van Gogh, Amsterdam   (d) SELF PORTRAIT, 1888. Courtesy of the Fogg
Art Museum, Harvard University. Bequest — Collection of Maurice Wertheim, class of 1906

13
examining
a desire

The greatest religious leaders have consistently advised us that the way to happiness lies not in attaining the objects of our desires, but in ridding ourselves of desire. While most of us admire such wisdom, few follow it.

If we are not ready to renounce our desires, it does us no harm to examine them. Some secret part of us keeps whispering that fulfillment of our desires isn't really going to make us happy. But we go on chasing after the toy balloon anyway. Perhaps desire itself is our way of life. We know that as soon as we get that new car we're going to start dreaming about the next one. Some people, as soon as they get a new husband or wife, start thinking about the next one. Maybe desire is just a kind of wound up spring that keeps us running.

A good job, status, and security—these are the common desires examined by the authors in this unit. But these desires shouldn't go unexamined. We needn't sleepwalk through life.

class discussion

State your most serious, long-term desire. Then let others ask you such questions as "Why?" "What do you mean by that?" and "What do you expect to get out of it?" Try to answer seriously, without giving up or falling back on generalities like "Everybody wants that." Why do *you* want it?

generalization

As we have said under "giving specifics" in the Introduction, a general statement is one that covers many specific instances. To *generalize* is to observe what a number of specific examples have in common. It is the same process that in science is called "inductive thinking."

Before you can generalize, you must find and observe the examples. And when you offer a generalization to others, you must support it by giving these examples.

There are many *levels* of generalization. Let's say you have observed your dog, Truffles, overturning garbage cans, begging from the neighbors, jumping on a child carrying an ice cream cone, stealing hamburger from the kitchen table, running home at feeding time, and doing tricks for a scrap of meat. From this evidence you can state a *low-level* generalization: "Truffles will go through a lot to get food." You can*not* make a generalization about dogs until you have seen many other dogs do the same things. Then you can go up another step on the ladder and say, "Dogs will go through a lot to get food." Add more observations and you can make it "animals." Keep broadening the scope, and eventually you can work your way up to "Nourishment is essential to living things."

The point is, don't jump to conclusions. Keep your generalization down to the level where your evidence supports it solidly.

writing assignment

1. What is your desire for an occupation or career? What do you hope to get out of it in happiness or satisfaction? Make a clear economical statement answering these questions.
2. As an example, describe at least one person you know who has attained the same object. In specific terms, tell what each does and what satisfaction each person seems to get from doing it. (If you don't know anybody like this, possibly you are not serious in your desire. No one should become a surgeon on the basis of watching Dr. Welby alone.)
3. What do you want to be doing on the afternoon of November 30, 2000? For example, if you answered the first question, "I want to be a good auto mechanic," then describe in concrete, hour-by-hour terms what you would expect to be doing. Not, "I expect to own my own garage," but, "I expect to be removing and cleaning a carburetor, replacing the worn jets, and reinstalling it," and so on through the specific activities of a working day. Project yourself into the here and now of your future.
4. Formulate a two-part generalization covering the evidence in questions 1 and 2. It might go something like, "I want most to be (or do) so and so, first because . . . , and second because . . ."

class writing assignment

Organize the material you have written into an essay with an introductory statement, two or more paragraphs of examples, and a conclusion that is in the form of a generalization.

from Invisible Man

RALPH ELLISON

It goes a long way back, some twenty years. All my life I had been looking for something, and everywhere I turned someone tried to tell me what it was. I accepted their answers too, though they were often in contradiction and even self-contradictory. I was naïve. I was looking for myself and asking everyone except myself questions which I, and only I, could answer. It took me a long time and much painful boomeranging of my expectations to achieve a realization everyone else appears to have been born with. That I am nobody but myself. But first I had to discover that I am an invisible man!

And yet I am no freak of nature, nor of history. I was in the cards, other things having been equal (or unequal) eighty-five years ago. I am not ashamed of my grandparents for having been slaves. I am only ashamed at myself for having at one time been ashamed. About eighty-five years ago they were told they were free, united with others of our country in everything pertaining to the common good, and, in everything social, separate like the fingers of the hand. And they believed it. They exulted in it. They stayed in their place, worked hard, and brought up my father to do the same. But my grandfather is the one. He was an odd old guy, my grandfather, and I am told I take after him. It was he who caused the trouble. On his deathbed he called my father to him and said, "Son, after I'm gone, I want you to keep up the good fight. I never told you, but our life is a war and I have been a traitor all my born days, a spy in the enemy's country ever since I give up my gun back in the Reconstruction. Live with your head in the lion's mouth. I want you to overcome 'em with yeses, undermine 'em with grins, agree 'em to death and destruction, let 'em swoller you till they vomit or bust wide open." They thought the old man had gone out of his mind. He had been the meekest of men. The younger children were rushed from the room, the shades drawn and the flame of the lamp turned so low that it sputtered on the wick like the old man's breathing. "Learn it to the younguns," he whispered fiercely; then he died.

But my folks were more alarmed over his last words than over his dying. It was as though he had not died at all, his words caused so much anxiety. I was warned emphatically to forget what he had said and, indeed, this is the first time it has been mentioned outside the family circle. It had a tremendous effect upon me, however. I could never be sure of what he meant. Grandfather had been a quiet old man who never made any trouble, yet on his deathbed he had called himself a traitor and a spy, and he had spoken of his meekness as a dangerous activity. It became a constant puzzle which lay unanswered in the back of my mind. And whenever things went well for me I remembered my grandfather and felt guilty and uncomfortable. It was as though I was carrying out his advice in spite of myself. And to make it worse, everyone loved me for it. I was praised by the most lily-white men of the town. I was considered an example of desirable conduct— just as my grandfather had been. And what puzzled me was that the old man had defined it as *treachery*. When I was praised for my conduct I felt a guilt that in some way I was doing something that was really against the wishes of the white folks, that if they had understood they would have desired me to act just the opposite, that I should have been sulky and mean, and that that really would have been what they wanted, even though they were fooled and thought they wanted me to act as I did. It made me afraid that some day they would look upon me as a traitor and I would be lost. Still I was more afraid to act any other way because they didn't like that at all. The old man's words were like a curse. On my graduation day I delivered an oration in which I showed that humility was the secret, indeed, the very essence of progress. (Not that I believed this—how could I, remembering my grandfather?—I only believed that it worked.) It was a great success. Everyone praised me and I was invited to give the speech at a gathering of the town's leading white citizens. It was a triumph for our whole community.

It was in the main ballroom of the leading hotel. When I got there I discovered that it was on the occasion of a smoker, and I was told that since I was to be there anyway I might as well take part in the battle royal to be fought by some of my schoolmates as part of the entertainment. The battle royal came first.

All of the town's big shots were there in their tuxedoes, wolfing down the buffet foods, drinking beer and whiskey and smoking black cigars. It was a large room with a high ceiling. Chairs were arranged in neat rows around three sides of a portable boxing ring. The fourth side was clear, revealing a gleaming space of polished floor. I had some misgivings over the battle royal, by the way. Not from a distaste for fighting but because I didn't care too much for the other fellows who were to take part. They were tough guys who seemed to have no grandfather's curse worrying their minds. No one could mistake their toughness. And besides, I suspected that fighting a battle royal might detract from the dignity of my speech. In those pre-invisible days I visualized myself as a potential Booker T. Washington. But the other fellows didn't care too much for me either, and there were nine of them. I felt superior to them in my way, and I didn't like the manner in which we were all crowded together into the servants' elevator. Nor did they like my being there. In fact, as the warmly lighted floors flashed past the elevator we had words over the fact that I, by taking part in the fight, had knocked one of their friends out of a night's work.

We were led out of the elevator through a rococo hall into an ante-room and told to get into our fighting togs. Each of us was issued a pair of boxing gloves and ushered out into the big mirrored hall, which we entered looking cautiously about us and whispering, lest we might accidentally be heard above the noise of the room. It was foggy with cigar smoke. And already the whiskey was taking effect. I was shocked to see some of the most important men of the town quite tipsy. They were all there—bankers, lawyers, judges, doctors, fire chiefs, teachers, merchants. Even one of the more fashionable pastors. Something we could not see was going on up front. A clarinet was vibrating sensuously and the men were standing up and moving eagerly forward. We were a small tight group, clustered to-gether, our bare upper bodies touching and shining with anticipatory sweat; while up front the big shots were becoming increasingly excited over some-thing we still could not see. Suddenly I heard the school superintendent, who had told me to come, yell, "Bring up the shines, gentlemen! Bring up the little shines!"

We were rushed up to the front of the ballroom, where it smelled even more strongly of tobacco and whiskey. Then we were pushed into place. I almost wet my pants. A sea of faces, some hostile, some amused, ringed around us, and in the center, facing us, stood a magnificent blonde—stark naked. There was dead silence. I felt a blast of cold air chill me. I tried to back away, but they were behind me and around me. Some of the boys stood with lowered heads, trembling. I felt a wave of irrational guilt and fear. My teeth chattered, my skin turned to goose flesh, my knees knocked. Yet I was strongly attracted and looked in spite of myself. Had the price of looking been blindness, I would have looked. The hair was yellow like that of a circus kewpie doll, the face heavily powdered and rouged, as though to form an abstract mask, the eyes hollow and smeared a cool blue, the color of a baboon's butt. I felt a desire to spit upon her as my eyes brushed slowly over her body. Her breasts were firm and round as the domes of East Indian temples, and I stood so close as to see the fine skin texture and beads of pearly perspiration glistening like dew around the pink and erected buds of her nipples. I wanted at one and the same time to run from the room, to sink through the floor, or go to her and cover her from my eyes and the eyes of the others with my body; to feel the soft thighs, to caress her and destroy her, to love her and murder her, to hide from her, and yet to stroke where below the small American flag tattooed upon her belly her thighs formed a capital V. I had a notion that of all in the room she saw only me with her impersonal eyes.

And then she began to dance, a slow sensuous movement; the smoke of a hundred cigars clinging to her like the thinnest of veils. She seemed like a fair bird-girl girdled in veils calling to me from the angry surface of some gray and threatening sea. I was transported. Then I became aware of the clarinet playing and the big shots yelling at us. Some threatened us if we looked and others if we did not. On my right I saw one boy faint. And now a man grabbed a silver pitcher from a table and stepped close as he dashed ice water upon him and stood him up and forced two of us to support him as his head hung and moans issued from his thick bluish lips. Another boy began to plead to go home. He was the largest of the group, wearing dark red fighting trunks much too small to conceal the erection which projected from him as though in answer to the insinuating low-registered moaning of the clarinet. He tried to hide himself with his boxing gloves.

And all the while the blonde continued dancing, smiling faintly at the big shots who watched her with fascination, and faintly smiling at our fear. I noticed a certain merchant who followed her hungrily, his lips loose and drooling. He was a large man who wore diamond studs in a shirtfront which swelled with the ample paunch underneath, and each time the blonde swayed her undulating hips he ran his hand through the thin hair of his bald head and, with his arms upheld, his posture clumsy like that of an intoxicated panda, wound his belly in a slow and obscene grind. This creature was completely hypnotized. The music had quickened. As the dancer flung herself about with a detached expression on her face, the men began reaching out to touch her. I could see their beefy fingers sink into the soft flesh. Some of the others tried to stop them and she began to move around the floor in graceful circles, as they gave chase, slipping and sliding over the polished floor. It was mad. Chairs went crashing, drinks were spilt, as they ran laughing and howling after her. They caught her just as she reached a door, raised her from the floor, and tossed her as college boys are tossed at a hazing, and above her red, fixed-smiling lips I saw the terror and disgust in her eyes, almost like my own terror and that which I saw in some of the other boys. As I watched, they tossed her twice and her soft breasts seemed to flatten against the air and her legs flung wildly as she spun. Some of the more sober ones helped her to escape. And I started off the floor, heading for the anteroom with the rest of the boys.

Some were still crying and in hysteria. But as we tried to leave we were stopped and ordered to get into the ring. There was nothing to do but what we were told. All ten of us climbed under the ropes and allowed ourselves to be blindfolded with broad bands of white cloth. One of the men seemed to feel a bit sympathetic and tried to cheer us up as we stood with our backs against the ropes. Some of us tried to grin. "See that boy over there?" one of the men said. "I want you to run across at the bell and give it to him right in the belly. If you don't get him, I'm going to get you. I don't like his looks." Each of us was told the same. The blindfolds were put on. Yet even then I had been going over my speech. In my mind each word was as bright as flame. I felt the cloth pressed into place, and frowned so that it would be loosened when I relaxed.

But now I felt a sudden fit of blind terror. I was unused to darkness. It was as though I had suddenly found myself in a dark room filled with poisonous cottonmouths. I could hear the bleary voices yelling insistently for the battle royal to begin.

"Get going in there!"

"Let me at that big nigger!"

I strained to pick up the school superintendent's voice, as though to squeeze some security out of that slightly more familiar sound.

"Let me at those black sonsabitches!" someone yelled.

"No, Jackson, no!" another voice yelled. "Here, somebody, help me hold Jack."

"I want to get at that ginger-colored nigger. Tear him limb from limb," the first voice yelled.

I stood against the ropes trembling. For in those days I was what they called ginger-colored, and he sounded as though he might crunch me between his teeth like a crisp ginger cookie.

Quite a struggle was going on. Chairs were being kicked about and I could hear voices grunting as with a terrific effort. I wanted to see, to see more desperately than ever before. But the blindfold was as tight as a thick skin-puckering scab and when I raised my gloved hands to push the layers of white aside a voice yelled, "Oh, no you don't, black bastard! Leave that alone!"

"Ring the bell before Jackson kills him a coon!" someone boomed in the sudden silence. And I heard the bell clang and the sound of the feet scuffling forward.

A glove smacked against my head. I pivoted, striking out stiffly as someone went past, and felt the jar ripple along the length of my arm to my shoulder. Then it seemed as though all nine of the boys had turned upon me at once. Blows pounded me from all sides while I struck out as best I could. So many blows landed upon me that I wondered if I were not the only blindfolded fighter in the ring, or if the man called Jackson hadn't succeeded in getting me after all.

Blindfolded, I could no longer control my motions. I had no dignity. I stumbled about like a baby or a drunken man. The smoke had become thicker and with each new blow it seemed to sear and further restrict my lungs. My saliva became like hot bitter glue. A glove connected with my head, filling my mouth with warm blood. It was everywhere. I could not tell if the moisture I felt upon my body was sweat or blood. A blow landed hard against the nape of my neck. I felt myself going over, my head hitting the floor. Streaks of blue light filled the black world behind the blindfold. I lay prone, pretending that I was knocked out, but felt myself seized by hands and yanked to my feet. "Get going, black boy! Mix it up!" My arms were like lead, my head smarting from blows. I managed to feel my way to the ropes and held on, trying to catch my breath. A glove landed in my mid-section and I went over again, feeling as though the smoke had become a knife jabbed into my guts. Pushed this way and that by the legs milling around me, I finally pulled erect and discovered that I could see the black, sweat-washed forms weaving in the smoky-blue atmosphere like drunken dancers weaving to the rapid drum-like thuds of blows.

Everyone fought hysterically. It was complete anarchy. Everybody fought everybody else. No group fought together for long. Two, three, four, fought one, then turned to fight each other, were themselves attacked. Blows landed below the belt and in the kidney, with the gloves open as well as closed, and with my eye partly opened now there was not so much terror. I moved carefully, avoiding blows, although not too many to attract attention, fighting from group to group. The boys groped about like blind, cautious crabs crouching to protect their mid-sections, their heads pulled in short against their shoulders, their arms stretched nervously before them, with their fists testing the smoke-filled air like the knobbed feelers of hypersensitive snails. In one corner I glimpsed a boy violently punching the air and heard him scream in pain as he smashed his hand against a ring post. For a second I saw him bent over holding his hand, then going down as a blow caught his unprotected head. I played one group against the other, slipping in and throwing a punch then stepping out of range while pushing the others into the melee to take the blows blindly aimed at me. The smoke was agonizing and there were no rounds, no bells at three minute intervals to relieve our exhaustion. The room spun around me, a swirl of lights, smoke, sweating bodies surrounded by tense white faces. I bled from both nose and mouth, the blood spattering upon my chest.

The men kept yelling, "Slug him, black boy! Knock his guts out!"

"Uppercut him! Kill him! Kill that big boy!"

Taking a fake fall, I saw a boy going down heavily beside me as though we were felled by a single blow, saw a sneaker-clad foot shoot into his groin as the two who had knocked him down stumbled upon him. I rolled out of range, feeling a twinge of nausea.

The harder we fought the more threatening the men became. And yet, I had begun to worry about my speech again. How would it go? Would they recognize my ability? What would they give me?

I was fighting automatically when suddenly I noticed that one after another of the boys was leaving the ring. I was surprised, filled with panic, as though I had been left alone with an unknown danger. Then I understood. The boys had arranged it among themselves. It was the custom for the two men left in the ring to slug it out for the winner's prize. I discovered this too late. When the bell sounded two men in tuxedoes leaped into the ring and removed the blindfold. I found myself facing Tatlock, the biggest of the gang. I felt sick at my stomach. Hardly had the bell stopped ringing in my ears than it clanged again and I saw him moving swiftly toward me. Thinking of nothing else to do I hit him smash on the nose. He kept coming, bringing the rank sharp violence of stale sweat. His face was a black blank of a face, only his eyes alive—with hate of me and aglow with a feverish terror from what had happened to us all. I became anxious. I wanted to deliver my speech and he came at me as though he meant to beat it out of me. I smashed him again and again, taking his blows as they came. Then on a sudden impulse I struck him lightly and as we clinched, I whispered, "Fake like I knocked you out, you can have the prize."

"I'll break your behind," he whispered hoarsely.

"For *them?*"

"For *me*, sonofabitch!"

They were yelling for us to break it up and Tatlock spun me half around with a blow, and as a joggled camera sweeps in a reeling scene, I saw the howling red faces crouching tense beneath the cloud of blue-gray smoke. For a moment the world wavered, unraveled, flowed, then my head cleared and Tatlock bounced before me. That fluttering shadow before my eyes was his jabbing left hand. Then falling forward, my head against his damp shoulder, I whispered,

"I'll make it five dollars more."

"Go to hell!"

But his muscles relaxed a trifle beneath my pressure and I breathed, "Seven?"

"Give it to your ma," he said, ripping me beneath the heart.

And while I still held him I butted him and moved away. I felt myself bombarded with punches. I fought back with hopeless desperation. I wanted to deliver my speech more than anything else in the world, because I felt that only these men could judge truly my ability, and now this stupid clown was ruining my chances. I began fighting carefully now, moving in to punch him and out again with my greater speed. A lucky blow to his chin and I had him going too—until I heard a loud voice yell, "I got my money on the big boy."

Hearing this, I almost dropped my guard. I was confused: Should I try to win against the voice out there? Would not this go against my speech, and was not this a moment for humility, for nonresistance? A blow to my head as I danced about sent my right eye popping like a jack-in-the-box and settled my dilemma. The room went red as I fell. It was a dream fall, my body languid and fastidious as to where to land, until the floor became impatient and smashed up to meet me. A moment later I came to. An hypnotic voice said FIVE emphatically. And I lay there, hazily watching a dark red spot of my own blood shaping itself into a butterfly, glistening and soaking into the soiled gray world of the canvas.

When the voice drawled TEN I was lifted up and dragged to a chair. I sat dazed. My eye pained and swelled with each throb of my pounding heart and I wondered if now I would be allowed to speak. I was wringing wet, my mouth still bleeding. We were grouped along the wall now. The other boys ignored me as they congratulated Tatlock and speculated as to how much they would be paid. One boy whimpered over his smashed hand. Looking up front, I saw attendants in white jackets rolling the portable ring away and placing a small square rug in the vacant space surrounded by chairs. Perhaps, I thought, I will stand on the rug to deliver my speech.

Then the M.C. called to us, "Come on up here boys and get your money."

We ran forward to where the men laughed and talked in their chairs, waiting. Everyone seemed friendly now.

"There it is on the rug," the man said. "You get all you grab."

"That's right, Sambo," a blond man said, winking at me confidentially.

I trembled with excitement, forgetting my pain. I would get the gold and the bills, I thought. I would use both hands. I would throw my body against the boys nearest me to block them from the gold.

"Get down around the rug now," the man commanded, "and don't anyone touch it until I give the signal."

"This ought to be good," I heard.

As told, we got around the square rug on our knees. Slowly the man raised his freckled hand as we followed it upward with our eyes.

I heard, "These niggers look like they're about to pray!"

Then, "Ready," the man said. "Go!"

I lunged for a yellow coin lying on the blue design of the carpet, touching it and sending a surprised shriek to join those rising around me. I tried frantically to remove my hand but could not let go. A hot, violent force tore through my body, shaking me like a wet rat. The rug was electrified. The hair bristled up on my head as I shook myself free. My muscles jumped, my nerves jangled, writhed. But I saw that this was not stopping the other boys. Laughing in fear and embarrassment, some were holding back and scooping up the coins knocked off by the painful contortions of the others. The men roared above us as we struggled.

"Pick it up, goddamnit, pick it up!" someone called like a bass-voiced parrot. "Go on, get it!"

I crawled rapidly around the floor, picking up the coins, trying to avoid the coppers and to get greenbacks and the gold. Ignoring the shock by laughing, as I brushed the coins off quickly, I discovered that I could contain the electricity—a contradiction, but it works. Then the men began to push us onto the rug. Laughing, embarrassedly, we struggled out of their hands and kept after the coins. We were all wet and slippery and hard to hold. Suddenly I saw a boy lifted into the air, glistening with sweat like a circus seal, and dropped, his wet back landing flush upon the charged rug, heard him yell and saw him literally dance upon his back, his elbows beating a frenzied tattoo upon the floor, his muscles twitching like the flesh of a horse stung by many flies. When he finally rolled off, his face was gray and no one stopped him when he ran from the floor amid booming laughter.

"Get the money," the M.C. called. "That's good hard American cash!"

And we snatched and grabbed, snatched and grabbed. I was careful not to come too close to the rug now, and when I felt the hot whiskey breath descend upon me like a cloud of foul air I reached out and grabbed the leg of a chair. It was occupied and I held on desperately.

"Leggo, nigger! Leggo!"

The huge face wavered down to mine as he tried to push me free. But my body was slippery and he was too drunk. It was Mr. Colcord, who owned a chain of movie houses and "entertainment palaces." Each time he grabbed me I slipped out of his hands. It became a real struggle. I feared the rug more than I did the drunk, so I held on, surprising myself for a moment by trying to topple *him* upon the rug. It was such an enormous idea that I found myself actually carrying it out. I tried not to be obvious, yet when I grabbed his leg, trying to tumble him out of the chair, he raised up roaring with laughter, and, looking at me with soberness dead in the eye, kicked me viciously in the chest. The chair leg flew out of my hand and I felt myself going and rolled. It was as though I had rolled through a bed of hot coals. It seemed a whole century would pass before I would roll free, a century in which I was seared through the deepest levels of my body to the fearful breath within me and the breath seared and heated to the point of explosion. It'll all be over in a flash, I thought as I rolled clear. It'll all be over in a flash.

But not yet, the men on the other side were waiting, red faces swollen as though from apoplexy as they bent forward in their chairs. Seeing their fingers coming toward me I rolled away as a fumbled football rolls off the receiver's fingertips, back into the coals. That time I luckily sent the rug sliding out of place and heard the coins ringing against the floor and the boys scuffling to pick them up and the M.C. calling, "All right, boys, that's all. Go get dressed and get your money."

I was limp as a dish rag. My back felt as though it had been beaten with wires.

When we had dressed the M.C. came in and gave us each five dollars, except Tatlock, who got ten for being last in the ring. Then he told us to leave. I was not to get a chance to deliver my speech, I thought. I was going out into the dim alley in despair when I was stopped and told to go back. I returned to the ballroom, where the men were pushing back their chairs and gathering in groups to talk.

The M.C. knocked on the table for quiet. "Gentlemen," he said, "we almost forgot an important part of the program. A most serious part, gentlemen. This boy was brought here to deliver a speech which he made at his graduation yesterday . . ."

"Bravo!"

"I'm told that he is the smartest boy we've got out there in Greenwood. I'm told that he knows more big words than a pocket-sized dictionary."

Much applause and laughter.

"So now, gentlemen, I want you to give him your attention."

There was still laughter as I faced them, my mouth dry, my eye throbbing. I began slowly, but evidently my throat was tense, because they began shouting, "Louder! Louder!"

"We of the younger generation extol the wisdom of that great leader and educator," I shouted, "who first spoke these flaming words of wisdom: 'A ship lost at sea for many days suddenly sighted a friendly vessel. From the mast of the unfortunate vessel was seen a signal: "Water, water; we die of thirst!" The answer from the friendly vessel came back: "Cast down your bucket where you are." The captain of the distressed vessel, at last heeding the injunction, cast down his bucket, and it came up full of fresh sparkling water from the mouth of the Amazon River.' And like him I say, and in his words, 'To those of my race who depend upon bettering their condition in a foreign land, or who underestimate the importance of cultivating friendly relations with the Southern white man, who is his next-door neighbor, I would say: "Cast down your bucket where you are"—cast it down in making friends in every manly way of the people of all races by whom we are surrounded . . .' "

I spoke automatically and with such fervor that I did not realize that the men were still talking and laughing until my dry mouth, filling up with blood from the cut, almost strangled me. I coughed, wanting to stop and go to one of the tall brass, sand-filled spittoons to relieve myself, but a few of the men, especially the superintendent, were listening and I was afraid. So I gulped it down, blood, saliva and all, and continued. (What powers of endurance I had during those days! What enthusiasm! What a belief in the rightness of things!) I spoke even louder in spite of the pain. But still they talked and still they laughed, as though deaf with cotton in dirty ears. So I spoke with greater emotional emphasis. I closed my ears and swallowed blood until I was nauseated. The speech seemed a hundred times as long as before, but I could not leave out a single word. All had to be said, each memorized nuance considered, rendered. Nor was that all. Whenever I

uttered a word of three or more syllables a group of voices would yell for
me to repeat it. I used the phrase "social responsibility" and they yelled:
    "What's that word you say, boy?"
    "Social responsibility," I said.
    "What?"
    "Social . . ."
    "Louder."
    ". . . responsibility."
    "More!"
    "Respon—"
    "Repeat!"
    "—sibility."
    The room filled with the uproar of laughter until, no doubt, distracted
by having to gulp down my blood, I made a mistake and yelled a phrase I
had often seen denounced in newspaper editorials, heard debated in private.
    "Social . . ."
    "What?" they yelled.
    ". . . equality—"
    The laughter hung smokelike in the sudden stillness. I opened my
eyes, puzzled. Sounds of displeasure filled the room. The M.C. rushed
forward. They shouted hostile phrases at me. But I did not understand.
    A small dry mustached man in the front row blared out, "Say that
slowly, son!"
    "What, sir?"
    "What you just said!"
    "Social responsibility, sir," I said.
    "You weren't being smart, were you, boy?" he said, not unkindly.
    "No, sir!"
    "You sure that about 'equality' was a mistake?"
    "Oh, yes, sir," I said. "I was swallowing blood."
    "Well, you had better speak more slowly so we can understand. We
mean to do right by you, but you've got to know your place at all times. All
right, now, go on with your speech."
    I was afraid. I wanted to leave but I wanted also to speak and I was
afraid they'd snatch me down.
    "Thank you, sir," I said, beginning where I had left off, and having
them ignore me as before.
    Yet when I finished there was a thunderous applause. I was surprised
to see the superintendent come forth with a package wrapped in white
tissue paper, and, gesturing for quiet, address the men.
    "Gentlemen, you see that I did not overpraise this boy. He makes
a good speech and some day he'll lead his people in the proper paths. And
I don't have to tell you that that is important in these days and times. This

is a good, smart boy, and so to encourage him in the right direction, in the name of the Board of Education I wish to present him a prize in the form of this . . ."

He paused, removing the tissue paper and revealing a gleaming calf-skin brief case.

". . . in the form of this first-class article from Shad Whitmore's shop."

"Boy," he said, addressing me, "take this prize and keep it well. Consider it a badge of office. Prize it. Keep developing as you are and some day it will be filled with important papers that will help shape the destiny of your people."

I was so moved that I could hardly express my thanks. A rope of bloody saliva forming a shape like an undiscovered continent drooled upon the leather and I wiped it quickly away. I felt an importance that I had never dreamed.

"Open it and see what's inside," I was told.

My fingers a-tremble, I complied, smelling the fresh leather and finding an official-looking document inside. It was a scholarship to the state college for Negroes. My eyes filled with tears and I ran awkwardly off the floor.

I was overjoyed; I did not even mind when I discovered that the gold pieces I had scrambled for were brass pocket tokens advertising a certain make of automobile.

When I reached home everyone was excited. Next day the neighbors came to congratulate me. I even felt safe from grandfather, whose deathbed curse usually spoiled my triumphs. I stood beneath his photograph with my brief case in hand and smiled triumphantly into his stolid black peasant's face. It was a face that fascinated me. The eyes seemed to follow everywhere I went.

That night I dreamed I was at a circus with him and that he refused to laugh at the clowns no matter what they did. Then later he told me to open my brief case and read what was inside and I did, finding an official envelope stamped with the state seal; and inside the envelope I found another and another, endlessly, and I thought I would fall of weariness. "Them's years," he said. "Now open that one." And I did and in it I found an engraved document containing a short message in letters of gold. "Read it," my grandfather said. "Out loud."

"To Whom It May Concern," I intoned. "Keep This Nigger-Boy Running."

I awoke with the old man's laughter ringing in my ears.

1. What desire has the narrator been acting on? Define it as accurately as you can.

2. What caused him to begin developing doubts about this desire? Analyze the events in order to identify the elements that cause him to question his desire.

3. State as precisely as you can the generalization that seemed to be implied by these elements.

4. Is this the only possible generalization? See if it can be qualified with an *if* or *but*.

5. This is the first chapter in a book about the narrator's "running." In the end he decides that he lives in an alienated culture, that the principle "Keep This Nigger-Boy Running" applies to the way most people, black and white alike, treat each other: everyone is exploited. He retreats from society, literally crawling into a hole. The reader is confronted with a dilemma: Ralph Ellison, in effect, advises you to drop out of society because it's hopeless; others, such as the Reverend Jesse Jackson, advise you to accept society on its own terms and be a winner. From observing their surroundings, different people come up with opposite generalizations. What would your choice be? On what evidence do you base it, and what are your reasons? In terms of your own action, is any compromise possible between the two generalizations? Be realistic: talk about *specific* actions.

6. Do you ever feel that you are being kept running for someone else's purposes? Or do you ever feel that your desires are not really your own, that they have been fed to you by others? Explain. If you have such feelings, what do you feel you should do about them? Are there practical ways to live the life you want to live?

The Unknown Citizen

W. H. AUDEN

To JS/07/M/378
This Marble Monument Is Erected by the State

He was found by the Bureau of Statistics to be
One against whom there was no official complaint,
And all the reports on his conduct agree
That, in the modern sense of an old-fashioned word, he was a saint,
For in everything he did he served the Greater Community.
Except for the War till the day he retired
He worked in a factory and never got fired,
But satisfied his employers, Fudge Motors Inc.
Yet he wasn't a scab or odd in his views.
For his Union reports that he paid his dues,
(Our report on his Union shows it was sound)
And our Social Psychology workers found
That he was popular with his mates and liked a drink.
The Press are convinced that he bought a paper every day
And that his reactions to advertisements were normal in every way.
Policies taken out in his name prove that he was fully insured,
And his Health-card shows he was once in hospital but left it cured.
Both Producers Research and High-Grade Living declare
He was fully sensible to the advantages of the Installment Plan
And had everything necessary to the Modern Man,
A gramophone, a radio, a car and a frigidaire.
Our researchers into Public Opinion are content
That he held the proper opinions for the time of year;
When there was peace, he was for peace; when there was war, he went.
He was married and added five children to the population,
Which our Eugenist says was the right number for a parent of his generation,
And our teachers report that he never interfered with their education.
Was he free? Was he happy? The question is absurd:
Had anything been wrong, we should certainly have heard.

---

1. What is the purpose of serving "the Greater Community"? What is the purpose of the community?
2. What was the desire of the person who became the Unknown Citizen? Do you know anyone like him? Does such a person exist?
3. What does "normal" mean?
4. What is the meaning of "And our teachers report that he never interfered with their education"? Have you ever interfered with the education offered by your teachers?
5. Can you answer the questions "Was he free? Was he happy?" in specific terms? Are the questions absurd?
6. Is the Unknown Citizen in any way like the narrator of *Invisible Man*? If so, how? How is he different?

1. Surely the most common desire is to be wealthy, or at least comfortably well-off. Has the woman in the fish bowl achieved this goal? What evidence do you find in the picture?
2. Why is she unhappy?
3. A fish bowl can be seen out of as well as into. Which is the woman's problem—seeing, or being seen?
4. How is her problem related to that of the narrator of *Invisible Man*?
5. What is the answer to the problem?

PLATE XIII

THE FISH BOWL: Pavel Tchelitchew. The Metropolitan Museum of Art, Gift of
Constance Atwood Askew in memory of R. Kirk Askew, Jr., 1974

Drawing by Lorenz; © 1973 The New Yorker Magazine, Inc.

14

seeing the
whole
picture

The ultimate generalization is some sort of conclusion about the nature of the universe. Only philosophers attempt such generalizations; however, any of us can try to see some aspects of the world as a whole. We can also contribute our own unique observations to the general picture. For example, the "whole picture" of humanity's suicidal assault on the natural environment is one we are all beginning to see, and it is one to which we can all bear witness: the pollution of the river our fathers and mothers swam in, the dimming of the night skies from increasing air pollution in our own lifetime, the despoiling of the countryside around us with badly planned suburbs.

For that matter, we don't have to wait until we are issued philosopher's licenses to have our own ideas about the meaning of human life and death. We can all listen to our own hearts and feel how things are. But we should be sure that we *are* hearing our own hearts and not the thumping on the pulpit next door. We don't want our feelings to be no more than other people's clichés or stereotypes. We want to find our own voices and speak for ourselves.

class discussion

Throughout this book you have been asked to organize your thoughts, stay close to observation, employ careful reasoning processes. By now, at least to some degree, these disciplines should be part of you. Even in discussing large philosophical questions, you should be able to relate them to your own experience and, rather than accepting the reasons of others, look at them freshly from your own viewpoint. With this in mind, try kicking around some of the big questions: What are we? What are we doing here? What is the meaning of life and death? What can we be sure about, and what can we probably never know? And—why do you think so?

writing assignment

What do you think you are? In relation to the universe as a whole, what is your part? How do you define yourself? In other words, what is a human being, and how should one live, and why? As far as possible, support your answers with material from your own observation and experience. Make some attempt to persuade your reader that you are right.

argument

Argument is the art of getting others to agree with you. There are three good ways to do this: presenting evidence, reasoning, and persuading. Evidence consists of facts that support your view. Reasoning is giving reasons, theorizing about the advantages your view has. Persuading is enhancing your view with appeals to emotion.

Evidence is the best kind of argument. If you have enough facts, you have a sound case. Reasoning is a weaker technique, but often effective. If you can demonstrate clearly, for example, just how the introduction of one-way streets will ease the flow of traffic in your town, you may convince the city legislators to adopt your plan. Persuasion is mainly useful in calling attention to the importance of your point. If you describe vividly the horrors and frustrations of congested traffic on two-way streets and then the delights of driving on unobstructed one-way streets, you may get people to pay more attention to your plan. But nothing replaces evidence. If you can prove that several other cities have solved similar problems with one-way streets, you will probably win your argument.

class writing assignment

This last writing session can be used to rework the material from the above writing assignment into better form, with attention to unity, coherence, emphasis, good paragraphing, and so on.

Or it can be used to air some idea you have not had a chance to express in previous assignments. If you and your instructor agree, you might even want to discuss what benefits you may have gained from sharpening your perceptions as a result of previous assignments.

Dexter

SYDNEY FRANCIS ORONSAY

I know a man named Dexter who is a heroin addict. He lives in a deserted apartment building that has been left standing in the midst of an industrial wasteland. When you go to visit him, you are likely to find him asleep on the floor, or rather draped over a kind of compost heap made up of burst cushions, tattered blankets, dirty clothes, greasy rags, crumpled papers, battered books, split shoes, dry bread crusts, bowls of moldy breakfast cereal, empty milk cartons, crumbled dog food, cigarette butts, burnt paper matches, and other less easily identifiable detritus. If his dog, an enthusiastic wire-haired terrier, knows you, it will sniff you and then run in barking to wake its master. Dexter will open his eyes, stretch, and sit up with a crooked grin. He is in his twenties and has a physique that would stimulate the hopes of any track coach. I have twice watched him vault from the ground to the roof of a house in seconds. Roof-climbing and sprinting are Dexter's most regular exercises.

It is not because Dexter is lazy that his home is such a mess, but because he works so hard. He is the hardest working man I know. He has to be. He can't keep a steady job, and he needs at least forty dollars a day plus food money to keep going. Sometimes he has to walk miles before he finds a house with a "For Sale" sign on it, and then he still has a whole night's work ahead of him, disassembling and removing the air conditioner, detaching light fixtures and door knobs, cutting loose copper pipe, unscrewing faucets and drainpipes, wrestling with the range and refrigerator and sometimes a washing machine, collecting thermostats, regulators and switch boxes, and dragging off hoses. Everything has to be gathered in one place near the alley, the smaller items safe in the garbage cans. Then it all has to be loaded into a friend's pickup truck and, before the sun rises, delivered to the dealer who will offer it for sale at the local flea market.

As a businessman Dexter has a certain distinction in his community. Though of course they are not aware of his identity, property owners think of him as Genghis Khan or Attila the Hun. There is an aura of romance about his way of life, as there is about the role of Errol Flynn in the old swashbuckling movies. Unhappily, Dexter doesn't see it that way. To him it's just a job. He works with tunnel vision, and the light at the end of the tunnel is the glint of a hypodermic needle. Though he is an accomplished artist, he does not live for his art. He is a junkie.

A junkie is a person with a desire that can never be satisfied for more than a short time. Dexter exists from day to day, from rush to rush. He remains forever infantile, a slave to instant gratification, a consumer. Withdrawal is not his problem. Whenever Dexter gets up to four bags a day he quits for a few days, sometimes for as long as a month. He sweats and sniffs and can't sleep for a few nights, but his suffering is not all that bad. What is significant is that he always goes back to heroin.

Dexter buys his heroin from an enormously fat pusher named Della. Most dealers despise the junkies they sell to, and Della is no exception. "All junkies are animals that deserve to die," she will say. She keeps the works—the apparatus for shooting—at her house, and Dexter goes there to use them. Usually they are dirty, and from time to time he gets cotton fever or hepatitis from them. Sometimes she sells him heroin cut with poisonous substances or poison that has no heroin in it. At such times Dexter will perform the joyous ritual that is always a part of getting down, full of anticipation of the rush and the following hours of cool pleasure; then, almost immediately, he will begin to feel the poison spreading through his veins and will stagger out of Della's house, hoping he can get home in time to fall on his bed of trash, where he will be miserably sick for twelve or twenty-four hours. When this happens Della laughs at him. He is a sucker. Though he knows that one day he will die of the stuff she sells him, he always comes back for more.

Heroin is not a natural substance. It is a derivative of morphine, which in turn is a derivative of opium. By the time it reaches the user, it is heavily adulterated as well. It is not taken in a natural way, but is injected directly into the bloodstream.

The addict is not a natural person. During the past two decades, when many different kinds of people have been experimenting with drugs, it has been discovered that most of us are not potential heroin addicts. Most who try it don't like it. Most who do find it rewarding have one characteristic in common: they have never been able to form loving relationships with other people. Apparently it is not heroin that makes the addict unable to love, but the incapacity to love that makes the addict. Heroin seems to be a substitute for love.

When the addict shoots heroin, he experiences what he calls the "rush." This is a sensation that cannot be described, but only praised in the most extravagant language. Dexter insists that it is the ultimate pleasure anyone can feel, something like orgasm times ten. The rush is followed by several hours of delightful detachment during which troubles fade into insignificance and the user feels a cool, god-like superiority to life's problems. He is able to think with greater than normal clarity, he feels at one with the world, and he is incapable of experiencing pain. He seems to exist outside of time. He is happy wherever he is and does not want activity or company. He is content to be.

The third stage comes only after years of use. The addict becomes accustomed to his euphoric detachment so that it is now his ordinary mode of life. As a result, straight life without heroin becomes confused, ugly and painful, completely intolerable. The addict must now have his drug not for pleasure, but for escape from the straight world. Heroin is no longer rewarding but only necessary. He is hooked for life, and his life is a relentless, frantic struggle for money to support his habit. Other people no longer have much meaning for him except as potential sources of money.

After ten years of use Dexter is between the pleasure and necessity stages. The pleasure is dimming and the need growing. He could still kick the habit if he could find something better than heroin. He still looks for love, but in a pathetically infantile way. He has never learned to give and can only take. When he is straight he is disoriented, a different person from one minute to the next. Sometimes he will cling to a friend's hand for a moment and look into his eyes as if to say, "Can't you love me enough to pull me out of this hell?" But a minute later he is thinking about money again.

The trouble is, Dexter *can't* find anything better than heroin. When he looks at the straight world, he is dismayed by what he sees. He does not see the beauty of nature, but the ugliness of industry. He does not see people loving one another, but people exploiting one another. He cannot believe in love because he has never seen a convincing example. Heroin has not caused Dexter's predicament. It has only given him a cell to crawl into, a poor shelter in the world of the neutron bomb.

I wish there were something I could say to Dexter. Should I try to convince him it is better to be hooked on possessions instead of heroin? I cannot believe that it is. Heroin addiction does not destroy forests, devastate the countryside, fill the air with smoke, pollute rivers, and poison seas, as does the excessive consumption of manufactured goods. Dexter steals only what he needs. He is not greedy. He does not steal the resources of the earth from future generations.

Addiction is a strong attachment to a short-lived sensation, an attachment that persists after the sensation has ceased to be rewarding.

But that definition is not complete. It leaves out the most significant aspect of addiction, one we may fail to perceive at all because it has become so much a part of ourselves, our culture, and our way of looking at life. It is this: the addict believes that the sensation he experiences within himself comes from a source outside himself.

Dexter worships needles and the ritual of shooting. No human being has ever received the look of love he directs toward a needle. When he was getting clean I have seen him avidly shoot a hypodermic of warm water into his vein and get at least the semblance of a high from it. Even when that clue is pointed out to him, he does not understand that his pleasure comes from within himself. He believes it comes from heroin. Most of us believe it comes from possessions. Most of us are not even potential heroin addicts, but we are hard-core possession addicts.

The disease of materialism is this belief that pleasure is in things and not in ourselves. We are all like Dexter. We vainly seek joy in things and, in order to acquire those things, waste our lives in useless work and joyless scheming. We rob and plunder the earth and each other as Dexter robs houses and hustles his friends. We too have accepted artificial things as substitutes for love. We fool ourselves with empty symbols, as Dexter does with his syringe of water. As a result, we have reduced much of our world to a trash pile that is like Dexter's room, and we live in an industrial wasteland.

A great share of the trash we have accumulated is in the form of machines and of machines to make and control machines. We not only slave to acquire them, but we then allow the machines themselves to enslave us. We obey their signals, tend them, repair them, cramp our actions to their time and space, submit to being charged and taxed and officiously watched by them. We even allow machines to dream for us.

Once in a motel where I was staying the fuses blew out in the separate circuit that served the television sets. The lights stayed on and the air conditioners kept working. Nevertheless, there was nearly a riot. People poured out of their rooms as though a fire alarm had sounded. They formed a furious mob around the unfortunate night clerk, who didn't know where to find the fuses. They all had that look in their eyes of being lost, deprived, frightened by emptiness, the look of the sick junkie who can't find a fix and doesn't know what to do, the look I have seen in Dexter's eyes. They believed they would suffer without their nightly input. Their plugs had been pulled.

We are all junkies as long as we persist in believing that fulfillment comes from something outside ourselves, something manufactured. If we cherish this belief, we will plug into anything that promises a rush and leave the plug in after the rush is gone. We will remain the slaves of things and of machines.

We watch television because we have forgotten how to dream without it. We let its shoddy dreams, adulterated and sold to us by contemptuous pushers, usurp our own, killing the time that is the substance of our lives. We buy car after car, dissatisfied with each because the thrill we felt the first time we drove one does not return; we have forgotten that the thrill was inside us, not in the car. When marriage fails to bring the bliss we felt in its beginning, we blame our mates, get divorced, and try another with the same result. Or we become sex junkies, trying to recapture our first rush by repeating the mechanics of the act over and over with different partners. We buy possessions, become bored with them, and buy more; then, instead of enjoying them, we worry about losing them, insure them, pay taxes on them, and make our homes into fortresses to protect them from our neighbors. Our dreams stagnate inside us while we lay waste our lives for the watered syringes of fatter bank accounts, bigger houses, more expensive club memberships.

Have you noticed in your neighborhood one of those dogs that barks incessantly all day long? It is lonely and neurotic because it belongs to someone who neglects it and leaves it tied up by itself. When its owner was a child, he experienced joy in the company of a dog. Now he keeps replacing the first dog compulsively, wondering why he does not feel that joy again. Because the joy does not return he blames the dog; it's just not the dog the first one was, they don't make dogs like that any more. He has forgotten that his joy came from loving the dog, not from the dog. And because he has forgotten how to love his dog it annoys his neighbors, who shake their heads and think about calling the police. He has forgotten how to love his neighbors too.

Most of us have forgotten how to love our neighbors. We quarrel over boundaries. We resent people crossing our property. We build fences. We isolate ourselves with property and tie ourselves up in our own yards with the rope of property addiction, and we are lonely. We have let unnatural, manufactured things replace the natural love in our lives. Nobody loves a junkie, whether he is a heroin junkie or a possession junkie, because neither kind knows how to love.

How can we love our neighbors? We do not love life. We are dedicated to its destruction. We kill living things to create dead things. We are consumers. We consume the earth to surround ourselves with dead things, make it into a desert with lumbering and strip mining, build hideous industrial cities where there were once woods and meadows full of flowers, and poison rivers and lakes and seas. We work in factories and offices where, except for other workers, there is not a living thing in sight, and we wonder why we do not feel alive. We imprison our children in schools that have no windows so they will not be tempted by life and will become good consumers. We invent bombs that kill people and leave their property intact.

Dexter hates to be reminded of the mess heroin has made of his life. He does not like to face that reality. Nor do the rest of us care to face the reality of the world we have destroyed. We do not choose to live among our steel mills and chemical factories or amid the stumps of our devastated forests and the chaos of our strip-mined hills or in the hopeless slums of our central cities; those places are for the poor. On weekends we create traffic jams escaping from the cities we have built, to crowd ourselves into what little is left of the forest, the lakes and the rivers, the seashore. Least of all do we like to be reminded of the vanity of our materialistic yearning: of the same automobile we found so beautiful ten years ago, now, in the junkyard, an eyesore to be hidden from our vision.

As a heroin addict rather than a possession addict, Dexter has two advantages over the rest of us. At least during the first years of his drug use, he derives an unquestionably keen pleasure from it; and he can live with a clear conscience, knowing that nothing has to be destroyed to provide his pleasure. While it is true he is a consumer, he consumes far less than most of us. Even his stealing, he can tell himself, is necessary only because of drug laws supported by those he steals from: legal heroin would cost about ten cents a bag. In other respects we have everything in common with him. We too are in a vicious circle: the more we are dissatisfied with our world, the more we demand the artificial drug of possessions; and the more the world is laid waste for the production of possessions, the less satisfying it becomes. The circle tightens, and at its center is death, death by war, death by starvation, death by poison. Like Dexter, we stupidly continue in the same suicidal spiral until we die of overdosing or, poisoned victims of a neutron bomb, expire upon our heap of artifacts.

Most of us know we're hooked. Most of us are at least dimly aware that we are unhappy as the slaves of dead things. But few of us have any idea how to go about kicking the habit.

It is often hardest to see the most obvious. The most obvious aspect of our lives, that which contains everything we can ever know or experience or imagine, is our own consciousness. It is that overwhelming fact of life that the scientist, the materialist, can do nothing with. Ask a scientist what consciousness is. His eyes will dart about evasively and he will mutter something that sounds like "epiphenomenon." He is conscious, we assume, but he doesn't want to think about it. He can only try to explain it as a byproduct of physical processes. The truth is he *can't* think about it. Nobody can. Thinking about consciousness is like putting your feet in your mouth and trying to swallow yourself. You *are* consciousness.

We can't think about consciousness, but we can develop it. If an athlete sets out to develop his muscles, he doesn't have to think about them; all he has to do is practice exercises that have worked for other people. Many well-tested disciplines for expanding consciousness are available: Zen, yoga, karate, a hundred different techniques of meditation. But before we are willing to give them our attention, we have to believe that they will lead to something better than we have now. The way to kick a habit is to find something better.

We all have the clue, like Dexter getting high on his syringe of water. Who has not awakened from a dream, full to the brim with happy feeling? We can never remember just what it was about the dream that made us so happy, but there was no mistaking the feeling. We were experiencing a natural high, and it was all in the mind. Who has not suddenly felt a rush of well-being for no reason at all and stretched and grinned and maybe danced a little and hugged the person nearest him? Who has not washed his consciousness clean with hiking or running or dancing and then felt the cool suffusion of peace and optimism flow through him? It is there, with us all the time, inside ourselves. It is this feeling of natural happiness, not the economy, that we need to develop.

It is possible that the American Indian or, for that matter, our own primitive ancestors felt this natural happiness most of the time. Most primitive people use some sort of drug now and then, but there are no addicts among them. They accept the earth and live with it. They live among living things, not dead things, consuming only what they need. They respect the earth and leave it as it is and thus do not need to escape from it.

How many times have we heard that sour judgment, "He thinks the world owes him a living"? It comes from the person who thinks everybody should work for a living. But what we call work is mischief and destruction. The earth gives us a living freely if we don't bite the hand that feeds us; by now we've nearly bitten it off. Our primitive ancestors did not work for a living, they played. They hunted and fished, gathered nuts and roots and berries, and tended animals and plants. They needed no possessions, for they possessed a world that was better than any manufactured thing. They had more leisure than we dream of, and they did not consume it with busyness and worry. They were not junkies. They were not in love with junk.

People who don't know what they're talking about often fall back on meaningless familiar sayings. One of these is, "You can't go back." It is nonsense. Sometimes the only way to go is back. When you have hiked into a box canyon with walls you can't climb, you don't bang your head against the rock; you go back. That's where we are now, boxed in by materialism. Depending on science to make a ladder for us is like trusting the guide who put us on the wrong trail in the first place. Rational, scientific thinking—materialistic thinking—is what has led us into the trap. What we need now is to develop our consciousness, listen to our intuition, expand our sense of what life really is. We need to get back in touch with the nature that is inside us.

We do not need all the things we have gathered around us; what we do need is life around us, other living beings to teach us what our own nature is. We have lost touch. We are children of the earth, a link in what was once called the Great Chain of Being. We have tried to unlink ourselves and have nearly succeeded in breaking the chain, destroying the living part of being and, with it, our own consciousness. But what we really are is still there inside us. We need to silence the babble of our busy minds and listen until it speaks to us.

We have to find our way step by step back to the fork where we took the wrong trail. There are steps that each of us, as individuals, can begin with.

We can unplug our television sets and get our own dreams back. Television is the most sterile and unrewarding of all addictions. Besides blocking our inner receptivity with meaningless static, it is the tool of those pushers who profit from our weakness, our disease of consumerism.

We can stop reading the news every day. News frightens us with phantoms and makes us paranoid. It clutters the brain with irrelevant fact and disturbs the emotions with crises that in a month will have been forgotten. Democracy thrives not on knowledge of daily incident, but on independence of mind. More than we need to be overinformed, we need to clear our minds.

We can stop consuming more than we need. Conspicuous consumption advertises that we love neither the earth nor other people, but that we love junk. Luxuries and status symbols make it obvious that we have no independence of mind, but are suckers for the pushers who want us to stay hooked. An expensive home or car shows that we desire the envy of fools, not the love of our neighbors.

We can learn to question the value of such ideals as hard work, competition, and an expanding economy. This is the propaganda of pushers. What we need is more leisure and fairer distribution of necessities. The world owes us all a living. Most "production"—the killing of live things to produce dead things—is destruction of that living and of those people whose lives must be used up in work.

We can stop abusing our leisure by filling it up with the frenetic mechanical activities of consumerism and use it to cultivate quietness of mind. Happiness is our natural state. We need only stop frightening it with noise and it will come shyly out.

We have allowed things to become more important to us than lives. We have used people, animals, plants, and the living soil itself to provide our manufactured dosages. Now we need to stop playing the part of the missing link in the chain of life, to reach out our hands to the life on either side of us and reestablish the fundamental connection. We can begin with people. We can begin with our own children, who, in quietness of mind, may have something to teach us, or with our parents, or with our husbands or wives or lovers, or with our neighbors.

Like Dexter, we have been addicts too long. We have accepted material things in place of love and have forgotten how to love. We have forgotten that joy is inside ourselves, not in things outside. We have become so addicted to material things that we are dependent on steadily increasing supplies of them, in spite of knowing that they are adulterated, shoddy, and often poisonous, in spite of knowing that we are the prideless dupes of manufacturers, advertisers and sellers who despise us and label us consumers, and in spite of knowing that our blind greed is destroying our only home, the earth. Like Dexter shooting poison into his veins, we have let our consciousness atrophy to the point where we are completely unrealistic about what we are doing to ourselves. Though we know our greed is killing us, we keep going back to the pushers for more. Like Dexter, we have become a little less than human. As it will be hard for Dexter to find his way back, so it will be hard for all of us. But we have to try. It is the only way.

---

1. What is the theme or central idea of "Dexter"? Try to state it in one sentence.
2. "Dexter" is an argument. The author is trying to win the reader to his way of thinking. Why do you believe he wants you to think as he does?
3. Does the author employ reasoning as a technique of argument? If so, point out sentences or paragraphs in which reasoning is used.
4. Where does he use persuasion? What persuasive images does he offer? Where does he employ emotional language?
5. Evidence is the soundest kind of argument. Does Oronsay offer any evidence that his ideas are right? If so, does he use his evidence well, or could the same evidence be used to support a contradictory argument? If you believe it could, demonstrate how.
6. An author who argues well anticipates the reader's objections. Do you find any places in the essay where Oronsay has done this?

Powwow

W. D. SNODGRASS

(Tama Reservation, Iowa, 1949)

They all see the same movies.
    They shuffle on one leg,
        Scuffing the dust up,
    Shuffle on the other.
They are all the same:
    A Sioux dance to the spirits,
    A war dance by four Chippewa,
    A Dakota dance for rain.
        We wonder why we came.
Even tricked out in the various braveries—
    Black buffalo tassels, beadwork, or the brilliant
    Feathers at the head, at the buttocks—
Even in long braids and the gaudy face paints,
        They all dance with their eyes turned
    Inward, like a woman nursing
A sick child she already knows
    Will die. For the time, she nurses it
    All the same. The loudspeakers shriek;
        We leave our bleacher seats to wander
    Among the wickiups and lean-tos
In a search for hot dogs. The Indians
        Are already packing; have
    Resumed green dungarees and khaki,
    Castoff combat issues of World War II.
        (Only the Iroquois do not come here;
They work in structural steel; they have a contract
        Building the United Nations
    And Air Force installations for our future wars.)
These, though, have dismantled their hot-dog stand
        And have to drive all night
To jobs in truck stops and all-night filling stations.

We ask directions and
They scuttle away from us like moths.
Past the trailers,
Beyond us, one tepee is still shining
Over all the rest. Inside, circled by a ring
Of children, in the glare
Of one bare bulb, a shrunken fierce-eyed man
Squats at his drum, all bones and parchment,
While his dry hands move
On the drumhead, always drumming, always
Raising his toothless, drawn jaw to the light
Like a young bird drinking, like a chained dog,
Howling his tribe's song for the restless young
Who wander in and out.
Words of such great age,
Not even he remembers what they mean.
We tramp back to our car,
Then nearly miss the highway, squinting
Through red and yellow splatterings on the windshield,
The garish and beautiful remains
Of grasshoppers and dragonflies
That go with us, that do not live again.

---

1. While the author of the poem does not employ irony in the sense of saying the opposite of what he means, he does point out ironies in the scene. What are some of his ironic contrasts?
2. What is the point of the poem?
3. What means of persuasion does the poet use to argue this point? Does he offer evidence?
4. In the last five lines the poet reinforces his argument with a *symbol*— a thing that stands for something else. What is the image that stands for something else? What does it stand for?
5. How is this poem related to "Dexter"? How is it related to the Don Ivan Punchatz' illustration on the next page?
6. Form a generalization that would sum up what the poet is saying. Then examine the poem more closely, and see if you can find a broader meaning implied in the contrasting images.

---

1. This illustration can be seen as an argument in paint. What is the argument?
2. What techniques of argument have been used: presentation of evidence, reasoning, or persuasion?
3. To what extent does the painting show "the whole picture" of humanity's destruction of the environment? What is omitted, if anything?
4. Can you compose an effective argument against what is implied by the picture? What evidence can you offer to support your argument?
5. What might be the function of a picture such as this one? How might it achieve practical effects?
6. What relationships do you find between this picture and "Dexter"? Between this picture and "Powwow"?

PLATE XIV

Cover painting for *America the Raped,* Courtesy of Avon Books. Don Ivan
Punchatz, Ilustrator; Barbara Bertoli, Art Director.

Index of Authors and Titles

Index of Artists and Plates

A	9
B	0
C	1
D	2
E	3
F	4
G	5
H	6
I	7